D1258336

Massachusetts in the Gilded Age

Massachusetts
in the Gilded Age

selected essays

Edited by Jack Tager and John W. Ifkovic

The University of Massachusetts Press   Amherst   1985

Library of Congress Cataloging in Publication Data

Main entry under title:

Massachusetts in the Gilded Age.
Includes index.
1. Massachusetts—History—1865–   —Addresses,
essays, lectures. I. Tager, Jack. II. Ifkovic, John W.
F70.M45   1985   974.4′041   84–23970
ISBN 0–87023–480–3
ISBN 0–87023–481–1 (pbk.)

The Institute for Massachusetts Studies and the University of
Massachusetts Press gratefully acknowledge financial support from
the following corporations and foundations, whose generosity
helped make this publication possible.

Bank of New England/West
BayBank Valley Trust Company
Community Savings Bank
Easco Hand Tools, Inc.
Frank Stanley Beveridge Foundation
Massachusetts Mutual Life Insurance Company
Shawmut First Bank and Trust Company
Systems Engineering and Manufacturing Corporation
Totsy Manufacturing Company
Westfield River Paper Company

Contents

Preface

In October 1982, and February and March 1983, the Institute
for Massachusetts Studies sponsored a series of three symposia on Massachusetts in the Gilded Age, hosted by the
John Fitzgerald Kennedy Library in Boston. In planning and
organizing the sessions, the institute's staff recognized that
far too little scholarly research has been done on Massachusetts history after the Civil War, and they hoped to encourage research and promote an understanding of what had
largely been a hidden phase of Massachusetts history. The
programs brought together historians with a diverse range
of interests. Some were experts on the period from 1876 to
1900; others specialized in Massachusetts history, or in state
and local history; still others were interested in immigration
and the development of urbanization. Those who presented formal papers received constructive criticism from
such specialists as Stephan Thernstrom in social history,
Gerald McFarland in political history, Robert O'Leary in
religious history, Bruce Stave, Jack Tager, and Sam Bass
Warner in urban history. Some of these historians served in
an official capacity at the symposia, as commentators or or-
ganizers. Others lectured on their most recent research, and
still others attended the sessions and provided insights and
ideas by their thoughtful questions.

Out of these scholarly discussions came common agreement that there was a need to correlate the broad general-
izations that characterize an historical epoch such as the
Gilded Age, with the specific data provided by case study

analysis of state and local history. The symposia served to increase our knowledge of Massachusetts history from 1865 to 1900, and in the process enabled the participants to compare developments on the national scene with parallel events in Massachusetts. It seemed appropriate to publish the revised papers, both to illuminate the significance of Massachusetts historical studies for the generalist and to enhance the knowledge of the public.

Jack Tager, professor of history at the University of Massachusetts, Amherst, prepared the introductions to each section of this volume. His introductory essay describes the economic transformation of Massachusetts during the nineteenth century, from a basically rural, agricultural society to an urban, industrial one. This account of the emerging factory system, the demographic consequences of immigration, and the process of urbanization, sets the stage for the subsequent essays that offer further insight into the changes that occurred during the Gilded Age.

Part two of the book focuses on political change and the impact of ethnicity upon post-Civil War Massachusetts. The essay by Dale Baum, of Texas A and M University, provides a statistical analysis of how party loyalty and voter preferences affected the outcome of state elections and altered party ideology. Peter Haebler, of Merrimack Valley College, offers a case study of the French-Canadian struggle to gain political power in Holyoke by their alliance with Republicans. Thomas McMullin of the University of Massachusetts, Boston, examines New Bedford, the attitude of its various ethnic groups toward unions, and the evolving class structure within that industrial city.

Part three studies social change and social mobility in the Gilded Age. Alexander Keyssar, of Brandeis University, explores the effect of urbanization upon social relationships and concepts of community, citing the general sources of both discord and cohesion in Massachusetts life. The connection between industrialization and social mobility is the subject of the essays by Francis R. Walsh, of the University of Lowell, and Ronald A. Smith, of Pennsylvania State University. Professor Walsh investigates the case of one highly mobile immigrant, John Boyle O'Reilly, editor of the *Boston Pilot* and spokesman for the Irish, who tried to bridge the gap between Boston's two societies. Professor Smith, on the other hand, looks at the controversy over the nature of college athletics at Harvard University between 1869 and 1909. The debate on collegiate sports as either gentlemanly recreation or competitive excellence illustrates the Brahmin reluctance to accept meritocracy in the place of class and tradition.

Part four turns to social reform in Boston and its relationship to machine politics. The essay by Ivan D. Steen, of the State University of New York at Albany, delves into the reform activities of a prominent Boston minister and founder of Goodwill Industries, the colorful Reverend Henry Morgan. Marilyn Thornton Williams, of Pace University, illuminates the motives of reformers interested in moral uplift, by discussing the public bath movement of Boston and the pivotal role played by the city's Brahmin mayor, Josiah Quincy. The final essay by Jack Tager compares the accomplishments of both the ministerial reformers and the public bath movement reformers with the social reform successes of the Irish mayors, John F. Fitzgerald and James Michael Curley. These essays examine the ideas of Boston social reformers, whose notions of social improvement inevitably clashed with those held by the Irish party bosses and their followers.

This book could not have been completed without the assistance of a great many individuals and organizations. First and foremost, we must express our appreciation to those who presented the results of their research at the three sessions of the Symposium on Massachusetts in the Gilded Age. The commentators were willing to share their knowledge and understanding of the subject, and in the process they assisted the authors in the subsequent revisions of their papers. We also thank the staff of the John Fitzgerald Kennedy Library, and especially Dan Fenn, the director, and John Stewart, the director of education. John Stewart provided great support at every stage of the project, and he deserves much of the credit for the success of the symposium's three sessions. We would like to express our appreciation to the Lowell Institute for the kind and generous financial assistance required for the public sessions of the meetings. Finally, we acknowledge the contribution of Joseph Carvalho III of the Springfield City Library, and of Martin Kaufman, director of the Institute for Massachusetts Studies, who with John Ifkovic, associate director of the Institute, helped plan the symposia.

Jack Tager
John W. Ifkovic

ONE

Massachusetts and the Age of Economic Revolution

Massachusetts and the Age of Economic Revolution

JACK TAGER

Mark Twain's christening of post-Civil War America as the "Gilded Age" has masked the period's true identity. Twain acted as spokesman for those disaffected with the questionable morality and driving acquisitiveness of the age's robber barons and party bosses. Patricians like Henry Adams felt that the cult of materialism foretold the doom of civilization itself. "Hating vindictively, as I do, our whole fabric and conception of society . . . I shall be glad to see the whole thing utterly destroyed and wiped away. . . . My view of the case is always to encourage the big thieves and to force the pace. Let's get there quick! I'm for Morgan, McKinley and the Trusts! They will bring us to ruin quicker than we could do it ourselves." Yet for all the scandals and bribery, one would be hard put to find much difference between the Gilded Age and other periods of American history. For example, the early national period produced the Yazoo land scandal and Aaron Burr; the twentieth century had Teapot Dome and Albert Fall and Watergate and Richard Nixon. The exaggerated response of outraged gentlemen and the "honest" middle classes of the Gilded Age may have been due to a pervasive Victorian "cultural absolutism" that rejected any deviation from an elevated morality. On the other hand, complaints about corruption and the loosening ties of civilization might well have been the rationalizations of fading elites faced with a successful "parvenu challenge." Perhaps the most appropriate rejoinder to the popular myth of Gilded Age venality was Carl Degler's characterization of the period as the "Age of Economic Revolution."[1]

From 1865 to 1900 the redirection of economic life from farm to factory spawned a new urban society that transformed the lives of all Americans by the twentieth century. This economic revolution was the result of the complex interweaving of a growing factory system; gigantic boosts in farm output due to mechanization; the development of a national transportation system that ended the reliance upon local markets; and the migration of peasants from American farms and European villages to the mushrooming, chaotic urban centers of America. The result was social dislocation, and both discontent and satisfaction with the fruits of industrial productivity.

Technology gave man the power, skill, and precision to expand productivity beyond expectation. However, the capitalist system, affected by the vagaries of the market, fostered seemingly capricious cycles of prosperity and depression. The reduction of the farm labor force provided the initial workers for the new factories, thus gestating a system that required the production of raw materials, the provision of services, the building of cities, the construction of transportation networks, the modification of the structure of trade and business, and the reorganization of financial and governmental institutions. New population groupings were based on class, ethnicity, and religious affiliation. Special interest groups were organized to protect, change, inform, hate, and exclude. A small articulate upper class felt threatened by these social changes. Old local loyalties gave way because of demographic instability, creating a need to reorder the traditional rural visions of family and home. As the propertyless class of urban proletariat grew, the breach between the few very rich and the many poor threatened the tenuous social order.

The technology of the age stimulated the creation of new business organizations able to amass enormous amounts of capital, eradicating the old communal workplace; in its stead burgeoned the national corporation based upon absentee ownership and a new urban bureaucracy of managerial elites. The gargantuan growth of cities, with their ethnic ghettoes and class-based residential segregation, completed the social replacement that affected every spectrum of society. This profound economic change of the second half of the nineteenth century saturated the nation at large. Massachusetts, one of the first states to industrialize, typified the painful metamorphosis from rural society to urban commonwealth.

Certain characteristics of preindustrial Massachusetts made it uniquely suitable for an economic revolution. A shaky and perilous agricultural base encouraged the possibilities for other economic activities. Between 1810 and 1830, a short boom in dairy farming, vegetables, and fruits in the eastern part of the state, and cattle and sheep in the western areas, collapsed because of the post-1840 transportation revolution. Inexpensively priced goods from the west virtually destroyed the profitability of local and state farming. Dairy and truck farming continued, but on a smaller scale, as farmers faced rising costs of operation and the need for greater capital expansion.[2] Involvement in trade, fishing, and crafts marked an already diversified economy that welcomed new investments and capital ventures. With abundant capital from shipping, well supplied with untapped sources of labor—impoverished farmers—and blessed with a major port in Boston, Massachusetts was ready to shift to manufacturing.

The people of Massachusetts were the first in the nation to experience and cope with the industrial revolution. Measured by overall productivity, Massachusetts was third to New York and Pennsylvania, but per capita by 1880 it "was the most thoroughly industrialized state." In 1880 three-quarters of the work force in the state could be considered members of the working class.[3] The factory system began in Waltham in 1813 with the textile industry that was to dominate the state's economy throughout the century. From the 1820s on, new mills and factory towns multiplied—textiles, woolens, and papers in Lowell, Lawrence, Fall River, New Bedford, Chicopee, Holyoke; shoes in Lynn, Brockton, Haverhill, and Randolph. Between 1850 and 1880, manufacturing flourished in Massachusetts.

The decade of 1860 was a period of the greatest growth of manufacturing; the number of manufacturing establishments jumped from 8,176 in 1860 to 13,212 in 1870, a rise of 61.8 percent. Capital investment expanded in this period by 74.5 percent. In the next decade, although the number of manufacturing units grew only by a modest 8.6 percent, capital investment rose by 31.1 percent. Population increases of 23.8 percent in 1860, 18.4 percent in 1870, and 22.4 percent in 1880, provided the necessary labor to man the new factories. By 1880, 42 percent of the labor force was in manufacturing, 14 percent in trade and finance, 8 percent in construction, 19 percent in service areas (including public administration and household work), 7 percent in transportation, only 10 percent in agriculture, and 1 percent in fisheries.[4] The majority of Massachusetts residents were now either involved in industry or in areas supportive of industry—the definitive sign of an industrialized society.

An integral component of the trend to the factory system was the development of an effective transportation network. Though dwarfed by New York, by 1877 the port of

Boston eclipsed Philadelphia and Baltimore combined. Easy access to overseas and coastal markets and to raw materials provided a natural incentive for capital investment in manufacturing. After 1877 the viability of the port was to decline as New York, Philadelphia, and Baltimore increased their share of trade because of larger port facilities and greater accessibility to important railroad connections.[5] The railroad was vital to any industrial buildup. After a slow start in the 1840s, the 1850s brought major railroad construction to Massachusetts, the most in the Union. By the end of the decade every Massachusetts town of 5,000 or more had a railroad connection.

Following the Civil War a new spurt of railroad building began. The creation of the consolidated Boston and Albany Railroad in 1867, the wealthiest corporation in the state, and the completion of the Hoosac Tunnel route in the 1870s, finalized the state-wide railroad network and opened up trade with the West. Reaching all corners of the state, the railroads brought in the cotton, wool, iron, coal, livestock, wheat flour, and corn, and on return carried westward and southward the finished manufactured goods.[6] The railroads carried more than goods; the ability to move considerable numbers of workers, foreign and native-born, was to alter significantly the nature of both the population density and mix of the state of Massachusetts.

Except for tiny Rhode Island, Massachusetts was the Union's most densely populated state of the nineteenth century. The abundance of jobs attracted large numbers of displaced farmers and peasants. Continuous and heavy rural/urban migration was the prime factor in the redistribution and reallocation of the labor force, serving constantly changing industrial needs in various geographic areas. Historian Stephan Thernstrom focused on the remarkable population fluidity of Boston and the state, contending that migration into Boston was much greater than reported, even though many people left the city in search of work: "Thus the actual volume of movement into Boston during the 1880's was approximately *twelve* times larger than estimated net in-migration, because huge numbers of people were leaving the city at the same time that huge numbers of others were entering it." This turnover took place in the face of population increases in Boston of from 20 to 25 percent for each decade from 1880 to 1910. Thernstrom wrote: "The country had an enormous reservoir of restless and footloose men, who could be lured to new destinations when opportunity beckoned."[7] The population of the state as a whole advanced by 22.4 percent, 25.6 percent, and 25.3 percent, respectively, in the three decades from 1870 to 1900, almost directly comparable with the overall percentage growth rate of the entire United States. In addition, an intraregional migration from northern New England did much to replace the number of native-borns who left Massachusetts."[8]

An important segment of the population movement to the cities was from overseas. According to historian Carl Siracusa, the proportion of foreign-born increased from 1 percent in 1830, to 25 percent in the 1870s; this number does not consider the children of immigrants born in the United States. The first to come were the Irish peasants escaping from potato blight and English oppression. By 1846, 1,000 per month were entering an already overcrowded Boston. They spread throughout the state in the 1850s, working in the railroad camps, the construction crews, and, finally, in the mills.[9] French Canadians, Germans, and others followed the Irish after the Civil War. The *Holyoke Transcript* of March 29, 1879, described the arrival of poverty-stricken French Canadians from the agrarian depression of Quebec: "They come with all their wordly goods packed in boxes and bundles, and the gents' room at the Connecticut River

Railroad depot is packed with their effects till it looks like a wholesale warehouse. . . . Some have friends or relatives here, expecting to find plenty of work on their arrival."[10] Of a population of 1,783,085 in 1880, 439,341 had at least one foreign-born parent.[11]

The big surge in immigration occurred from 1890 to 1910, when over a million foreigners came to New England cities from eastern and southern Europe.[12] These immigrants were to become the cliff dwellers of Massachusetts's new urban civilization; as early as 1875 the census revealed that for the first time a majority of the people (50.6 percent) lived in the nineteen incorporated cities of the state.[13] The end of the century bore witness to the transformation from a rural to an urban Massachusetts, with 76 percent of the state's 2,805,346 residents living in cities.[14]

These urban centers were the product of the greed and paternalism of elite Boston entrepreneurs, who initiated the industrialization process by creating the factory towns. These Boston Brahmins were the sons of the maritime patricians of eighteenth-century New England. Taking advantage of overseas commerce, as well as investing in land, these men constructed a "Brahmin ethos"—a set of ideas, attitudes, and institutions dominated by economic needs and kept exclusive by intermarriage—that was to dominate Massachusetts banking, politics, and professions.[15] Their sons were able to overcome the financial disaster wrought by the Embargo of 1807 and the War of 1812 by investing in a profitable new commercial venture—textile manufacturing. Slavishly adhering to the business ethic, "the Brahmins developed from a maritime elite into a ruling class."[16] The so-called golden years from 1820 to 1860 witnessed the introduction of the company town and absentee ownership.

These merchant shippers, shipowners, captains, traders, importers, exporters, and agents were to consolidate their capital and establish the modern corporation. Known as the "Boston associates," these corporate pioneers started a new industry on a large scale, developed new techniques of manufacture, devised a system to sell their products, recruited, trained, and housed a labor force, built virtually new communities, and contributed heavily to the construction of a transportation system vital to their own needs.[17] Furthermore, they triggered a massive demographic movement with enormous social consequences; because sizable numbers of farm women and children were brought into the factory system, the family structure was seriously affected. In the process, housing and health problems were created that gave rise to the need for new urban services. The Boston associates also introduced substantial numbers of foreign workers to inhospitable communities, a measure that generated xenophobia, ethnic tension, and group conflict. Their efforts indirectly promoted new forms of social mobility in spite of often deplorable treatment of workers; when they cut wages during times of depression, they unknowingly stimulated union organization and fostered ethnic politics. In other words, the Boston associates began the process of transforming Massachusetts into an industrial commonwealth.

The names of the Boston associates—the likes of Edmund Dwight, Kirk Boott, Patrick T. Jackson, William Sturgis, Harrison Grey Otis, T. H. Perkins, Israel Thorndike, Abbott and Amos Lawrence, Nathan Appleton, the Lowells, the Cabots, the Lymans, the Quincys, the Eliots, the Blisses—can be found on the boards of directors, or as major stockholders, in virtually all of the cotton mills of 1850.[18] They managed or owned one-fifth of the entire U.S. textile industry with a complex array of interlocking directorates. These men controlled production by exchanging information on costs, posting similar bids for raw cotton, fixing the price of finished products, owning the water power sites and sub-sidiary manufacture of textile machinery, and even owning the houses of workers. To reach new markets they invested in the first Massachusetts railroads, building the Boston and Lowell road (1835), and by the late 1840s they shared inter-est in 25–35 percent of the railroad mileage in the state. Their "financial/industrial integration" was completed in their in-volvement with 40 percent of Boston's banks by 1848, and 38 percent of the state's insurance industry.[19] The number of textile workers had grown from 27,600 in 1837, to 93,000 in 1880. Similarly, the shoe industry, catapulted to change by the introduction of the sewing machine in 1852, grew from 35,300 workers in 1837, to 61,500 in 1880.[20] The efforts of Boston's capitalist elite made Massachusetts first in the nation in the high proportion of workers involved in manu-facturing and nonagricultural pursuits.

Whereas the early factory towns were built upon the availability of water power and local farm labor, the con-tinued flow of cheaper unskilled labor eventually resulted in the replacement of farmers' daughters with Irish immi-grants in the 1840s. After the Civil War, new migrants began pouring into these towns, and, with all pretension of pater-nalism gone, the factory towns were to become modern in-dustrial cities. Waltham—developed by Francis Lowell and friends in 1813 with the establishment of the Boston Manu-facturing Company—by 1890 was a city of 18,707. With 44 percent of the population Irish Catholic, engaged mainly in blue-collar, low-paying work, and with Yankee Protestants in higher status jobs, the city was divided into fairly distinct ethnic, class-oriented neighborhoods. By 1894 the presence of significant numbers of French Canadians necessitated a separate Catholic church—a sign of ethnic divisiveness. Waltham's workers in the Gilded Age were not subject to the grinding poverty common to other factory towns. They did experience a measure of material success, but not enough to move them from blue-collar to white-collar ranks. The evidence suggests that these antagonistic and often warring ethnic and religious groups hammered out a reasonable accommodation within a "markedly stratified society."[21] However, this was not the case in Lowell and Lawrence.

In an attempt to duplicate the financial success of Waltham, the Boston associates created Lowell in 1822 on the banks of the Merrimack River. The Merrimack Massachusetts Company mill was quickly followed by the Boott Mills, the Tremont Mills, and the Lawrence, Appleton, Suffolk, Hamilton, Massachusetts, and Prescott manufacturing companies. The Lowell mills were the first to use power looms and were the first factories in which all processes, from raw cotton to finished cloth, were completed in a single mill. Incorporated in 1826 with a population of 2,500, by 1895 Lowell had a population of 84,387 (28,260 employed in industry). With the continuous expansion of the cotton industry, Lowell reigned supreme until 1890, when it was surpassed by Fall River.

As in Waltham, the farmers' daughters first gave way to the flood of Irish immigrants in the late 1840s and 1850s, and then to the French Canadians. After 1890 Lowell's Irish and French Canadians (23,000 by 1900) were the most extensive foreign groups, to be followed by new arrivals from Portugal, Greece, Poland, Lithuania, and Italy. The immigrants crowded into the central area of the city while native-borns fled to the outer districts. All attempts at corporate housing ceased, and high land costs led to the inevitable rise of slums and tenements. Health and sanitation became serious problems, and ethnic conflicts were heightened.[22]

Lawrence, chartered in 1847, was not significantly different. At first, it was heralded as a model town boasting wide streets, planted trees, and corporation-owned boarding houses. The *Merrimack Courier* described it as "the loveliest city in the world." Lawrence was transformed when the Irish began arriving in large numbers. While they provided cheap labor—less than one dollar for a twelve-hour day by 1850—they lived in makeshift shanties and were plagued by typhoid fever epidemics and tuberculosis. Historian Donald Cole wrote, "The 1850s was one of the worst decades in the history of the city, a decade notorious for its disease, its tragedies, and its attacks on the immigrants." By 1875, 8,000 poverty-stricken Irish had inundated the town. The squalor of Irish life, coupled with high rates of illiteracy and drinking, led to the rise of an intense nativism that divided the community for years.

The revival of the cotton industry after 1865 marked the opening of new mills, which in turn spurred another wave of migration, this time from Canada. By 1900 one-fifth of the immigrants were French Canadians who were treated miserably by both native-born and Irish. This steady in-migration of different ethnic groups altered Lawrence's political structure. The Irish moved toward the Democratic party and scored some political successes. John Breen, the first Irish-born Catholic mayor in the Commonwealth, was elected in 1881. Breen served for three one-year terms, but internal party squabbles kept the Irish divided till the 1890s. In the last decade of the century the city made some general progress with efforts to improve housing, reduce mortality rates, and provide some needed municipal services.[23]

Located some fifty miles south of Boston, Fall River has been referred to as the "Queen City of Cotton." Its natural advantages of water power, a coastal location, and a humid climate good for cotton attracted investors from Providence and Boston. Ten mills were set up by 1837. With the change-over from water power to steam, Fall River had the advantage of cheaper transportation costs for coal, and more mills were built. The mix of workers was somewhat different than that of Lowell and Lawrence. A mainly Yankee work force was augmented by large numbers of English mill workers from Lancashire. The 1870s and 1880s saw an influx of Irish workers, but these also were mill workers who had migrated previously to Lancashire, and thus were already urbanized and familiar with the English trade union movement. By 1875, 13,000 of the population of 43,000 came from Lancashire, the next largest group being 5,000 French Canadians. In 1900 Fall River had forty-two industrial corporations with a working force of 26,371, in a total population of 104,863.

Fall River's workers lived in densely packed clusters of slum "villages" surrounding the mill sites. Very low wages forced entire families to work, and Fall River had the highest proportion of child laborers (25 percent), as opposed to other company towns (8 percent). The workers themselves were divided into the skilled—earning $524 a year in 1875—and the unskilled, largely French Canadians, earning $395 a year. Dispersed slum villages kept the urbanized English/Irish apart from the peasant French Canadians. A work style based on plentiful labor, excessive job pressure, a machine-tending technology, and many women and child laborers all prevented workers from successfully organizing.[24] Throughout the century, Fall River's workers suffered through periodic dislocations and the hardships of constant wage-cutting, as well as periods of unemployment and labor conflict.

Success in promoting worker solidarity, and thus some measure of worker prosperity, was more possible in the shoe industry, particularly in Lynn. In the nineteenth century Lynn was the country's leading shoe manufacturing center. In 1880 the city had over 170 shoe factories, employing 10,700 workers out of an overall population of 38,274. Close to, and financed by Boston capital, the shoe industry was dramatically affected by the introduction of the sewing machine in 1852 and the automated stitcher in 1862. Casting aside individual shoe-sewing, labor had become so specialized by 1880 that it took thirty-three different jobs to complete one pair of shoes. Unlike the textile industry, three-fourths of all shoe workers were native-born and were to remain so until the end of the century. (By 1920, 62 percent of the work force was immigrant.)

Largely seasonal work, declining wage rates, and living in densely packed tenements surrounding warehouse factories in the central area of the city contributed to generally harsh living conditions. Nevertheless, because there were many small manufacturers and one-loft shops that required limited capital investment, some workers could rise in status. Moreover, centralization of work and residence, easily assimilated new workers, and integrated working-class neighborhoods all promoted interaction and cohesion among workers. This interrelatedness molded a class consciousness and solidarity that gave Lynn workers the distinction of being the first to join or form successful unions, with the result that they were less susceptible to the vicissitudes of employer/industry demands.[25]

The financiers of Boston did not totally ignore the western portion of the state—Chicopee and Holyoke were to become depressing replicas of the factory towns in the east. Boston associates Harrison Grey Otis, Samuel Eliot, George Bliss, and Edmund Dwight built the area's first cotton mill in 1825 on a Connecticut River tributary named Chicopee. As in other factory towns between 1840 and 1860, increased competition and rising production costs resulted in a search for cheaper supplies of labor. The bulk of the Yankee laborers were displaced by Irish and French-Canadian immigrants. By 1875, 35 percent of the population was foreign-born (21 percent Irish, 9.6 percent French Canadian). In 1885, the French Canadians had increased to 11.8 percent of the population, and a new set of arrivals from Poland made up 8.8 percent of the immigrant population. The Yankees maintained control over the skilled jobs, and the usual separation of workers by religion, language, class, and customs fragmented all efforts at unified labor organization.

Finding textiles overly competitive, Chicopee's outside investors began diversifying. An expansion of industry between 1890 and 1910, including bicycles and automobiles, furthered the factory system in the community. Finally incorporated as a city in 1891, 43 percent of the total population was now foreign-born. The city had a large working class earning low wages, and a miniscule middle class. Relying upon commercial Springfield for retail services, and lacking its own newspaper, Chicopee had become a typical one-dimensional satellite industrial city.[26]

Holyoke had to struggle for many years to attain the dubious distinction of becoming a full-fledged factory town. The antebellum period witnessed numerous local attempts to establish industry, but all failed. Even some Boston investors went bankrupt after the panic of 1857 forced closure of the Hadley Falls Textile Company. Not until the Civil War and after, particularly with the trend to establishing paper mills instead of cotton factories, did investors achieve some measure of financial success. The depression of 1873 had little impact upon the growing prosperity of the newly incorporated city. A boom in the paper industry led to great expansion, and Holyoke's population zoomed from 14,000 in 1873, to 21,961 in 1880. Constant growth of the paper industry was followed by a construction boom in housing and the establishment of subsidiary paper factories—blank books, pads, boxes, envelopes, and paper mill machinery.

By 1895 Holyoke ranked eighth in factory production in Massachusetts.

Unfortunately, the workers, again largely Irish and French Canadian, did not fare as well as outside investors. Wages were always lower than in other factory towns, and workers faced constant wage cuts, frequent mill accidents, high fire risk, long hours, and a century-old shortage of decent low-cost housing. The 1875 Report of the State Bureau of Labor Statistics recorded: "Holyoke has more and worse tenement houses than any manufacturing town of textile fabrics in the state. . . . It is no wonder that the death rate in 1872 was greater in Holyoke than in any large town in Massachusetts, excepting Fall River." Historian Constance Green called it a "hell hole." By 1900 Holyoke was a company town of paper mills, with sixteen independent firms combined into one large monopoly, the Consolidated Paper Company. This paper-industry colossus thwarted further economic growth of the city and made its population totally dependent upon the decisions wrought in boardrooms elsewhere in the state.[27]

Springfield, largely dismissed by Boston associates as lacking industrial potential, was to grow and flower as a commercial/financial metropolitan center. An early development there was the construction in 1794 of the United States Armory, which attracted a wide range of artisans, skilled workers, and merchants. The creation of a railroad link with Boston via Worcester in 1839, and the building of the Hartford and Springfield Railroad in 1844, opened a direct route to New York City. Springfield became the transportation terminus of the western part of the state.[28] Incorporated in 1852, Springfield slowly built up a balance between trade, manufacturing, and professional activity. The Civil War gave further impetus to weapons production, and firms of less than twenty workers produced a variety of goods and services: railroad cars, paper products, books, toys, subsidiary textile corporations, and, finally, automobiles and motorcycles in the 1890s. A center for the wholesale trade of paper, wool, flour, cotton, and provisions, Springfield became the region's retailing and financial capital.[29] Its economic diversity engendered a stability uncommon for the period. *Springfield Republican* editor, Solomon Griffin, remarked, "Fortunately, not to this day has the city developed any one manufacturing interest so dominant . . . thereby to become a crushing liability in periods of financial distress."[30]

Springfield's variety of commercial/industrial enterprises, coupled with moderate economic growth, produced relatively benign demographic consequences. Griffin described the Springfield of 1872 as "a homogeneous municipality of the best New England sort."[31] Springfield did not have the disproportionately large immigrant population so common to the factory towns. Only 25 percent were foreign-born in 1875, and 10 percent of these were the easily assimilated English and Scottish;[32] there were 15,000 Irish and some 1,500 Germans in 1885. Irish men were manual laborers, and the women were usually domestics. The Germans were skilled workers for the most part, tradesmen, teamsters, gunmakers, brewers, and cigar makers. The Irish did not achieve political influence until 1900, when they also owned twenty-two of the city's thirty-five saloons. The period of major immigration of Italians, Russian Jews, and Poles was not to come until the turn of the century.[33] Thus, Springfield—remarkably similar to Worcester, another variegated commercial/industrial center[34]—was to attain a measure of urban prominence. Yet it would always be dwarfed and eclipsed by the metropolitan giant of the east, Boston.

Post-Civil War Boston was suffused with the smug confidence embodied in Emerson's praise of the city "as the town which was appointed in the destiny of nations to lead the civilization of North America." Describing William Dean Howells's arrival in 1866, twentieth-century author Van Wyck Brooks commented that Boston was "ripe for invasion," signifying the "commanding influence" of New England ideals in a city that was "a hallowed ground for thousands of the rising generations."[35] Actually, the invasion was to occur on a much different plane than that of the intellect. The Gilded Age was the period when Boston shed its small-scale, walking-city image to become the indecorous, sprawling, volatile metropolis of the present century.

Historian Sam Bass Warner chronicled the story of the "physical rearrangement" of Boston from a tightly packed merchant city of 200,000 in 1850, to an "industrial metropolis" in 1900 of over a million people in thirty-one cities and towns around a ten-mile radius.[36] The search for land to develop resulted in tons of gravel being dumped into the waters between Boston and Roxbury, creating the South End; the landfill of the area south of Beacon Street became the Back Bay. From an original 780 acres, by 1870 Boston extended over 24,000 acres, thirty times its previous size. The land grab continued with the political annexation of Roxbury (1867–68), Dorchester (1869–70), Charlestown, Brighton, and West Roxbury (1873–74); by 1875 the population tripled to 341,000.[37]

The "privatistic" urges of streetcar magnates and land speculators were not hindered by a city lacking zoning ordinances. Developments in sanitary engineering and the extension of municipal services motivated large financial institutions, small investors, and thousands of prospective home buyers to build new residences. Between 1870 and 1900, 22,500 homes went up for 167,000 suburbanites. By 1900 Boston became the typical metropolis of the twentieth century: an inner city of work and low-income residences, dotted with pockets of more affluent neighborhoods, and ringed by middle- and upper-income suburbs. The consequences of a metropolis built by accidental traffic patterns and unregulated capitalism was class segregation of the suburbs and confinement of the poor to the inner city slums.[38] For the most part, of course, the vast majority of Boston's poor in the Gilded Age were the city's newcomers.

Boston's first immigrants, largely the poorest peasants from southern Ireland, came in the 1840s and 1850s and found an inhospitable, anti-Catholic, already densely packed merchant/commercial city with few jobs available. With Boston's investors building factory towns, the unskilled, illiterate Irish peasants scrambled for positions as day laborers and domestics in a city economy that did not require great accumulations of labor. Before the Civil War, 35,000 Irish accounted for one-third of a total population of 160,000, and they remained, wrote historian Oscar Handlin, "a massive lump in the community, undigested, undigestible."[39] Arriving penniless and facing massive unemployment, whole families were forced to seek work at low-paying, temporary jobs. Many left the city to work in railroad construction or the new factory towns. Interestingly, the continued presence of large numbers of cheap Irish laborers stimulated an industrial boom in Boston proper.

By 1865 Boston had become the nation's fourth-largest manufacturing city. The sewing machine revolutionized the clothing industry, and the division of labor at cheap rates made Boston, by 1870, the center for the manufacture of low-cost, ready-made clothing. Various industries followed, among them piano factories, ironworks, shipyards, and distilleries.[40] Years later, a successful Irish politician, James Michael Curley, recalled his first factory job in 1889 at the age of fifteen in a piano works: "We slaved away in overalls and undershirts in the blistering temperatures required in those days in the manufacture of pianos. . . . During the nine months I worked there my weight dropped from 134 pounds to eighty. I was paid $7.50 a week until put on piecework, and when my pay increased to as much as $16 a week the boss put me back on the former schedule."[41] Curley complained and was fired.

New industry meant more jobs, and jobs meant more people flocking to the city in even greater numbers. The rate of population increase was well over 20 percent per decade from 1880 to 1900. The steady and continuous flow of Irish immigrants, 14.3 percent of the population in 1880, converged with that of migrant Yankee farmers; also 25,000 French Canadians arrived by that same year.[42] After 1890, record numbers of Jews, Italians, and others from southern and eastern Europe contributed to the rising material prosperity of the city.

Prosperity, however, was difficult to achieve for many of Boston's migrants. Sam Bass Warner speculated that whereas 40 to 50 percent of Boston's families were middle class in 1900, at least one-third were poor. It was to take two or three generations before an immigrant family could advance to the middle class. They faced job shortages due to seasonal layoffs, depression, and intense job competition. Immigrants lived in congested neighborhoods rife with disease and plagued by substandard living conditions. Furthermore, these ethnic groups tended to coalesce into clannish enclaves, a situation that bred nativism, resentment, and intergroup hostility.[43]

Middle-class social reformers feared that the immigrants "would depress the wage standard" for native-born workers, and that their alien lifestyles would "degrade family life."[44] As late as 1903, even after years of Puritanlike toil, the Irish were still regarded as inferior in the opinion of

Boston settlement-house reformers such as Frederick A. Bushee:

> It cannot be said that the ordinary Irishman is of a provident disposition; he lives in the present and worries comparatively little about the future. He is not extravagant in any particular way, but is wasteful in every way; it is his nature to drift when he ought to plan and economize. This disposition, combined with an ever-present tendency to drink too much, is liable to result in insecure employment and a small income. And to make matters worse, in families of this kind children are born with reckless regularity. So long as these children are wholly dependent, they are of course a burden upon their parents; but when children arrive at a wage-earning age, large families among the shiftless are better off than small families, because improvident families, if they had no children would not save the amount which the rearing of the children costs. The high rate of mortality among Irish children, however, makes the economic burden heavier.[45]

The intensity of slum life, combined with the Yankee middle- and upper-class dread of alien hordes violating moral codes and democratic principles, gave rise to exaggerated notions of rampant crime and vice in the city's streets. The evidence, however, suggests otherwise.

Serious crime in metropolitan Boston declined sharply from the mid-nineteenth to the mid-twentieth century. Two significant studies analyzing police arrest statistics in Boston relating to murder, forcible rape, robbery, assault, burglary, and larceny demonstrated that these crimes dropped off by nearly two-thirds. On the other hand, overall recorded crime rates increased. The crimes involved, however, were minor—drunkenness, truancy, unlicensed peddling, and traffic violations. The industrial revolution, historian Roger Lane contended, "demanded regularity of behavior, a life governed by obedience to the rhythms of clock and calendar."[46]

The autonomy and unrestricted personal freedom of rural life became intolerable, both in crowded urban centers and in a factory economy that insisted upon advanced forms of social control to maximize efficiency. Minor crimes, such as drunkenness, became objectionable and disruptive, and arrests rose markedly because of attitudinal changes and because the police and penal forces were enlarged and made more professional. Another factor in the peaceful assimilation of peasants into city life was a gradual but steady rise of the standard of living due to more permanent employment opportunities. Contrary to popular belief, urbanization was a major force in "civilizing" Boston's urban masses during and after the Gilded Age.[47]

Contributing to the process of social cohesion and peaceful coexistence in the new industrial commonwealth were the initial attempts of the state legislature to ameliorate the worst excesses of urban and factory life. Robert Woods, the pioneering settlement-house founder and social reformer, wrote that the immigrant "incursion" had precipitated "sanitary, industrial and moral problems so threatening that it became necessary to call upon the state for new and unprecedented forms of legislative action."[48] In general, legislators of both parties never doubted the beneficial aspects of the industrial revolution. Even so, Massachusetts was the first state to undertake some measure of regulation of competition and to enact early forms of factory legislation to protect helpless workers.

One historian of Gilded Age Massachusetts even suggested that the state legislature's reform efforts in the area of industrial legislation predated the Progressive Era. Lord Bryce's comment that the General Court in 1888 was "substantially pure and does its work well" seems an overstatement, yet by the end of the century the legislature's actions were impressive.[49] In 1869 the state established a railroad commission to mediate between railroads and the public interest. They created a Board of Gas and Electric Light Commissioners in 1885, with added powers in 1887, 1893, and 1894, allowing for rate fixing, the control of competition, and the governing of stock sales. Commissions on hospitals, asylums, libraries, charities, penal institutions, and a Bureau of Labor Statistics followed.

A summary list of laws relating to labor regulation and governing political practices were the first passed in the nation: the 1866 Factory Inspection Act, a ten-hour limit for women and children in 1874, an 1886 weekly payments measure, an employers' liability act, a law outlawing contract labor, an 1887 act making Labor Day a holiday, the Secret Ballot Act of 1888, the 1890 Lobby Regulation Act, the 1891 abolition of the poll tax for voting, and the 1892 Corrupt Practices Act.[50] The motivation behind these legislative measures remains obscure. That some historians view these activities as pure political pandering to special interest groups, or as ineffective "show pieces of conservative reform," begs the issue.[51] The salient fact is that the state legislature of Massachusetts faced up to the realities of the age well before the rest of the nation.

The end of the century brought more changes to Massachusetts. The economy seemed to be in an advantageous competitive position because of its early start. However, competition from other regions, such as the South with its lower labor and transportation costs, and New York and Philadelphia with their major ports and financial dominance, soon spelled the end to Massachusetts's preeminence. Conspicuous in this economic demise was the defusion of the capitalistic drives of Boston's elite and their increased commitment to an aristocratic tradition that looked askance at trade. The "twilight of Brahmin entrepreneurship coincided with the economic decline of Boston and New England."[52] Professor Barrett Wendell of Harvard lamented on this loss of Brahmin power: "We are vanishing into provincial obscurity . . . America has swept from our grasp. The future is behind us."[53] Happily, not many shared this morbid vision, and the continued immigrant flood of Italians, Jews, Poles, and hosts of others demonstrated that Massachusetts still offered viable and attractive economic opportunities. The prosperity of Massachusetts in the twentieth century would lean heavily on the economic foundations built in the Gilded Age.

This economic survey of the last thirty-five years of nineteenth-century Massachusetts leaves much unexplored. How individuals and groups in the population responded to momentous economic change is the subject of this book. Politicians, laborers, immigrants, elites, ministers, social reformers, and countless others all have a story to be told. What is fascinating is both the variety and commonality of their experiences—a sharing of the turmoil of change and a resolution to seek personal and collective improvement. The following essays examine the complexity, confusion, and sensitivity of the people of Massachusetts during their confrontation with the Age of Economic Revolution.

Notes

* I wish to thank David Cantor, Edwin Gabler, John Ifkovic, and Martin Kaufman for reading and criticizing this essay.

1. Henry Adams, from letters of 1893 and 1895, quoted in Van Wyck Brooks, *New England: Indian Summer 1865–1915* (New York, 1940), p. 494 n.15. For an interpretation of late nineteenth-century America as a "heterogeneous polyarchy, a network of accommodation and compromise" in an era of Victorian "cultural absolutism," see Jon C. Teaford, *The Unheralded Triumph: City Government in America, 1870–1900* (Baltimore, 1984), p. 9. For a discussion of the "twilight of the Brahmins," see Frederic C. Jaher, *The Urban Establishment: Upper Strata in Boston, New York, Charleston, Chicago, and Los Angeles* (Champaign/Urbana, 1982), pp. 88, 89; Carl N. Degler, *The Age of the Economic Revolution, 1876/1900* (Glenview, Ill., 1977), p. iii.

2. Carl Siracusa, *A Mechanical People: Perceptions of the Industrial Order in Massachusetts, 1810–1880* (Middletown, Conn., 1979), pp. 16–18, 23–24.

3. Ibid., pp. 10, 22, 36.

4. Ibid., table 1, table 2, p. 22.

5. The decline of Massachusetts industrial growth in the twentieth century may be related to the diminishing significance of the Port of Boston. Robert W. Eisenmenger, *The Dynamics of Growth in the New England Economy* (Middletown, Conn., 1967), p. 19.

6. Edward C. Kirkland, *Men, Cities and Transportation: A Study in New England History, 1820–1900* (Cambridge, Mass., 1948), pp. 284–85, 362, 368, and chaps. 11, 12.

7. Stephan Thernstrom, *The Other Bostonians: Poverty and Progress in the American Metropolis, 1880–1970* (Cambridge, Mass., 1973), pp. 221, 228, 11.

8. Eisenmenger, *Dynamics of Growth*, pp. 60, 75.

9. Siracusa, *Mechanical People*, table 4, p. 29; Richard D. Brown, *Massachusetts: A Bicentennial History* (New York, 1978), p. 188.

10. *Springfield's Ethnic Heritage: The French and French-Canadian Community* (Springfield, Mass., 1976), p. 9.

11. Siracusa, *Mechanical People*, p. 260 n. 24.

12. Eisenmenger, *Dynamics of Growth*, p. 63.

13. Michael H. Frisch, *Town into City: Springfield, Massachusetts, and the Meaning of Community, 1840–1880* (Cambridge, Mass., 1972), p. 123.

14. Roger Lane, "Urbanization and Criminal Violence in the Nineteenth Century," in *American Urban History*, ed. Alexander Callow, 2d ed. (New York, 1973), p. 196.

15. Jaher, *Urban Establishment*, pp. 20, 22, 23, 25, 37, 38.

16. Ibid., p. 86.

17. Vera Shlakman, *Economic History of a Factory Town: A Study of Chicopee, Massachusetts* (Northampton, Mass., 1935), pp. 14, 15, 24, 31, 35–37; Jaher, *Urban Establishment*, pp. 50–53.

18. Shlakman, *Economic History*, tables on pp. 39–42.

19. Ibid., pp. 37–38, 42–44.

20. Siracusa, *Mechanical People*, table 8, p. 38.

21. Howard M. Gitelman, *Workingmen of Waltham: Mobility in American Urban Industrial Development, 1850–1890* (Baltimore, 1974), pp. 164–68, 169, 170, 180.

22. Margaret Parker, *Lowell: A Study of Industrial Development* (New York, 1940), pp. 59–69, 89–99, 172.

23. Donald Cole, *Immigrant City: Lawrence, Massachusetts, 1845–1921* (Chapel Hill, 1963), pp. 20–22, 27–32, 41–43, 56, 67.

24. John T. Cumbler, *Working-Class Community in Industrial America: Work, Leisure, and Struggle in Two Industrial Cities, 1880–1930* (Westport, Conn., 1979), pp. 8, 99–105, 108–10, 113, 118, 120. See also Thomas R.

Smith, *Cotton Textile Industry of Fall River, Massachusetts: A Study of Industrial Localization* (New York, 1944).

25. Cumbler, *Working-Class Community,* pp. 5–8, 16, 17, 22, 36–40, 61. See Alan Dawley, *Class and Community: The Industrial Revolution in Lynn* (Cambridge, Mass., 1976); and Paul G. Faler, *Mechanics and Manufacturers in the Early Industrial Revolution: Lynn, Massachusetts, 1780–1860* (Albany, 1981).

26. Shlakman, *Economic History,* pp. 15, 26, 39, 98, 138, 195, 211, 226.

27. Constance M. Green, *Holyoke, Massachusetts: A Case History of the Industrial Revolution in America* (New Haven, 1939), pp. 12–16, 64, 116–17, 148–50, 163, 175–87, 195.

28. Writer's Program, Massachusetts, *Springfield, Massachusetts* (Springfield, Mass., 1941), p. 17.

29. Ibid., pp. 50–54; Frisch, *Town into City,* pp. 6, 78, 118, 121.

30. Solomon B. Griffin, *People and Politics, by a Massachusetts Editor* (Boston, 1923), p. 14.

31. Ibid., p. 3.

32. Frisch, *Town into City,* p. 124.

33. *Springfield's Ethnic Heritage,* pp. 12, 15, 22, 25.

34. The history of Worcester still needs to be done. Aside from the work of boosters and antiquarians, the one satisfactory study that partly fills the vacuum is that of Roy Rosenzweig, *Eight Hours for What We Will: Workers and Leisure in an Industrial City, 1870–1920* (New York, 1983). In addition, several other cities and factory towns not discussed have yet to find scholarly biographers. A fine study of the industrial revolution in antebellum southern Worcester County is that of Jonathan Prude, *The Coming of Industrial Order: Town and Factory Life in Rural Massachusetts, 1810–1860* (New York, 1983).

35. Brooks, *New England,* p. 5.

36. Sam Bass Warner, *Streetcar Suburbs: The Process of Growth in Boston, 1870–1900* (Cambridge, Mass., 1962), p. 1.

37. Andrew J. Peters, "Boston—The Municipality, 1890–1930," in *The Commonwealth History of Massachusetts,* ed. Albert B. Hart, vol. 5 (New York, 1930), p. 70; Thomas O'Connor, *Bibles, Brahmins and Bosses: A Short History of Boston* (Boston, 1976), pp. 84–85.

38. Warner, *Streetcar Suburbs,* pp. 2–4, 17, 92, 98, 160–62.

39. Oscar Handlin, *Boston's Immigrants, 1790–1880: A Study in Acculturation,* rev. and enl. (Cambridge, Mass., 1972), p. 55.

40. Ibid., pp. 74–77.

41. James Michael Curley, *I'd Do It Again: A Record of All My Uproarious Years* (Englewood Cliffs, N.J., 1957), p. 43.

42. Handlin, *Boston's Immigrants,* pp. 212–13; Thernstrom, *Other Bostonians,* pp. 10–11.

43. Warner, *Streetcar Suburbs,* pp. 8, 9, 11.

44. Robert A. Woods, ed., *Americans in Process* (Boston, 1903), p. 8.

45. Frederick A. Bushee, *Ethnic Factors in the Population of Boston* (New York, 1903), p. 93. This analysis of the "shiftlessness" of the Irish raises disturbingly familiar connections with some present-day social science interpretations of poverty. See, for instance, Edward Banfield, *The Unheavenly City* (Boston, 1968), pp. 53, 229.

46. Lane, "Urbanization," p. 196.

47. Ibid.; Theodore Ferdinand, "The Criminal Patterns of Boston since 1849," *American Journal of Sociology* 73 (July 1967): 84–99.

48. Woods, *Americans in Process*, p. 7.

49. Richard Abrams, *Conservatism in a Progressive Era: Massachusetts Politics, 1900–1912* (Cambridge, Mass., 1964), pp. 3, 5.

50. Ibid., pp. 5–9, 11–13; Richard Harmond, "Troubles of Massachusetts Republicans during the 1880s," *Mid-America* 56 (April 1974): 89–90; Geoffrey Blodgett, *The Gentle Reformers: Democrats in the Cleveland Era* (Cambridge, Mass., 1966), p. 118.

51. Ibid., p. 118; Siracusa, *Mechanical People*, pp. 151–81.

52. Jaher, *Urban Establishment*, p. 93.

53. Brooks, *New England*, p. 419.

TWO

The Response to Economic Change: Politics and Ethnicity

Introduction

The new industrial society created a multitude of problems for Massachusetts. Massive demographic change and the redistribution of the population into urban communities forced the political parties to reevaluate their ideological positions and to reconsider the basis of their political constituencies. The industrial worker was either catered to or attacked, depending upon the possibilities of obtaining pluralities. In turn, workers perceived that politics was a possible avenue by which to improve the conditions affecting their lives. To promote economic and social betterment through politics, however, was to follow a path fraught with difficulty. Deeply felt antagonisms based upon whether one was an artisan or a machine-tender, a Yankee, an Irishman, or a French Canadian, a Protestant or a Catholic, limited the possibility of achieving political success. More immediate concerns such as wages and working conditions divided the skilled and unskilled workers and prevented compromise and political coalition building. Discontented workers sought redress by strikes and by attempts to unionize. These labor struggles occurred within a turbulent political scenario and represented a major response by workers and politicians to the "Age of Economic Revolution" in Massachusetts.

The post-Civil War period saw the state's Republicans in power, a condition of ascendancy that would last well into the twentieth century. They controlled the congressional seats with large majorities and monopolized the Senate.

They dominated both houses of the General Court from 1865 to 1948. They retained the governship until 1905, with the exception of the years 1874–75, 1883–84, 1891–94; the only time the Republican vote dropped below 50 percent was in the divisive days of the Mugwump revolt in 1884.[1] Although the Civil War left the Democrats in ruins, they re-emerged as a substantial political force through their alliance with the Irish masses, who viewed the Republican party as both anti-Catholic and anti-Irish.

The Republican domination graphically illustrated the fragmented and pluralistic electorate in industrialized Massachusetts. Diversity of interests among special groups, and apathy among voters, kept Republican politicians in office even though they no longer held clear-cut majorities. Both parties attempted to act as brokers among the contending forces that made up the electorate.[2] Issues such as civil service reform, the tariff, nativism, temperance, economic depression, and controversies over state control of municipal services, had important consequences for party strategy and voter preference. In his essay on the Massachusetts voter, Dale Baum analyzes the impact of these issues on the voter. He argues that "in narrow terms of the underlying distribution of partisan loyalties, the voting alignments forged in war persisted into the twentieth century," but "the ideological division which originally shaped these alignments did not survive." With the Irish wed to the Democrats, the opportunistic Republicans took a more open-ended, pluralistic political approach. Senator George Frisbee Hoar, aged leader of Massachusetts Republicans, wrote to the newly prominent Henry Cabot Lodge in 1883: "Unless we can break this compact foreign vote, we are gone, and the grand chapter of the old Massachusetts history is closed."[3]

Whereas Republicans equivocated as to proper strategy

—fluctuating on the dubious issues of temperance and nativism to sway blocs of voters[4]—they welcomed the growing affiliation of one Catholic working-class group, the
French Canadians. Arriving after the Irish, willing to work
at lower wages, and hostile to labor unions, the French-
Canadian peasants were treated miserably by Yankee Protestant and Irish Catholic alike. State Labor Commissioner
Carroll D. Wright characterized them as "the Chinese of the
Eastern states." He went on to say: "These people have one
[sic] good trait. They are indefatigable workers and docile."[5]
The French Canadians, on their part, hated the Irish, not
only because of ill-treatment at their hands, but also because of the Fenian raids on Canada between 1866 and 1871.
Thus, the French Canadians saw themselves as outside any
one particular party, and were constantly vigilant as to
which party would respond to their special ethnic/religious
needs. An example of the French-Canadian struggle to gain
political power is illustrated in Peter Haebler's essay on ethnic politics in Holyoke. His conclusion is that although the
French Canadians had become politically involved, "they
were still not able to make significant inroads into the political power structure and thus continued to take what they
could from the Republicans."

Doubting the potential for success in Republican-dominated state politics, most ethnic groups focused attention
on the more pressing economic issues of the day. Wages actually declined in Massachusetts from 1869 to 1909.[6] Wage
cuts, especially in textiles, occurred whenever overproduc-
tion brought prices down. Working long hours and facing
job speedups, affected by innovations in mechanization
that eliminated positions, living in unhealthy and crowded
tenements, workers responded with walkouts, strikes, and
union organization.

However, efforts at worker solidarity were made difficult

by a host of circumstances. The persistent rift between skilled and unskilled labor seemed bridged momentarily by the popular acceptance in 1885 of the Knights of Labor, with its call for one large, all-inclusive union. Nevertheless, the reverberations of Chicago's Haymarket affair of 1886, and the move to organize on more pragmatic trade lines, quickly put an end to the Knights' popularity and viability as a labor organization in Massachusetts and elsewhere. Because of the perennial oversupply of unskilled labor, workers' sporadic attempts at strikes were easily quelled by stubborn employers. Even when skilled workers successfully organized, such as the cotton mule spinners in 1889, they soon found their union useless when the owners introduced "ring spinning," which allowed the use of unskilled labor.[7] Wage and hour reductions in Fall River in 1875 encouraged large numbers of workers to join unions. The employers responded by a lock-out intended to break the unions; after holding out as long as possible, the workers surrendered and only those who would sign "yellow dog" contracts could return to work.[8]

Another serious threat to working-class unity was ethnic conflict. A typical tactic of employer union-busting was to pit immigrants against each other and against native-American workers through the use of scab labor. In the 1870s, Fall River owners actively recruited French Canadians to blunt the growing militant unionism of English and Irish workers; the strike of 1879 was broken by bringing in French Canadians as "knobsticks," or scabs.[9] Holyoke workers first organized in the 1880s because of fear of job competition from the newly arrived French Canadians.[10] By 1890 working-class Lawrence was characterized as a city in which "Irish and natives ruled French Canadians."[11]

The French-Canadian culture was already hostile to things English, with priests and shopkeepers in Quebec advising would-be migrants of the evils of joining unions. Retaining their language and religion, building their own churches and parochial schools, residing in tightly knit residential communities, they came into conflict with other working-class groups. Thomas A. McMullin tells the complicated story of worker response to industrialism in New Bedford, and of the many pitfalls encountered by workers' organizations because of ethnic differences. "The experience of textile workers in New Bedford," he wrote, "suggests that immigrants did not adjust to urban industrial conditions in a uniform manner." Although some concessions on wages and conditions were achieved, at the end of the century workers' groups accomplished little, except sharing the belief that unions were imperative for survival in industrialized Massachusetts.

Jack Tager

Notes

1. Alec Barbrook, *God Save the Commonwealth: An Electoral History of Massachusetts* (Amherst, Mass., 1973), p. 11; Peter Eisinger, "Ethnic Political Transition in Boston, 1884–1933: Some Lessons for Contemporary Cities," *Political Science Quarterly* 93 (1978): 236.
2. Richard D. Brown, *Massachusetts: A Bicentennial History* (New York, 1978), p. 186.
3. Barbrook, *God Save the Commonwealth*, p. 16.
4. Richard Harmond, "Troubles of Massachusetts Republicans during the 1880s," *Mid-America* 56 (April 1974): 89–91, 97–98.
5. *Springfield's Ethnic Heritage: The French and French-Canadian Community* (Springfield, Mass., 1976), p. 10.
6. Robert W. Eisenmenger, *The Dynamics of Growth in the New England Economy* (Middletown, Conn., 1967), p. 24.
7. George W. Coleman, "Labor and the Labor Movement, 1860–1930," *The Commonwealth History of Massachusetts,* ed. Albert B. Hart, vol. 5 (New York, 1930), pp. 433–36.
8. John T. Cumbler, *Working-Class Community in Industrial America: Work, Leisure, and Struggle in Two Industrial Cities, 1880–1930* (Westport, Conn., 1979), pp. 166–69.

9. Ibid., p. 120.
10. Constance M. Green, *Holyoke, Massachusetts: A Case History of the Industrial Revolution in America* (New Haven, 1939), p. 200.
11. Donald Cole, *Immigrant City: Lawrence, Massachusetts, 1845–1921* (Chapel Hill, 1963), p. 67.

The Massachusetts Voter:
Party Loyalty in the Gilded Age,
1872–1896

DALE BAUM

Most historians who write about nineteenth-century politics do not have the type of information supplied by modern
opinion polls and, as a consequence, have been forced to
develop rather complicated methods of statistical inference
to analyze and describe earlier American voters. Insofar as
much of this research has concentrated on the Midwest,
older eastern states such as Massachusetts may display a
quite different electoral history. The picture of the Bay State
voter in the Gilded Age presented here is based in part on
the observations of contemporaries of the period, but it is
also derived from a sophisticated quantitative analysis of
city and town voting returns and census data. Some aspects
of this picture may resemble voting patterns in the late
twentieth century. In other ways, however, the Gilded Age
was a startling, different political world, not always inferior
to our own.[1]

The most notable characteristic of Gilded Age politics was
the strength of party identification among the voters.
George S. Merriam, a firsthand observer of Massachusetts
politics for many years, explained in 1885 'that men were
bound to their parties ''by a tie not so much of reason as of
habit, sentiment, and finally of inheritance; so that John
Smith is a Republican or a Democrat because his father was

one before him; and hardly asks himself seriously why he prefers his party any more than he asks why he prefers Mrs. John Smith to other women, or John Smith, Junior, to other boys."[2]

This view of party loyalty is consistent with the interpretation of party identification advanced by a team of political scientists at the University of Michigan in their classic study, *The American Voter* (1960). What remains a matter of controversy is the measurement of stability and change in party loyalties. The prevailing model of electoral change is based on the concept of "critical elections" and party systems. Put briefly, this perspective divides the evolution of national politics into stable phases disrupted by infrequent, brief, and intense periods of realignment, resulting in five distinct party "eras." The first, so-called preparty system, spanning the years from 1789 to 1820, prefaced the creation of truly national and competitive partisan organizations such as the Democratic and Whig parties. These two parties flourished during the second period, from 1824 to the massive reshuffling of voters in the 1850s. The third party era was the Civil War party system, which was firmly entrenched by 1860 with the rise to power of the first purely sectional party, the Republicans. During the 1890s a new electoral era resulted from agrarian discontent in the South and West, coupled with urban dissatisfaction with the Democrats in the Northeast. Finally, the New Deal marked the last party system, issuing from the economic depression of the 1930s, and persisting until the Great Society of Lyndon Baines Johnson.[3]

According to "critical election" theory, each electoral era consists of a stable period which begins and ends with fluctuation and then realignment. During stability, individuals continually vote for the same party, and so party loyalty remains constant. Voters seldom cross party lines between elections and the political balance remains unchanged. The placid equilibrium is eventually shattered by one or a few "critical" or "realigning" elections in which many voters abruptly shift their party allegiance. This electoral reorganization results from many factors, the most important of which is that new issues arise which cut across old party alignments. Individuals then are aroused to reassess their political beliefs and party preferences, and new coalitions of voters are formed along with another political balance between the two parties. Realignment provokes changes in party platforms, legislative outputs, and approaches to issues. More important, the public may form different ideas or perceptions about the nation's political process.[4]

The idea of a Civil War party system is thus the central organizing motif for studying American electoral history during the second half of the nineteenth century. Historians have further divided this electoral era into two phases of stability: before and after 1874, the year in which national Republican hegemony was destroyed by Democratic congressional victories. Although the Democrats were not subsequently able to establish dominance, intense electoral competition with Republicans throughout the late 1870s and 1880s characterized the second phase of the Civil War party system. Minor parties, such as the Greenbackers and Prohibitionists, arose along with factions such as the Mugwumps, and contemporaries often perceived these groups as important because they might be able to tip the balance of power in closely contested elections.[5]

The methodology employed in this study—ecological regression estimation of voter transition probabilities in contingency tables—makes possible a subtle and precise assessment of the changing patterns of party preference in Massachusetts presidential politics in the late nineteenth century. By employing this technique, estimates of the proportions of voters moving across party lines, including Republican-to-Democrat and Democrat-to-Republican party switches, have been calculated for every sequential successive and alternative pair of presidential elections from 1864 to 1904 (see table 1). For all these Massachusetts elections, these are the first estimates that have ever been made based on a relatively sophisticated statistical procedure. These estimates reveal that Bay State voter behavior in the presidential elections of the late nineteenth century does not fit the predictions of "critical election" theory, for there is both more stability and volatility in electoral outcomes than this theory would suggest. In Massachusetts, no critical election or period shatters voter coalitions created by the Civil War experience; and yet there is instability in voter alignments throughout the period.[6]

According to the estimates in Table 1, at no time during the 1864 to 1904 period did more than 7 percent of the eligible voters switch from one party to another, even if third parties are included. In the seven presidential contests of the 1870s, 1880s, and 1890s, on the average over successive election pairs, slightly less than 5 percent of the electorate crossed party lines from one election to the next. The size of Republican-to-Democrat and Democrat-to-Republican party switchers over the span of these same successive elections was, on the average, equal to a very low 2 percent of the electorate.[7] Most of the volatility in the electoral process involved the entry of new voters or the departure of previous voters. In other words, voter turnout fluctuated from one election to the next, and turnout was as important in shaping the outcome of presidential elections as voters switching parties. Moreover, some of the total amount of shuffling across party lines was apparently temporary. According to the estimates of voting patterns over sequential alternative elections (or successive pairs of elections eight years apart), the second election—with two important exceptions—tended to reestablish the coalitions of eight years earlier, or at least wiped out some of the gains made previously by either major party at the expense of the other.

The intense and stable partisanship of the late nineteenth century sharply contrasted with the electoral volatility of the decade before the Civil War. The well-documented massive shuffling of voters between parties in the 1850s was a cumulative process, in that old coalitions of voters were never again reassembled.[8] This is significant, for, unlike in many other states when the shifting of voters largely ceased after the outbreak of civil war, the Massachusetts men who voted in 1864 for Abraham Lincoln did not represent a reconstitution of the old Whig party. Nor, for that matter, were those voting for the Republicans in the 1850s the same as those who a decade earlier supported the anti-Catholic and anti-immigrant Know-Nothing party. Likewise, the old Jacksonian Democratic party survived in name only as its mass constituency underwent fundamental realignment. In short, party affiliation in the late antebellum period, excluding, of course, Free Soilers and Liberty party men, was a poor predictor, at least in Massachusetts, of postwar voting alignments. Antislavery crusades and emotional years of civil war had etched a new line of cleavage into the Bay State electorate until the old lines dividing voters were thoroughly destroyed. And for at least a generation following Robert E. Lee's surrender at Appomattox, memories of the Civil War, its antislavery antecedents, and its Reconstruction aftermath helped forge the links of voter loyalty in the Bay State as well as in the entire nation.[9]

However, during the war years, one group among the Bay State Democrats had neither altered its partisan commitments nor temporarily shifted party allegiances throughout the electoral upheavals of the 1850s. These were

Table 1 Regression Estimates of Stability and Change in Party Preference: Massachusetts Presidential Elections, 1864–1904 (in percentages of electorate)

A. Sequential Successive Presidential Elections

Election Pair	Actual Number of Cities and Towns	Repeat Dem.	Repeat Rep.	Repeat 3rd Party	Repeat Not Voting	(Total Stability)	Rep. to Dem.	Dem. to Rep.
1864–1868	(332)	19	46	—	21	(86)	—	—
1868–1872	(334)	13	37	—	27	(77)	5	1
1872–1876	(338)	16	32	—	25	(73)	2	—
1876–1880	(341)	27	33	—	24	(84)	—	1
1880–1884	(344)	22	29	1	23	(75)	1	—
1884–1888	(346)	24	29	1	25	(79)	1	—
1888–1892	(350)	27	31	1	20	(79)	—	—
1892–1896[a]	(351)	16	36	2	22	(76)	—	3
1896–1900	(352)	15	39	—	25	(79)	—	—
1900–1904	(353)	22	35	2	30	(89)	—	—

B. Sequential Alternative Presidential Elections

Election Pair	Actual Number of Cities and Towns	Repeat Dem.	Repeat Rep.	Repeat 3rd Party	Repeat Not Voting	(Total Stability)	Rep. to Dem.	Dem. to Rep.
1864–1872	331	11	33	—	24	(68)	—	1
1868–1876	331	15	32	—	26	(73)	6	—
1872–1880	337	15	26	—	21	(62)	—	—
1876–1884	342	23	27	—	23	(73)	—	—
1880–1888	343	24	27	—	21	(72)	—	—
1884–1892	346	21	25	1	23	(70)	3	—
1888–1896[a]	350	16	30	—	24	(70)	—	2
1892–1900	350	26	33	—	30	(89)	—	—
1896–1904	352	14	35	—	26	(75)	—	—

NOTE: The estimates were computed by a multivariate version of ecological inference outlined in J. Morgan Kousser, "The 'New Political History': A Methodological Critique," *Reviews in American History* 4 (March 1976): 13, n. 11. Logically but not statistically impossible estimates which fell slightly outside the 0% to 100% range were set at their respective minimum or maximum limits, and values of the remaining estimates were then adjusted according to the restraints of the actual numbers of individuals within each category of the independent and dependent variables. This procedure eliminated a few negative estimates. In following this procedure, however, no modifications were made in the logical estimates of voters repeating a vote for the same party in both elections. Estimates of the percentage of abstainers in the first election who subsequently did not vote in the second election were also unaffected by this procedure, providing original esti-

New Dems.	New Reps.	Dem. Dropout	Rep. Dropout	3rd Party to Dem.	3rd Party to Rep.	Dems. to 3rd Party	Reps. to 3rd Party	(Total Insta-bility)[b]
4	7	—	3	—	—	—	—	(14)
2	6	6	3	—	—	—	—	(23)
11	10	—	3	—	—	—	—	(26)
2	8	—	4	—	—	—	1	(16)
5	5	1	6	—	—	3	2	(25)
3	8	2	—	4	2	—	1	(21)
7	6	2	4	—	1	—	1	(21)
—	10	8	—	—	—	4	—	(25)
9	—	—	5	2	—	—	1	(21)
3	4	2	1	—	—	—	—	(11)

New Dems.	New Reps.	Dem. Dropout	Rep. Dropout	3rd Party to Dem.	3rd Party to Rep.	Dems. to 3rd Party	Reps. to 3rd Party	(Total Insta-bility)[b]
8	10	4	9	—	—	—	—	(32)
9	10	1	—	—	—	—	—	(26)
13	16	—	7	—	—	—	1	(37)
6	7	—	5	—	—	2	3	(26)
8	11	—	6	—	1	—	2	(28)
7	12	2	—	3	2	—	—	(30)
—	16	4	2	—	1	4	—	(30)
—	5	3	—	—	1	—	—	(11)
8	4	—	6	3	1	—	1	(24)

mates fell similarly within the 0% to 100% range. For reasons to have more confidence in these estimates than others, see W. Phillips Shively, " 'Ecological' Inference: The Use of Aggregate Data to Study Individuals," *American Political Science Review* 63, no. 4 (December 1969): 1191.

[a]The Democratic vote in 1896 includes only those voting for William Jennings Bryan on the "regular" Democratic ticket.

[b]Total instability includes, in addition, a few other combinations of possible voter behavior between two elections not reported here, namely, segments of the electorate comprised of third-party supporters who were previous nonvoters, and former third-party voters who either subsequently abstained or voted for a different minor or third party.

the state's Irish-American citizens. Hostile to the antislavery cause on the one side and to the anti-Catholic nativist movement on the other, the Irish remained loyal to the Democrats. In 1864 they were the party's most important constituents casting, according to one estimate, over one-third of George B. McClellan's total vote. In presidential contests throughout the remainder of the nineteenth century, the Irish vote was disproportionately found in the Democratic column—even in the 1872 election when the Massachusetts Democratic ticket was laden with former Republicans.[10]

The 1872 presidential election has traditionally been viewed as a victory for the status quo, implying that party lines held firm in Ulysses S. Grant's crushing defeat of the eccentric Horace Greeley. Because of the lopsided Republican victory in Massachusetts, it has been seductively easy for historians to conclude that few rank-and-file Republicans bolted to the Liberal Republican and Democratic opposition. In short, most accounts of the Grant-Greeley contest agree that Republican defections did not amount to much, and were certainly less than the number of Republicans who would bolt in 1884 to protest their party's nomination of James G. Blaine.[11]

Yet bitter intraparty factionalism had wracked Bay State Republicans in 1872. Disillusioned with the Grant administration, an assortment of Republicans announced their support for any one or combination of the following: tariff reduction, free trade, civil service reform, efficient and honest government, and sectional harmony or reconciliation between North and South. These self-styled "Liberals" drew on the tenets of nineteenth-century "liberalism" that stressed laissez-faire economics and limited government. Few of them were concerned with the plight of immigrants living in crowded urban slums or with the grim daily lot of factory workers. Some were even hostile to the labor movement, believing it was an illegal conspiracy of workers determined to impose their terms on their employers. Thus, many found a refuge in the Liberal Republican movement from such reformist consequences of radical Republican ideology as the revitalization of the labor movement, which raised the specter of class conflict in their communities after the Civil War. These conservative Republicans were joined in an uneasy alliance with many anti-Grant radical Republicans. The refusal of many radicals to support Grant's reelection stemmed from their anger at the humiliating treatment that their leader, Senator Charles Sumner, had received from administration Republicans because of his opposition to Santo Domingo annexation. Many of Sumner's close political friends in the influential Bird Club, a dominant power in state politics since 1860, moved initially into the Liberal Republican movement when it became clear that Republicans would renominate Grant.[12]

By 1872 even former "Copperheads" realized that the Democratic party could not continue to fight the changes brought about by the Civil War. But the party was so disorganized that its only hope lay in exploiting divisions among Republicans. Only the most imaginative minds in 1871 could have predicted that in 1872 a radical Republican would be the gubernatorial candidate of the Massachusetts Democratic party. The "Liberal Republican and Democratic" nomination went to Frank Bird, the organizer of the club bearing his name and Sumner's close friend and political confidant. Bird was neither a favorite of the Democratic rank-and-file nor, for that matter, of many Liberals. At the Cincinnati convention that nominated Greeley, Bird had concentrated his efforts at preventing the selection of

Charles Francis Adams, the champion of the Massachusetts conservative Republicans and Sumner's arch-rival in state politics.[13]

Had Adams and not Greeley headed the 1872 anti-Grant coalition ticket, perhaps many more Republican leaders would have vented their displeasure with Grant through party revolt. Placing Massachusetts's own Henry Wilson on the ticket with Grant no doubt steadied many who wavered. Republican Congressman George Frisbie Hoar told his Worcester County constituents that by supporting Grant's reelection, he was reluctantly differing with the one person with whom he had been in complete agreement throughout his whole life. At the top of the Republican party pyramid relatively few prominent Republicans took the final step of actually casting a ballot for Greeley and the Liberal Republicans. Many Mugwumps or Independent Republicans who deserted their party in 1884 never considered voting for Greeley in 1872. Boston businessman John Murray Forbes was such an individual. The newer issues of tariff reform and honest government never took precedence in his mind over the need for continued protection of the southern blacks. Forbes warned that if Greeley were elected with Democratic votes, the new president would be drawn into the "reactionary vortex."[14]

Sumner's inability to convince many of his closest friends to vote for Greeley, and the landslide victory of the Grant-Wilson ticket should no longer be allowed to conceal the amount of shifting that occurred across party lines. For many rank-and-file Republicans the prospect of repudiating Sumner in their support of Grant proved troublesome. Republican party defections were far greater in 1872 than was the case twelve years later with the celebrated Mugwump revolt (see table 1). Slightly over one-tenth of the 1868 Republicans cast ballots for Greeley, thus directly repudiating the man they helped to elect to the presidency four years earlier. The reason why these bolters did not make the outcome closer is found in the high rate of Democratic nonvoting. About 30 percent of the 1868 Democrats sat out the balloting, demonstrating the reluctance of the Democratic rank-and-file to vote for a former Republican who had abused them for years in the editorial columns of the New York *Tribune*.[15]

A few 1868 Democrats were so repulsed by the 1872 coalition ticket that they voted for Grant (see table 1). This marked the first significant defection in twelve years in an otherwise solid Bay State Democratic coalition. A clue to the identities of these Democratic "bolters" is imbedded in the behavior of some prominent former Whig party men who, after the outbreak of the Civil War, protested radical Republican policies by joining the Democrats. But swallowing Greeley's candidacy proved too much for them. Former Whig party leader and Boston Brahmin Robert C. Winthrop felt that only "discord and confusion" would have resulted from the success of "so unnatural a combination as Greeley and the Democrats," and accordingly, he voted Republican in 1872 for the first time in his life.[16]

The 1872 election marked the eclipse of the emotional and ideological politics of the war and Reconstruction years. When Sumner, Bird, and Adams voted Democratic, they taught the Bay State electorate that political independence was not necessarily treasonable. At the state and local level the Massachusetts Democratic party gained a new respectability as it shook off its old wartime image as an outright friend of the rebelling South. Capitalizing on voter discontent caused by the economic depression, the local liquor issues, and the disclosures of scandals in the Grant administration, the Democrats in 1874 captured the governorship and destroyed the Republican monopoly on congressional seats. Although Democratic party chieftains hailed the "fresh accessions of strength" to their ranks, they were aware of the extremely tenuous hold their party had on the voters. Democrats had skillfully exploited newer issues and neutralized older ones relating to Reconstruction—at times even endorsing Grant's southern policy. Through this strategy the Democratic party allowed Bay Staters to vote against a Republican without forcing them also to reject the fourteen-year history of the Republican party's civil rights progress.[17]

The revival of Democratic party fortunes in Massachusetts presidential politics began with the 1876 election. As in 1872, the Democrats continued their efforts to woo disaffected Republicans by persuading a former Republican, Charles Francis Adams, to stand for governor on the ticket with presidential candidate Samuel J. Tilden. Bay State Democrats who had stayed away from the polls four years earlier under the stimulus of a Greeley candidacy now returned to their party. Although only about 65 percent of the 1868 Democrats voted for Greeley in 1872, about 94 percent voted for Tilden in 1876 (see table 1). Therefore, approximately 29 percent of the 1868 Democrats returned to the fold in 1876, making the Greeley-Grant contest of 1872 a deviating election for the Democrats.

Another look at voting patterns between 1868 and 1876 reveals that Tilden's vote represented more than a mere recovery from the Greeley debacle. Not only did Tilden's candidacy reunite many Democrats with their party, but about one-fifth of Tilden's vote consisted of former Grant voters, a group which included virtually all those Republicans who had bolted for Greeley four years earlier (see table 1). Thus the 1872 Liberal Republican defections were permanent, to the extent that the defectors continued to vote Democratic in 1876. Frank Bird, one of the most powerful radical Republicans in state politics before he bolted for

Greeley, acted with the Democratic party from 1872 until his death in 1894. Moreover, Bird was joined by additional former Grant supporters who moved into Democratic ranks in 1876. Whereas about 11 percent of the 1868 Republicans were in Greeley's column in 1872, approximately 16 percent of them voted for Tilden. Thus, an additional 5 percent abandoned their party in 1876, perhaps believing that it had been a mistake not to listen to Sumner in 1872. In net results, the Democratic party climbed seven percentage points higher in its share of the electorate than it had ever reached in any election since 1856 (see appendix).

Although the Republicans in 1876 continued their traditional dominance in presidential election years by carrying Massachusetts for Rutherford B. Hayes, the electoral changes of the 1870s created a more competitive party system which lasted until 1896 (see table 2). Not only had the Liberal Republicans' bolt created a minor realignment in the Republican party's mass constituency, but the party's leadership emerged from the decade transformed as well. The intramural fighting of the 1870s witnessed the defeat of the radical Sumner wing of the party along with the Liberals or Independents, for their fear that the party had degenerated into a mere vehicle for advancing ambitious and unprincipled politicians propelled them to make too direct an attack on the party organization. On the other hand, the leading exponent of "Grantism," the colorful Brahmin-baiter Benjamin F. Butler, was also defeated, for his sharp class rhetoric and unorthodox campaign style offended the respectable citizenry. With the Liberal faction held in check, if not alienated, and Stalwarts like Butler held at bay, power in the Republican party shifted to the so-called Half-Breeds. This group included such men as Hoar and Henry Dawes who were willing to curry favor with the state's businessmen and bankers, and yet were unwilling to wage intraparty wars on Liberals or Stalwarts.[18]

Table 2 Competitiveness and Turnout: Massachusetts Presidential Elections, 1860–1908

	Presidential Election Year					
	1860	1864	1868	1872	1876	1880
Percent of Turnout	76	73	76	64	72	72
David Index[a] of Competition	.49	.56	.60	.61	.84	.81

NOTE: Democratic party votes in 1860 and 1896 include only those votes received by Steven A. Douglas and William Jennings Bryan, respectively, on "regular" Democratic tickets. All calculations are my own, based on interpolations from lists of "legal" voters and the official returns for presidential electors on file in the Archives of the Commonwealth of Massachusetts, State House, Boston.

In 1878 Butler bolted to the Democrats to lead an insurrection of Irish-Americans and workingmen, but he failed to win the governorship on a "Democratic and Greenback" ticket and managed to fracture the Massachusetts Democrats in the bargain. Without the disruptive influence of a Butler gubernatorial candidacy in 1880, the Democrats easily united behind Winfield S. Hancock, a Civil War military hero free of any taint of disloyalty. The nomination of James A. Garfield by the Republicans was a victory for the Massachusetts Half-Breeds and met the approval of most members of the reform faction of their party. Although Garfield's assassination in 1881 elevated a Stalwart Republican, Chester A. Arthur, to the presidency, the reform element of the Republican party remained solidly in the Republican fold, mostly out of opposition to Butler, who as a Democrat finally won the governorship in 1882. In the following year Butler's hopes of winning the 1884 Democratic presidential nomination were quashed when he failed to win reelection

1884	1888	1892	1896	1900	1904	1908
70	72	75	70	68	67	65
.91	.90	.93	.49	.79	.78	.74

[a]The David Index expresses the vote of the runner-up (or, in this case, the Democratic candidate) as a percentage of the vote that would have been needed to win. See Paul T. David, *Party Strength in the United States: 1872–1970* (Charlottesville: University Press of Virginia, 1972), pp. 13–14.

to the governorship. He subsequently bolted from Democratic ranks to run for the presidency on the Greenback ticket.[19]

Why the righteous outrage of some reform-minded and issue-conscious Republicans superceded traditional party loyalty in 1884 remains a mystery. But one thing is certain: During their day the Mugwumps dominated political commentary to the extent that their own characterization of the 1884 election has been mistaken by many historians as an accurate description of politics in the Gilded Age. For example, the Mugwumps believed that a fundamental realignment of parties was under way in the 1880s. Some historians agree that the Mugwump revolt against Blaine produced "a sharp impact on party loyalties."[20] But this conclusion may better apply to prominent political elites than to the mass constituencies of the two major parties which did not experience fundamental realignment.

An analysis of voting patterns in the 1880 and 1884 elections reveals that few Republicans deserted their party and voted for Grover Cleveland and the Democrats. Only 3 percent of the 1880 Republicans—about 4,300 voters—bolted in 1884 and voted for Cleveland. Additional estimates of relationships between the high turnout 1883 gubernatorial contest—in which Mugwumps led efforts to crush Butler's bid for reelection—and the subsequent Blaine-Cleveland election suggest that the proportion of 1883 Republicans who bolted for Cleveland equalled about 5 percent—hardly as impressive as the Mugwumps' image of their own influence. In terms of presidential electoral politics, the major desertion of the 1884 election was not from Blaine to Cleveland through the Mugwump defection, but rather from Cleveland to Butler through defections in Democratic ranks. Butler, running on his People's party (Greenback and Anti-Monopoly) ticket, hurt the Democratic ticket far more than the Republican "bolters" helped it. For every 1880 Republican who voted for Cleveland, three 1880 Democrats cast ballots for Butler (see table 1).[21]

Butler ran exceedingly well among Irish-born citizens and Franco-Americans (see table 3). Estimates of the relationship between the birthplaces of eligible voters and voting patterns in 1884 suggest that Butler captured over one-fifth of the Irish-born voters and over two-fifths of the Franco-Americans. This hurt Cleveland's candidacy, in that he fared much worse than Hancock had in 1880 among these same groupings of voters. On the other hand, Blaine's penchant for twisting the British lion's tail cost him support among otherwise staunchly Republican party identifiers. Rather than vote for Cleveland, however, many British-Americans simply sat out the balloting altogether. Blaine also ran poorly among Massachusetts-born voters, a fact that shaped to a considerable degree the outcome of the 1884 election. On the average, in 1876 and 1880 the Republi-

Table 3   Estimated Relationships between Voting in the 1880, 1884, and 1888 Presidential Elections and the Birthplaces of Massachusetts Voters (by percent)

	Birthplace								
	Inside Massa-chusetts	Outside Massa-chusetts	Ireland	England	Germany	French Canada	British Canada	Other	All Voters
Democratic									
1880	18	14	83	0^a	68	13	10	0^a	28
1884	18	22	66	0^a	76	0^a	10	29	28
1888	20	20	94	0^a	55	95	11	0^a	32
Republican									
1880	48	45	14	63	0^a	0^a	0^a	35	42
1884	39	49	12	34	0^a	29	0^a	42	34
1888	44	56	6	40	0^a	0^a	0^a	64	39
Prohibition									
1880	0	0	0	0^a	0^a	0^a	0^a	2	0
1884	4	2	0^a	0^a	0^a	6	0^a	1	2
1888	4	2	0^a	0^a	0	5	0^a	0^a	2
Greenback									
1880	2	5	0^a	6	0^a	7	9	0^a	1
1884	5	0^a	22	0^a	0^a	46	16	0^a	6
Abstaining									
1880	31	40	3	31	32	80	80	63	28
1884	34	27	0^a	66	24	18	74	29	30
1888	32	22	0^a	60	44	0^a	89	36	27

NOTE: The 1885 state census contains information on the nativities of eligible voters in the entire state by city and town. In running multiple regressions with the party percentages as dependent, and the birthplace percentages as independent variables, the votes for each party in 1880 and 1884 were divided by the number of voters in 1885. Thus those abstaining in these two elections include those who were not yet eligible to vote in 1880. In analyzing the 1888 election, all statistics were calculated on the basis of 1888 voting populations in order to control for the influence of new voters.

[a] No estimate.

cans commanded the allegiances of approximately half the eligible voters born within the Commonwealth, whereas Blaine only attracted about 39 percent of them.

Blaine's weakness as a candidate in Massachusetts is revealed by the estimate that almost one-sixth of the 1880 Republicans did not vote in the 1884 presidential race (see table 1). Republican dropouts in 1884 constituted a larger proportion of the electorate than in any other election between 1864 and 1904. Although a disproportionate share of Republicans were repulsed by Blaine, they could not bring themselves to follow the Mugwumps, and cast a Democratic ballot. Not voting in 1884 was clearly the acceptable alternative to political apostasy. Voter apathy, not conversions to Democrats, continued to plague the Grand Old Party in the 1888 election. Slightly more former Garfield men abstained from voting in 1888 than in 1884. But Republican losses were balanced substantially in 1888 by the influx of new voters who had not voted in either 1880 or 1884 (see table 1). The subtle shifts in Republican party support reflected the decisions of the Republican leadership to offset defections and abstentions by former voters by appealing to the labor bloc, antiliquor forces, and the anti-Catholic vote. This strategy helped Republicans in the late 1880s win the competition with Democrats for previously uninvolved voters, but it also alienated some former party loyalists.[22]

Beginning in 1884, Republicans became more solicitous of the labor vote. Although the votes of native-born Protestant factory workers traditionally had been in the Republican column, and many Republicans in the state house had supported labor reform measures in the 1860s and 1870s, Republicans had subsequently taken the workingmen's ballots for granted. But in response to the rise in the 1880s of a new political awareness among industrial workers, Republicans pushed a rash of labor bills through the legislature in 1886 and 1887—even to the discomfiture of the state's corporate and banking interests. In seeking new acquisitions of voters, Republicans also wooed the prohibitionists and tried to capitalize on the resurgence of religious bigotry. In 1888 the party's gubernatorial candidate was a favorite among the antiliquor crusaders, and the party's platform defended the nonsectarian public school system against the perceived dangers from a growing Catholic school system. When a British-American political organization endorsed the anti-Catholic position on schools, Republicans omitted from their platform traditional words of sympathy for Ireland. Such a policy was sure to alienate what support Republicans had among Catholics, especially Irishborn and French-Canadian voters, and was bound to appeal to nativists and anti-Catholics.[23]

The estimates in Table 3 reveal that by stirring up ethnic and religious rivalries, the Republicans drove the Franco-Americans headlong into the Democratic column in 1888. Moreover, the traditional Republican grip on a small proportion of Irish-Americans was cut in half. In spite of Republican efforts to curry favor with the British-American vote, Republican standard-bearer Benjamin H. Harrison fared only slightly better than Blaine at the hands of this voting group. The English, however, either voted Republican or did not vote at all. Their behavior was mirrored by German-Americans who either voted Democratic or abstained. By dabbling in the waters of nativism and anti-Catholicism, the Republicans had intensified ethnic and religious differences in the late 1880s, making partisan lines more congruent with lines already separating cultural groups.[24]

In the "off-year" 1890 election the Democrats, by avoiding ethnocultural issues and continuing to emphasize the national question of tariff reform, won the governorship and captured four congressional seats. In the presidential contest of 1892 Cleveland again lost Massachusetts to Harrison, but the level of support for the Democrats reached a post-Civil War high. Voters turned out and voted in higher proportions than in any presidential election since 1868. The 1892 election was also the most competitive presidential election in the entire second half of the nineteenth century (see table 2). Cleveland in 1892 was the first Democrat since Tilden to outdistance the Republicans in attracting new voters and previous nonvoters (see table 1). Apathy in the ranks of former active voters continued to plague the Republicans: about 11 percent of the 1888 Harrison men failed to repeat a vote for the man they helped elect four years earlier. A few voters continued to shuffle between the Prohibitionist and the Republican parties, accounting for all those who switched between 1888 and 1892.

From the perspective of 1892, the switching that occurred between 1884 and 1888 is brought into better focus. Although there was a relatively high rate of voters switching parties between 1884 and 1888, almost half were 1884 Butler men returning to the Democratic party fold (see table 1). Thus, those who switched in 1888 tended to reestablish previous combinations of voters with one important exception: the few 1884 Republicans who voted Democratic in 1888 were joined by additional 1884 Republicans in the Democratic column in 1892. Thus in terms of Republican-to-Democrat switching, the eight years after 1884—in which Republicans mismanaged the liquor and school issues—represented the only long-term, significant Republican conversions to Democrats since the 1868–76 period, which had witnessed the anti-Grant Liberal Republican movement.

Nationwide the 1892 campaign, according to most historians, marked the beginning of the end of the Civil War party system, for the subsequent 1896 election radically transformed the coalitions of voters forged during the Civil War years. The grim economic hard times which followed the panic of 1893 set the stage once again for a permanent reshuffling of voters similar to that of the 1850s. Standard accounts of the realignment of the 1890s blame the economic depression for the erosion of Democratic support in the 1894 congressional elections, clearly a rebuke to the incumbent party. Voter disaffection crystalized in 1896 when the Democrats nominated an agrarian populist from Nebraska, William Jennings Bryan, for the presidency. Although differences in the 1896 campaign appeared to be geographical and economic—involving a deflationary gold policy favored largely in the industrial Northeast versus one of inflationist silver favored in the agrarian West and South—there were also social and religious issues. Bryan's fundamentalist Protestant zeal alienated many Catholics and other members of liturgical churches who traditionally voted Democratic. Although historians differ over the importance of sectional, economic, or ethnocultural issues, most agree that nationwide the 1896 election transformed both the anatomy and public image of the Democratic and Republican parties.[25]

What part did Massachusetts play in this national realignment? At the time few, if any, expected Bryan to carry the state, but the Democratic debacle went further than merely losing to William McKinley and the Republicans. The seeds of the 1896 Democratic destruction were sown before the election by former Mugwump George Fred Williams, the party's gubernatorial candidate. When Williams announced his conversion to Bryan and free silver, he split the Bay State Democratic delegation at the Chicago national convention and forced the issue of support for Bryan's economic proposals into state politics. As a consequence, the Democratic party divided into three groups: Williams supporters, gold or antisilver Democrats, and the Boston-Irish organization. Williams unleashed some terrifying amateurish and radical political forces in Boston where he converted the Bryan inflationary crusade into a party purge of his opponents.[26]

In November, Williams and the Bryanites plunged their party to its poorest showing since 1860. The "regular" party ticket attracted only slightly over half of the 1892 Democrats (see table 4). Not only did Bryan's candidacy fail to hold together the Massachusetts Democratic party which had flourished in the beginning of the decade, but it failed to win support from other segments of the electorate. Although Bryan won the support of the 1892 Populists, he picked them up on a separate People's Party ticket pledged to Tom Watson for vice-president. The People's ticket and the National (Gold) Democratic ticket together siphoned off about 13 percent of the 1892 Democrats. In spite of Bryan's evangelical style, he won no support from either Protestant Republicans or anti-Catholic Prohibitionists. The movement of voters across party lines, save for those 1892 Democrats voting in Bryan-Watson and Democratic Gold tickets, was a one-way march of 1892 Democrats into Republican ranks. Yet the 1896 outcome was shaped more by the failure of many 1892 Democrats to turn out and vote than by defections to the Republicans. Over one-fifth of the 1892 Democrats sat out the balloting for president in 1896, whereas, by way of comparison, virtually all the 1892 Republicans subsequently voted for McKinley.

Did the 1896 election set a new and enduring pattern in the state's presidential electoral politics? Apparently not. The Democratic defections in 1896 proved to be temporary (see table 1). Whereas about 52 percent of the 1892 Demo-

Table 4   Crossover Voting between the 1892 and 1896 Presidential Elections (in percentages of electorate)

Party in 1896:	Party in 1892:				Not Voting in 1892	Not Yet Eligible in 1892	Percent of 1896 Electorate
	Democratic	Republican	Prohibition	Populist			
Democratic	16	0	0	0	0	0	16
Republican	3	36	0	0	8	2	49
Prohibition	0	0	1	0	0	0	1
People's National (Gold)	2	0	0	1	0	0	3
Democrat	2	0	0	0	0	0	2
Not Voting in 1896	8	0	0	0	15	7	30
Percent of 1896 Electorate	31	36	1	1	23	9	100

NOTE: Actual N=351. In 1892 the Socialist Labor party received an inconsequential 871 votes, whereas in 1896 the Socialist Labor candidate polled 2,112 votes or about .4 percent of the potential electorate.

crats voted for Bryan on the "regular" Democratic ticket in 1896, about 90 percent voted for Bryan when he ran again for the presidency in 1900. Thus, roughly 38 percent of the 1892 Democrats returned to their party in 1900. Yet the Democratic party did not make a full recovery, as it failed in 1900 to receive any support from voters who were previously outside its ranks. Essentially reduced to a demoralized and disorganized rump party of old Cleveland style Democrats, the Massachusetts Democrats underwent a minor realignment in 1896. For the Republicans, however, the 1896 election proved to be a deviating one, as McKinley was unable to retain any of the Democratic voters who cast ballots for him under the stimulus of Bryan's first campaign. Virtually no one who either voted for Bryan on any ticket or went with the National (Gold) Democrats was found in McKinley's column in 1900. The enhanced Republican majorities in the elections of 1900 and 1904 were not due to Democratic conversions to the GOP or to Republican gains among urban workingmen, but to the persistence with which many former Democrats stayed away from the polls.[27]

The analysis of city and town election returns demonstrates that Bryan utterly failed, at least in Massachusetts, to attract Republican farmers and workers. Nor did his candidacy mobilize any elements of the previously uninvolved among the "toiling masses." Bryan's inflationary schemes made no sense to workingmen, for they were convinced that among the dollars that would decline in value were those in their pay envelopes. But even if workers had been more receptive, Bryan's appeal was too simplistic. The Bay State citizenry did not feel that their lives were as vulnerable to irresponsive political and economic power as Bryan's populist rhetoric seemed to claim. Massachusetts could thus appear "conservative" in the national political context only because the state had already accomplished by way of political and economic reforms in the post-Civil War period much of what Populists and subsequently Progressives elsewhere were just beginning to demand.[28]

In conclusion, during the Gilded Age the alignment of the Massachusetts party system created by the Civil War experience was modified initially by the Liberal Republican movement in the 1870s, then by the resurgence of ethnocultural conflicts in the 1880s, and finally by the Bryan campaign of 1896. Yet the resulting new line of cleavage by no means supplanted the old. From 1872 to 1896, Republicans became Democrats and Democrats became Republicans only under the emotional and psychological strain of abandoning the party of their youth or the party of their fathers. The barrier to crossing party lines was, in most instances, too formidable and voters were more likely to resolve the ensuing inner conflict by not voting than by switching parties. Thus, in narrow terms of the underlying distribution of partisan loyalties, the voting alignments forged in war persisted into the twentieth century.

Although the anatomy of electoral coalitions by and large endured, the ideological division which originally shaped these alignments did not survive. While stumping for McKinley on the eve of the 1896 election, Republican Senator Henry Cabot Lodge declared that "as the assault at Gettysburg rolled back from the gray stone wall and blue line," so would Republicans roll back the assault of the Bryanites.[29] To many in his audience who were in fact scared that Bryan was a dangerous demagogue seeking to inflame class conflict to the point of revolution, Lodge's single ritualistic reference to the Civil War must have seemed quaint, if not anachronistic. The transition from the political ambiance of 1863 to that of 1896 was gradual, but in the process Civil War issues had been thoroughly superceded by those associated with maintaining social harmony in a nation undergoing rapid industrialization. In this sense the Civil War party system of the Gilded Age had passed into history.

Appendix

Turnout and Proportion of Massachusetts "Legal" Voters Casting Ballots for Each Party in Presidential Elections, 1848–1908

Year	Democratic	Whig/Fillmore American/Consti- tutional Union	Free Soil/ Republican	Other	Abstained
1848	20.9%	36.1%	22.5%	.0%	20.6%
1852	23.8	28.1	15.0	1.0[a]	32.1
1856	19.0	9.5	52.4	.4	18.6
1860	15.4	10.0	47.7	2.9[b]	24.1
1864	20.2	——	52.4	.0	27.4
1868	22.9	——	52.8	.0	24.3
1872	19.5	——	44.0	——	36.5
1876	30.3	——	41.8	.2	27.8
1880	28.4	——	41.9	1.3[c]	28.4
1884	28.3	——	33.9	7.9[c]	29.9
1888	31.9	——	38.7	1.8[d]	27.6
1892	33.8	——	38.8	2.2[e]	25.2
1896	15.8	——	48.8	5.6[f]	29.8
1900	25.5	——	38.8	3.1[g]	32.5
1904	25.0	——	38.9	3.3[h]	32.8
1908	22.1	——	37.7	4.9[i]	35.2

SOURCE: All calculations are my own, based on interpolations from lists of "legal" voters and the official returns for presidential electors on file in the Archives Division of the Commonwealth of Massachusetts, State House, Boston.

[a]Constitutional Union ticket pledged to Daniel Webster, and scattered returns.

[b]Breckinridge Democrat, and scattered returns.

[c]Greenback, Prohibition, and scattered returns.

[d]Prohibition, and scattered returns.

[e]Prohibition, Populist, Socialist Labor, and scattered returns.

[f]People's National (Gold) Democrat, Prohibition, Socialist Labor, and scattered returns.

[g]Democratic Social, Socialist Labor, Prohibition, and scattered returns.

[h]Socialist, Prohibition, Socialist Labor, People's Party, and scattered returns

[i]Independent League, Socialist, Prohibition, Socialist Labor, and scattered returns

Notes

* Peyton McCrary, Gerald W. McFarland, and Stephan Thernstrom read an earlier draft of the manuscript and made helpful suggestions.

1. An excellent characterization of Gilded Age politics is contained in the first chapter of Robert D. Marcus, *Grand Old Party: Political Structure in the Gilded Age, 1880–1896* (New York: Oxford University Press, 1971), pp. 3–21. Two important behavioral studies examining midwestern politics are Paul Kleppner, *The Cross of Culture: A Social Analysis of Midwestern Politics, 1850–1900* (New York: Free Press, 1970), and Richard J. Jensen, *The Winning of the Midwest: Social and Political Conflict, 1888–96* (Chicago: University of Chicago Press, 1971). For an analysis of voting behavior in the Midwest which employs the same kind of information supplied by modern opinion polls, see Melvyn Hammarberg, *The Indiana Voter: The Historical Dynamics of Party Allegiance during the 1870s* (Chicago: University of Chicago Press, 1977).

2. George S. Merriam, *The Life and Times of Samuel Bowles,* 2 vols. (New York: The Century Co., 1885; reprint ed., 1970), 2:222.

3. Major works of the Michigan Survey Research Center group include: Angus Campbell, Philip E. Converse, Warren E. Miller, and Donald E. Stokes, *The American Voter* (New York: John Wiley & Sons, Inc., 1960); and Angus Campbell, Philip E. Converse, Warren E. Miller, and Donald E. Stokes, *Elections and the Political Order* (New York: John Wiley & Sons, Inc., 1966). The vast literature on critical realignment and party systems begins with the seminal article by V. O. Key, Jr., "A Theory of Critical Elections," *Journal of Politics* 17 (February 1955): 3–18, and culminates in the work of Walter Dean Burnham, *Critical Elections and the Mainsprings of American Politics* (New York: W. W. Norton and Co., 1970).

4. The best description of the realignment process is contained in James L. Sundquist, *Dynamics of the Party System: Alignment and Realignment of Political Parties in the United States* (Washington, D.C.: Brookings Institution, 1973).

5. Burnham, *Critical Elections*, pp. 18–21; Paul Kleppner, *The Third Electoral System, 1853–1892: Parties, Voters, and Political Cultures* (Chapel Hill, N. C.: University of North Carolina Press, 1979), pp. 26–32.

6. For a detailed discussion of the use of ecological regressions to construct voter transition probabilities in contingency tables, and for additional references to the methodological literature, see Laura Irwin Langbein and Allan J. Lichtman, *Ecological Inference*, Sage University Paper series on Quantitative Applications in the Social Sciences (Beverly Hills and London: Sage Publications, 1978). In several respects the methodology used in the analysis of Massachusetts voting during the 1860s presented here differs from that used in Dale Baum, "Know-

Nothingism and the Republican Majority in Massachusetts: The Political Realignment of the 1850s," *Journal of American History* 64, no. 4 (March 1978): 959–86. The estimates presented here were derived from a better specified model of determinants of voting patterns that took into account geographical population shifts between elections. Also I feel impelled to warn the reader that in the earlier analysis, the computer program I used failed at one point to execute the collapse of some of the voting units in Suffolk County into a single voting unit in order to solve problems caused by the annexation to Boston of several surrounding towns. This exaggerated the strength of the nonvoting elements in the country in 1864 and 1868, and rendered a few of the voting estimates unreliable. This error has been corrected in the analysis presented here.

7. These findings square with those found by Paul Kleppner for the North and Midwest in his essay on the third electoral system in Paul Kleppner, Walter Dean Burnham, Ronald P. Formisano, Samuel P. Hays, Richard Jensen, and William G. Shade, *The Evolution of American Electoral Systems* (Westport, Conn., and London: Greenwood Press, 1981), table 4.4, p. 130. To render comparable my estimates of Massachusetts party switchers with Kleppner's estimates for northern and midwestern regions, the sum of Democrat-to-Republican and Republican-to-Democrat party switchers must be divided by the sum of the proportions repeating Democratic or Republican preferences and proportions voting Democratic or Republican in the first election but abstaining in the second election.

8. See Baum, "Know-Nothingism," tables 16–21, pp. 980–82.

9. In the midwestern states most Whigs and Know-Nothings became Republicans, whereas Democrats continued to support their party. See Ray M. Shortridge, "The Voter Realignment in the Midwest during the 1850s," *American Politics Quarterly* 4, no. 2 (April 1976): 193–222. See also Michael F. Holt, *The Political Crisis of the 1850s* (New York: John Wiley & Sons, 1978), esp. pp. 101–217; and Sundquist, *Dynamics of the Party System*, pp. 63–91.

10. See Dale Baum, "The 'Irish Vote' and Party Politics in Massachusetts, 1860–1876," *Civil War History* 26, no. 2 (June 1980): 117–41.

11. Richard H. Abbott, "Massachusetts: Maintaining Hegemony," in *Radical Republicans in the North: State Politics during Reconstruction*, ed. James C. Mohr (Baltimore and London: Johns Hopkins University Press, 1976), pp. 20–21; and Charles Blank, "The Waning of Radicalism: Massachusetts Republicans and Reconstruction Issues in the Early 1870s" (Ph.D. diss., Brandeis University, 1972), pp. 87–122a. See also David Donald, *Charles Sumner and the Rights of Man* (New York: Alfred A. Knopf, 1970), p. 554; Fred Harvey Harrington, *Fighting Politician:*

Major General N. P. Banks (Westport, Conn.: Greenwood Press, 1948), pp. 201–3; and Richard E. Welch, Jr., *George F. Hoar and the Half-Breed Republicans* (Cambridge: Harvard University Press, 1971), p. 45.

12. A satisfactory explanation of the Liberal Republican movement has proven elusive. See Richard Allen Gerber, "The Liberal Republicans of 1872 in Historiographical Perspective," *Journal of American History* 62, no. 1 (June 1975): 40–73. Helpful works on the Liberal Republicans include Earle Dudley Ross, *The Liberal Republican Movement* (New York: H. Holt and Company, 1919); John G. Sproat, *"The Best Men": Liberal Reformers in the Gilded Age* (London and New York: Oxford University Press, 1968), esp. chap. 3. On the Republicans and the labor question, see David Montgomery, *Beyond Equality: Labor and the Radical Republicans, 1862–1872* (New York: Vintage Books, 1967). For involvement of leading Bay State Republicans, see Donald, *Charles Sumner and the Rights of Man*, pp. 498–555; Martin Duberman, *Charles Francis Adams, 1870–1886* (Stanford, Calif.: Stanford University Press, 1960), pp. 352–72; Harrington, *Fighting Politician*, passim; and [By his children], *Francis William Bird, A Biographical Sketch* (Boston: By the authors, 1897), p. 77.

13. Boston *Post*, Sept. 12, 1872; Boston *Globe*, Oct. 18, 1872. Looking back on the 1872 anti-Grant movement, Charles Francis Adams wrote: "Bird mainly contributed to the defeat of my nomination for the Presidency at Cincinnati from the jealousy of Sumner." Charles Francis Adams, "Diary," Feb. 8, 1876, Reel no. 86, Adams Family Papers, microfilm ed., Massachusetts Historical Society, Boston, Mass.

14. Welch, *George Frisbie Hoar*, pp. 43–45; John Murray Forbes to Charles Sumner, Aug. 10, 1872, in John Murray Forbes, *Letters and Recollections of John Murray Forbes*, ed. Sarah Forbes Hughes, 2 vols. (Boston and New York: Houghton, Mifflin and Co., 1899), 2:178–83.

15. This analysis of the 1872 election supports the contention of a few scholars that the schism in Republican leadership ranks had to have been reflected in some permanent crossing of party lines. See Sundquist, *Dynamics of the Party System*, p. 88 n. 49; Edith E. Ware, *Political Opinion in Massachusetts during Civil War and Reconstruction*, Columbia University Studies in History, Economics, and Public Law, vol. 74, no. 2 (New York: Columbia University Press, 1916), pp. 374–75.

16. Robert C. Winthrop to John H. Clifford, Aug. 8, 1872, Robert C. Winthrop Papers, microfilm ed., Massachusetts Historical Society, Boston, Mass.

17. Blank, "Waning of Radicalism," pp. 146–206.

18. Ibid., pp. 209–10.

19. Richard P. Harmond, "Tradition and Change in the Gilded Age; A Political History of Massachusetts, 1878–1893" (Ph.D. diss., Columbia

University, 1966), pp. 2–77; Welch, *George Frisbie Hoar*, pp. 59–98; Hans Louis Trefousse, *Ben Butler: The South Called Him Beast!* (New York: Twayne Publishers, 1957), pp. 252–53; Geoffrey Blodgett, *The Gentle Reformers: Massachusetts Democrats in the Cleveland Era* (Cambridge, Mass.: Harvard University Press, 1966), pp. 14–15; Welch, *George Frisbie Hoar*, pp. 104–5.

20. Harmond, "Tradition and Change," p. 130. See also Blodgett, *Gentle Reformers*, p. 54; and Gordon S. Wood, "The Massachusetts Mugwumps," *New England Quarterly* 33, no. 4 (December 1960): 435–51.

21. See Dale Baum, " 'Noisy but not Numerous': The Revolt of the Massachusetts Mugwumps," *The Historian* 41, no. 2 (February 1979): 241–56. Cf. Lee Benson, "Research Problems in American Political Historiography," in *Common Frontiers of the Social Sciences*, ed. Mirra Komarovsky (Glencoe, Ill.: Free Press, 1957), pp. 123–46.

22. Richard Harmond, "Troubles of Massachusetts Republicans during the 1880s," *Mid-America* 56, no. 2 (April 1974): 85–99.

23. Ibid., pp. 89–98.

24. Harmond argues persuasively that Republicans by the late 1880s "had exacerbated, rather than minimized group differences at a time when the electorate began increasingly to break up into various blocs." Ibid., p. 98.

25. On the national realignment of the 1890s, see Sundquist, *Dynamics of the Party System*, pp. 120–54; and Morton Keller, *Affairs of State: Public Life in Late Nineteenth-Century America* (Cambridge, Mass., and London: Belknap Press of Harvard University Press, 1977), pp. 565–87.

26. Blodgett, *Gentle Reformers*, pp. 205–39.

27. For other discussions of the 1896 election in Massachusetts, see William Diamond, "Urban and Rural Voting in 1896," *American Historical Review* 46 (March 1941): 281–305; Benson, "Research Problems," pp. 155–71; Key, "Theory of Critical Elections," p. 12; Sundquist, *Dynamics of the Party System*, pp. 147–48.

28. Richard M. Abrams, *Conservatism in a Progressive Era: Massachusetts Politics, 1900–1912* (Cambridge, Mass.: Harvard University Press, 1964), pp. 1–24.

29. Henry Cabot Lodge quoted in *Boston Daily Globe*, Oct. 8, 1896.

Liquor and Ethnicity: French Canadians in Politics, Holyoke, 1885–1910

PETER HAEBLER

During the last third of the nineteenth century, tens of thousands of French Canadians left Canada in search of economic opportunity. A disastrous agricultural decline in Quebec, together with the growing industrial activity of the nearby New England states, combined to lure French Canadians to the factory cities and towns of New England. By 1900 they comprised 10 percent of the population of New England.[1]

Although some French Canadians migrated to the upper Midwest and New York State, the largest numbers went to New England. The regional concentration of French Canadians is an important reason why they have, until recently, received comparatively little attention from students of ethnic history. As a result, stereotypes—cast in the nineteenth century by not always unbiased observers of the French-Canadian influx into New England—persisted. Typically, French Canadians were often viewed as clannish, priest-ridden, docile workers hostile to union activity, indifferent to education, and slow to assimilate.[2]

One area largely ignored by historians is the French Canadians' political behavior. The historic 1881 report of the Massachusetts Bureau of the Statistics of Labor declared that they care nothing for our institutions, civil, political, or educational. They do not come to make a home among us, to dwell with us as citizens, and so become a part of us; but their purpose is merely to sojourn a few years as aliens, touching us only at a single point, that of work, and, when they have gathered out of us what will satisfy their ends, to get them away to whence they came, and bestow it there. They are a horde of industrial invaders, not a stream of stable settlers. Voting, with all that it implies, they care nothing about. Rarely does one of them become naturalized.[3]

When they did participate in politics, nativists took a dim view. One nineteenth-century observer considered French Canadians

the bane of local and even state politics, particularly in New Hampshire, for many of the voters are purchasable at least once at each election and as they hold the balance of power in many small towns, purchasers for both parties are rarely wanting and prices rule high.[4]

These observations notwithstanding, French Canadians were actively and responsibly involved in political life in New England. This is especially true after 1885 when the French-Canadian population had become geographically more stable and endeavored to influence affairs in their adopted communities. There is, however, little agreement as to the nature of their political activity, especially their political affiliations in the late nineteenth and early twentieth centuries. Journalist Henry Loomis Nelson contended that French Canadians voted for Democrat Grover Cleveland in 1892 because the McKinley tariff had caused difficulties for Quebec farmers. Newspaper editor and novelist Jacques Ducharme agreed, arguing that the free trade principles of the Democratic party enticed the loyalties of those French Canadians who became naturalized. Ducharme argued, however, that the 1896 Free Silver campaign between McKinley and Bryan brought about a swing to the GOP.

Ducharme said that the debate over money touched the French Canadians' conservative nature, and the Republican party's desire to maintain the status quo won their allegiance in many cases.[5]

Writing in 1959, political scientist Duane Lockard said that because of their rivalry with the Irish, many of the early French Canadians voted Republican. However, Lockard contended that the liberalism with which William Jennings Bryan sought to win the Populist vote in 1896 changed the direction of the Democratic party and helped to bring Catholic ethnic minorities into the Democratic fold. By the 1920s, according to Lockard, the majority of French Canadians were Democrats. However, in a 1963 study of the French-Canadian presidential voting patterns, David Walker presented a different view. Walker maintained that, prior to 1896, the bulk of the French-Canadian presidential vote went to the Democrats, but he contended that French Canadians—like many other eastern, Catholic minority groups—were repelled by Bryan's unorthodox fiscal views and his fundamentalist, agrarian Protestantism. According to Walker, the preponderance of the French-Canadian presidential vote remained with the GOP from 1896 until the 1928 campaign of Al Smith. Walker also stressed the deep antagonism between the French Canadians and Irish which contributed to French-Canadian alienation from the Irish-dominated Democratic machines. But recognizing the difficulty in categorizing French-Canadian political behavior, Walker added that Yankee domination of the Republican party made it difficult for French Canadians to find a "completely satisfactory political domicile," and that local French-Canadian voting patterns often revolved around which of these two rival ethnic groups was the most powerful and feared.[6]

The most comprehensive study of French-Canadian po-

litical behavior to date has been conducted by Ronald
Petrin. In a study of forty-two Massachusetts cities and
towns with a sizable French-Canadian population, Petrin
created a typology based on the size of the towns and the
ethnic mix within them. Studying the gubernatorial elections between 1885 and 1915, he concluded that the French
Canadians did not identify strongly with either party, but
rather made pragmatic alliances as circumstances dictated.
However, he noted that in secondary, single-industry
towns where the French Canadians were usually the largest
ethnic group, the Democratic vote was generally higher
than in the larger cities. Petrin deemphasized the importance of French-Canadian conflicts with the Irish, and instead argued that unique local conditions, such as the spa-
tial alignment of ethnic groups within the community, were
important in determining political affiliations.[7]

Holyoke, Massachusetts, provides an example of the variegated nature of French-Canadian political behavior. The
Holyoke experience reinforces Petrin's view of the importance of residential patterns. But more important, the in-
terplay between French Canadians, Irish, and Yankees,
suggested by Walker, is a crucial element in determining
political alignments. Holyoke was established in 1848 as
a planned industrial town with the financial backing of Boston manufacturing interests. Located by a fifty-four foot
waterfall on the west bank of the Connecticut River several miles north of Springfield, Holyoke was originally con-
ceived as a center for textile manufacturing. After the Civil
War, the economic base of the town became more diversified and by the late nineteenth century, Holyoke was
a world center for the manufacture of paper and paper
products.

Early labor needs were filled by Yankee and Irish workers. French Canadians began to arrive in significant num-

bers in the years immediately following the Civil War. With the ebb and flow of immigration characteristic of the French-Canadian influx into New England in the last third of the nineteenth century, French Canadians numbered approximately 13,000 in 1900, making Holyoke the sixth largest French-Canadian community in New England. Although French Canadians comprised nearly 30 percent of the city's population, the Irish remained the numerically dominant ethnic group throughout the period. By 1900, Holyoke also contained smaller concentrations of English, Scots, Germans, and Poles. [8]

Although characterized by nativists as "Birds of Passage," it is evident that by the mid-1880s, the French-Canadian community in Holyoke and many other New England cities and towns had achieved a considerable degree of residential stability. Whereas the majority of French Canadians were factory operatives and day laborers, it is also true that the leadership in their communities was being assumed by a growing number of professionals, merchants, businessmen, and contractors anxious to influence affairs in the new homeland. [9]

Historian Samuel P. Hays has noted that the physical development and growth of American cities in the mid-nineteenth century produced a differentiation and decentralization in the social and economic life of the cities. In turn, the political structure was also decentralized. When each section and group demanded its own representation, the usual response was the political division of the cities into wards. The ward system resulted in a new type of political leader. Councilmen tended to reflect the concerns of their particular community, and the economic and social leaders in each ward began to gravitate toward politics as an extension of their leadership role. [10]

Hays's description of late nineteenth-century political life is a close approximation of the realities in Holyoke. In its original city charter of 1873, the city was divided into seven wards. The city executives—the mayor, treasurer, and clerk—were elected at large, whereas the bicameral legislative body was chosen by ward. The city council consisted of a seven-member board of aldermen, one from each ward, and a common council of twenty-one members, three per ward.[11] Through 1910, the major political rivals were the Irish and the Yankees. Although a distinct minority, the Yankees were usually able to rely on support from the Germans, English, and Scots. Both Yankees and Irish wooed the French Canadians, with varying success, especially in the post-1885 period when the number of French-Canadian voters was substantially increased. The local political system, until modified in 1897, worked to the advantage of the French Canadians, in that they could usually secure a nomination from both parties for at least one common council seat in wards with a large French-Canadian population. As their political strength increased, the French Canadians both used and were used by other political factions. On one hand, the French Canadians were able to secure elected and appointive office at least in proportion to their political strength. On the other, the extent of their influence was severely limited by other groups who used them to promote their own political advantage, a process that neutralized the French-Canadian impact.

After 1885 there was a dramatic increase in the number of French Canadians who chose to make Holyoke their permanent home and who became United States citizens. At the same time, French Canadians began to exhibit a degree of political power which reflected their increased prosperity and standing in the community. Their political participation was encouraged by both major political parties who sought their vote in order to control local government. By the end of the nineteenth century, local Republicans had succeeded in capturing the majority of the French-Canadian vote, which had previously been Democratic. The French Canadians had been unable to substantially influence or obtain recognition from the Democrats, a problem exacerbated by conflicts with the Irish who dominated the party. And Democratic leaders had been unable to assume a unified stand on the foremost local issue of the period: control of liquor selling. Irish Democratic misrule, combined with their exclusion of French Canadians from the political spoils, widened cultural differences and provided a rationale for French Canadians to turn to the GOP. In turn, the Republicans catered to French-Canadian desires for political and social recognition by insuring that they received a share of municipal jobs as well as places on the party ticket. Although French-Canadian political independence was circumscribed by Republican party leaders, the extent of French-Canadian participation and influence belies the commonly held notion of their widespread political apathy.

The growth of Holyoke in the 1870s produced demographic changes that altered the form of city government. By the 1880s the predominately Yankee manufacturing interests, which had controlled Holyoke since its incorporation in 1850, had been forced out of political power by immigrant groups, especially the Irish, who had come to work in the mills. Until the mid-1890s the political influence of the Irish was all-pervasive and produced a social and cultural upheaval of enormous proportions. By 1900, nativists—who were appalled by what they perceived to be the corrupting influence of Irish rule—were joined by other immigrant groups, including the French Canadians, to effectively challenge the Irish domination of City Hall. The successful "reform" machine, led by Mayors Arthur Chapin and Nathan Avery, soon came to terms with the Irish politicians, with the result that decorum became more apparent in city administration. However, the tenor of Holyoke politics changed little as the GOP mayors proved willing to seek political accommodations with the Democrats who usually controlled the board of aldermen.

The French Canadians' perception of politics in Holyoke changed considerably from 1885 to 1910. Although slower to naturalize and exercise their franchise than the Irish or Germans, they did significantly increase their proportion of the city's voters in the late nineteenth and early twentieth centuries. The French-Canadian vote, which was largely Democratic in local elections in the mid-1880s, became predominately Republican by the end of the century. At the same time, the willingness of French Canadians to vote with the GOP was an indication of important changes in the attitude of the French-Canadian community.[12]

Longstanding religious and economic rivalries with the Irish, and the belief that the Democratic party was not sufficiently accommodating, influenced the French Canadians' political decisions. It would be misleading, however, to imply that they voted as a bloc. In 1893 the *Holyoke Transcript* expressed the confusion of many Holyoke citizens when it asked, "Are Frenchmen Republicans or Democrats? Who can tell?"[13] At this time, there were important political divisions in the French-Canadian community, often centered around personality differences. The lack of political unanimity was both advantageous and disadvantageous for the French Canadians. In the late 1880s and 1890s, both parties actively solicited the important French-Canadian vote with political favors. But French-Canadian leaders were continually frustrated in their efforts to organize an effective ethnic voting bloc with which they hoped to exact even greater concessions from the major political parties.

It is difficult to determine precisely the size of Holyoke's

French-Canadian vote in any given year. After 1885 there were no statistical breakdowns of registered voters by ethnic origin. The problem of numbers is compounded by the fact that third-generation French Canadians, who became numerically important by 1900, were classified in the census returns as native-born of native parents, and are thus virtually indistinguishable as an ethnic bloc.

However, available evidence does indicate the relative growth of French-Canadian voting strength from 1885 to 1910. Naturalization records also support the idea that French-Canadian voters were increasing at a rate in excess of their population growth.[14] In 1885 they comprised 25.8 percent of the city's total population, but only 6.4 percent of its voters. By 1910 this imbalance was less severe, with French Canadians constituting more than 20 percent of the voters and 27 percent of the total population.[15]

Prior to 1897, the Holyoke City Council consisted of three common councilors and one alderman elected annually from each ward. Inasmuch as the bulk of the French-Canadian population lived in Wards Two and Four, and later Ward One, this system of geographic representation worked to their advantage. They were often able to secure two of the common council seats from Ward Two and one from Ward Four, and on occasion benefited from party attempts to bring an ethnic balance to the tickets in other wards. From 1887 to 1895, there were between three and six French Canadians on the twenty-one member common council. Before 1892, they were able to elect only three ward aldermen. However, from 1892 to 1910, every alderman that represented Ward Two was French Canadian, and in four of those years, a French Canadian was elected from Ward Six.[16]

In 1896, the city charter was altered, primarily because of the Yankee manufacturing elite's opposition to the abuses of the Irish Democratic-dominated city council. The re-vamping of the system of representation was not directed primarily against the French Canadians, but it worked to their disadvantage. The 1896 charter abolished the common council in favor of one board of aldermen. One representative was elected annually from each of the city's seven wards, and fourteen aldermen were chosen in city-wide elections every two years. Each party generally included French Canadians on their at-large slate, and between 1897 and 1910, two and sometimes three French Canadians held at-large seats.[17] However, because of their geographic concentration in three wards and the addition of fourteen at-large seats, the proportion of French Canadians on the board of aldermen decreased as their voting strength increased.

The 1896 charter was the result of social conflicts in Holyoke, but the principal issue in the city's political consciousness was the liquor license question. In 1892 the *Springfield Republican*, referring to Holyoke, accurately observed that "the [liquor] license question is the one thing that is on the minds of the politicians from one year's end to another."[18] The competition for licenses and control of liquor selling were paramount considerations in Holyoke's political life in the last decades of the nineteenth century, and the French Canadians played an important role in determining how these issues were resolved.

Until 1894 the power to grant liquor licenses was vested in the seven-member board of aldermen and, as a result, the aldermen's political leverage was considerable. In the 1880s, 100 to 160 licenses were issued annually and an unknown number of illegal saloons flourished. The police force, which until 1888 was appointed yearly by the mayor, was not large enough to enforce the license laws. It was also hampered by the power and interests of the mayor and council. The situation was made more acute by an 1889 Massachusetts law which linked the number of licenses to population, a step that reduced Holyoke's total to twenty-seven. The new law considerably increased the pressures on the aldermen, and led to the candidacy of individuals whose sole task was to balance their ward's competing liquor interests. Political careers were made or lost on an alderman's ability to deliver the promised number of licenses. The aldermen attempted to bring some order to the situation by raising license fees to over $1,000 annually, both as a revenue measure and as a means of discouraging potential applicants. Even with the high fees, the number of applicants usually exceeded the available licenses by three- or fourfold. The most effective method of awarding licenses was by means of a "ring" or "combination." A ring of four or five aldermen favorable to the liquor interests would meet privately in the weeks prior to the granting of licenses and work out a distribution that was mutually agreeable. If the ring, with a majority of votes on the board, remained intact—as was usually the case—the licenses were awarded with a minimum of public bickering. Critics of "ring rule" argued that this system bred the most unsavory sort of political maneuvering. The most flagrant abuses were committed by the political machine of Michael Connors, an alderman and cigar distributor. Connors's success was due to his control of liquor patronage, and after his election to the city council in 1891, he became the key element in the ring. Allegedly, saloon keepers who wanted a license were required to purchase a liberal supply of cigars from Connors.[19]

French Canadians, no matter what they felt about the merits of the liquor license distribution system, were generally opposed to the imposition of legal prohibition. Although some French-Canadian tavern owners personally benefited from traffic in liquor, the general sentiment among French Canadians was that total prohibition was impossible and that regulated liquor selling was preferable to abuses that might arise from widespread illegal selling.[20] Massachusetts law required an annual local option referendum of liquor selling, which was held in conjunction with the city election in December. The French-Canadian Ward Two usually returned a vote of at least two to one, and at times as high as five to one, against prohibition. On at least two occasions, in 1892 and 1898, French Canadians provided the margin that kept Holyoke from going dry.[21]

The liquor issue brought many French-Canadian businessmen into the political arena. It is true that between 1886 and 1892, a French Canadian served for only one term on the board of aldermen, the body which awarded licenses. However, French Canadians, particularly through their representatives on the common council, were able to obtain a respectable number of licenses. In 1889, when the license restriction law went into effect, the scramble and bargaining for permits became intense. A prime example of maneuvering concerned long-time saloon keeper Napoleon Aubertin, elected to the common council in 1888 from Ward Four. Aubertin was unable to secure one of the twenty-seven licenses issued in 1889, but he was successful in making an arrangement with an Irish liquor vendor, Thomas Lawler. Lawler received permission to move his tavern to Aubertin's premises. The saloon was operated by Aubertin, who reportedly paid Lawler $3,000 for this arrangement, three times the cost of a license.[22]

In 1891 French Canadians became even more successful in the quest for liquor licenses following the election of two of their number to the board of aldermen. Ward Two shoe dealer Antoine Marcotte and Ward Six trucker Mederic LaPorte, both Republicans, became members of the liquor ring. With Michael Connors, LaPorte—whose election campaign had been marred by charges that he promised licenses in return for political support—was one of the most aggressive aldermen in the combination. French Canadians secured seven of the thirty-five first-class licenses issued, causing the *Transcript* to remark, ''What an atmosphere of France and Canada there is about the licenses for 1892.''[23]

Alderman Marcotte was content to work his influence on behalf of two of his constituents, Labarre and Monat, who were seeking a joint license. Marcotte agreed to demolish a tenement he owned if Labarre and Monat succeeded, as they did, in getting a license. In return the saloon keepers erected a structure on the site, paid rent to Marcotte, and agreed to turn over its ownership to the alderman in three years. Marcotte's singlemindedness in the license game was a prime reason for his defeat in the next election to Democrat Frederick St. Martin, who prudently made many promises of licenses if elected. Reports that LaPorte had offered a license to an Irish alderman in return for the latter's acquiescence in the ring's decisions did not prevent his reelection.[24]

In 1893 LaPorte was again a leading figure in the ring and St. Martin replaced Marcotte. However, the harmony which usually prevailed in the ring was shattered, primarily because St. Martin would not or could not honor promises he had made during the campaign. The dissolution of the ring threw the license-awarding process into disarray. St. Martin was briefly able to take advantage of the confusion, and four licenses were granted to his French-Canadian constituents in Ward Two. However, through the efforts of Connors and LaPorte a new unity was soon achieved. Within a week the aldermen reconsidered the licenses that had already been granted and gained a measure of revenge for the turmoil St. Martin had instigated, withdrawing approval for three of the Ward Two licenses he had sponsored.[25]

Although the liquor issue crossed party lines, the Irish

Democratic domination of Holyoke's elected offices in the late 1880s and early 1890s was the major factor in perpetuating ring rule. The efforts of both Democratic and Republican mayors to enforce strictly the liquor-selling laws proved futile. Two mayors took the drastic step of refusing to sign licenses approved by the aldermen until those previously convicted of license violations were purged from the list. But political pressures and the need for the license revenue eventually forced these mayors to relent and sign the permits.[26] To predominantly Yankee manufacturing leaders in Holyoke, manipulation of the liquor licenses was the most irritating aspect of Irish Democratic rule. Their moralistic opposition to the abuses of the license system masked much of their resentment at being replaced as the city's political leaders. The Yankee elite dominated the local Republican party, although numerical necessity required that they seek political support from the English, Scotch, German, and part of the French-Canadian communities. Within the GOP, some voters called for total prohibition. On a few occasions, usually in conjunction with state-wide efforts, the prohibitionists—as noted—came very close to their goal in the annual liquor referendum. By and large, however, the dominant figures in the Republican party used the liquor issue to gain support and break Irish political control. Although Holyoke usually returned a respectable majority for the Democratic candidates in state elections, local Republicans were not without victories at the state level. In 1888 they were able to persuade the Republican-dominated General Court to amend the city charter. The revision was a tenure bill which made permanent all police appointments, except that of chief. But the 1889 license reduction law made enforcement of illegal selling most difficult, and some of the police force were inclined to overlook violations.[27]

The unsavory aspects of the license distribution in

1893 gave Republicans an opportunity to make structural changes in city government. The Democrats nominated an associate of ring boss Connors for mayor, while the GOP put forth a former police chief, Marciene Whitcomb, who had long opposed ring rule. Whitcomb was elected by a margin of nine votes, and once in office directed the police to enforce the laws concerning liquor selling. At the same time, Republicans in the General Court introduced legislation to create municipal liquor commissions—appointed by the mayor—to act on matters of license approval. As the bill was making its way through the legislature, the 1894 ring was formed by Connors and St. Martin. St. Martin had apparently mended his political fences, for half of the applicants from his ward received licenses. Mayor Whitcomb delayed signing the licenses until the liquor commission bill was enacted. Whitcomb then appointed the commission, which took new applications and subsequently rescinded the licenses of many tavern owners, including some French Canadians who had been aided by St. Martin.[28]

It soon became apparent that neither the liquor commission nor the revised 1896 city charter, which increased Republican strength in the city, could control the Irish machine. In 1895, Whitcomb, who had been elected to the state senate, was able to maneuver a bill through the General Court which would have permitted the governor to appoint a police commission, which in turn would control the granting of licenses. But opposition from the city council and pressure from state-wide liquor interests induced Republican Governor Frederick T. Greenhalge to veto the Whitcomb Bill in the name of home rule.[29]

With the board of aldermen now removed from liquor license distribution, the Democratic machine focused on recapturing the mayor's chair and the patronage that went with it. In 1895 Connors's lieutenant, James Curran, and in 1897, Connors himself, won election as chief executive, and both received overwhelming support from the French-Canadian wards. Connors's one-year administration was the high point of Democratic influence in Holyoke prior to 1910. The ring boss gave lip service to the enforcement of the liquor laws, but his opponents soon charged bribery and corruption in the awarding of licenses, and two liquor commissioners resigned in disgust. Ironically, the Connors machine was destroyed not by its own malfeasance, but as a result of a scandal not directly related to his organization. In the summer of 1898, it was discovered that the city tax collector, James Keough, had embezzled $150,000 of city funds.[30] The Keough scandal proved to be the catalyst that brought the bulk of the French-Canadian vote into the Republican party and helped insure GOP domination of city politics for the next twelve years.[31]

The Republican machine was put together by William F. Whiting, son of a former Holyoke mayor and congressman. Whiting was a paper manufacturer and later a member of Calvin Coolidge's cabinet. Whiting's brother-in-law, Arthur Chapin, was the successful Republican mayoral candidate in 1898 and he occupied the mayor's office until 1904, when he was elected state treasurer. Chapin's successor as mayor was Nathan Avery, who also served six terms and was closely allied with the Whiting organization. The twelve years, 1899–1910, of unbroken Republican control of the mayor's office were marked by a business-oriented approach to city government. The most flagrant abuses in the license system were controlled. On the surface, Republican rule was efficient and honest, although the Republicans used patronage to come to an accommodation with the city's Democratic politicians who normally controlled the board of aldermen.[32]

An important part of the Republicans' success was their

ability to capture the larger proportion of the French-Canadian vote. The French Canadians had generally voted Democratic in both state and city elections, but by the late 1880s and during the 1890s there were signs that a shift was taking place. The McKinley-Bryan campaign momentarily disrupted past voting patterns in Holyoke. For the first time since the Civil War, the GOP carried Holyoke in a presidential race, and in the heavily French-Canadian Ward Two, which had supported Cleveland in the past three elections, voters supported McKinley by a margin of almost 2 to 1.[33] Yet it was not national or state politics, but local issues which put the French Canadians solidly in the Republican camp.

As with the size of the French-Canadian voting bloc, the nature of their vote is equally difficult to determine. Only in Ward Two, and there not until the 1890s, did the French Canadians constitute a majority of residents. In 1900, Wards One and Four had a French-Canadian population of 30–35 percent, and 15–18 percent, respectively. Therefore, only in Ward Two are French-Canadian voting patterns somewhat discernible. From 1886 to 1898, in the annual election for mayor, Ward Two—which was divided into two precincts in 1895—generally returned a majority of 60–65 percent for the Democratic candidate. The French Canadians of Ward Two were closely tied to the Irish patronage machine, as indicated by Michael Connors's 2-to-1 and 3-to-1 margins in his 1896 and 1897 mayoral campaigns. The scandal of 1898 and the growing realization on the part of many French Canadians that they had been receiving short shrift from the Irish Democrats altered their voting habits.[34]

The French-Canadian switch to the Republican party was made more difficult because of their longstanding opposition to prohibition, which found its strongest political voice in the GOP. The events of 1898 had revived the hopes of the antiliquor forces, as well as those who simply wanted an honest city administration. However, in casting their votes for the Republican "reform" candidate for mayor and against the elimination of liquor sales, the French Canadians made it clear that they perceived reform as strict control of liquor, not as prohibition.[35] By using the liquor issue and that of political appointments, the Republicans were able to consolidate their gains among the French Canadians. As a result, from 1899 to 1910, with one exception, Precinct 2A—with a population nearly two-thirds French Canadian—was in the GOP column in the mayoral elections.

The French-Canadian vote in Wards One and Four is more difficult to determine. Ward One was a former Irish enclave into which the French Canadians had begun to move in the 1890s. Both precincts generally went 55–70 percent for the Democratic mayoral candidate, and the French-Canadian vote, indicated by activities on behalf of each party, appeared to be split. Most French Canadians in Ward Four lived in Precinct 4A, a section that included the Lyman Mills tenements. Ward Four had been the original French-Canadian area of Holyoke, but in the 1890s they were being replaced by Polish immigrants who took over the lowest-paying jobs in the cotton textile mills. By 1900 approximately one-fourth to one-third of 4A was French Canadian. Precinct 4B was largely Irish, and although both precincts in Ward Four were Democratic, there were significant differences in their voting patterns. In the Irish 4B, the Democratic margin was always greater than in the other precinct, suggesting that the Republicans were the recipients of a good share of 4A's French-Canadian vote.[36]

There were major differences not only in the ethnic make-up of the three French-Canadian wards, but also in the economic structure. Tax records clearly indicate a movement of major French-Canadian property holding into Ward One in the 1890s, and especially into Ward Two, and the decline of property holding in Ward Four. By 1898, there were many French Canadians in Ward Two to whom the idea of an honest, businesslike government would appeal. But their growing affinity for the Republican party was not simply a by-product of their increased affluence. The change in voting patterns, evident after 1898, indicates that the revelation of the Democratic scandal gave some French Canadians a moral rationale for abandoning their old political allegiances. In addition, they could no longer rely on Democratic largess. The political change was not complete, as evidenced by the importance of local issues in Precinct 2A: although 2A still continued to return a Democratic majority in the annual gubernatorial races from 1898 to 1910, it voted for the city's Republican mayoral candidates.[37]

The most influential French-Canadian Democrat in Holyoke was Pierre Bonvouloir, a successful grocer who was later instrumental in establishing the French-Canadian-owned City Cooperative Bank in 1889. Bonvouloir harbored political ambitions and had made a number of unsuccessful attempts to gain election to the common council. In 1886, in an effort to oust an incumbent, antiliquor Republican mayor, the Democrats nominated Bonvouloir for a school committee at-large seat in order to attract French-Canadian votes. He was only the second French Canadian to run city-wide, and his nomination began a period in which the French-Canadian vote became a valued commodity in Holyoke. At the nominating caucus Bonvouloir stressed the nature of his voter appeal, claiming that he was representative of a "race" the Democrats should recognize. Bonvouloir ran considerably ahead of his party's ticket in the French-Canadian wards and was elected by a narrow margin, while the Democratic mayoral candidate lost by 58 votes.[38]

Bonvouloir was reelected to the school committee in 1888 by a city-wide margin of almost 2 to 1. The next year he sought the office of city treasurer. He had the misfortune to encounter a popular Republican incumbent, and his candidacy was hurt by intraparty feuds with the Irish. Special efforts were made by the French-Canadian community to forget party differences and unite behind Bonvouloir, the first of their nationality to run for a municipal administrative position.[39] Their efforts moved the Republican *Transcript* to remark that "the disadvantage of having to run against a Frenchman in this city is apparent. The Frenchmen have drawn the line of nationalism very foolishly and every man of the men who vote at all may be relied upon to vote for Bonvouloir. It is not too much to expect every American to rebuke such an assumption by placing his ballot where it belongs."[40]

Bonvouloir was defeated by more than 300 votes, while the Democratic candidate for mayor won by approximately the same margin, a result which caused considerable resentment among Holyoke's French Canadians. The *Transcript* accurately observed that "Mr. Bonvouloir has been the victim of a scheme and the imprudence of his friends."[41] Many French Canadians believed that the scheme was hatched by the Irish Democratic leaders who had engineered Bonvouloir's nomination to get French-Canadian support, but then failed to help him in the general election. This speculation was borne out in part by the election returns which showed Bonvouloir running slightly ahead of the Democratic ticket in the French-Canadian areas, but considerably behind in otherwise Democratic sections of the city. The campaign left a legacy of bitterness, and some French Canadians vowed to be more careful before giving their support again to the Democratic party.[42]

The Republicans tried to capitalize on this disaffection in

1890, by running a French Canadian, Ophir Genest, for city clerk. They succeeded to the extent that, although losing, Genest ran as much as 2 to 1 ahead of other Republicans in the French-Canadian wards. The following year the Republicans even approached Bonvouloir, whose stature had been enhanced by his association with the newly established City Cooperative Bank, and offered to support him for the school committee race in order to dissuade him from making another attempt for the office of city treasurer. But Bonvouloir proved loyal to the Democrats and ran strongly for city treasurer, losing by only sixty votes. In 1892, with the Republican city treasurer running for mayor, Bonvouloir won the post capturing 60 percent of the votes. Bonvouloir remained city treasurer until 1932. He became a political institution in Holyoke and was rarely challenged at the polls. His ability and reputation for honesty were unmatched in Holyoke politics during this period. In 1901, when he did face opposition, the Republican *Transcript* urged voters to return Bonvouloir, for he was "safe, sound and conservative."[43] In 1898, without his knowledge, the Democratic State Convention nominated him for state treasurer. The Democrats had little chance of capturing any office on the lower part of the state ballot during these years, and the nomination, which Bonvouloir declined, was in large part a goodwill gesture toward the French-Canadian vote. Bonvouloir remained active in Holyoke politics and his influence helped hold some French Canadians in the Democratic party.[44]

The importance of Bonvouloir's political rise was not lost on the Republicans and they dutifully courted the French-Canadian vote, especially through appointments to various city commissions. In the 1880s French Canadians had been appointed to the park commission, board of assessors, and registrar of voters, but in the 1890s the custom became institutionalized. Unofficially there was a "French-Canadian seat" on the board of registrar of voters, park commission, board of assessors, fire commission, board of public works, the overseers of the poor, and various less important positions. French-Canadian vacancies were, with few exceptions, filled by other French Canadians. Most of the appointees were Republican because from 1893 through 1910, the GOP controlled the mayor's office for all but two years. But even the two Democratic mayors found it expedient to reappoint Republican French Canadians or replace them with Democratic French Canadians. The Republicans used these appointments to consolidate support among French Canadian business interests, reward politically faithful French Canadians—whom they had used to balance the GOP ticket—and sidetrack the careers of ambitious politicians. Commenting on businessman Daniel Proulx's appointment in 1898 as fire commissioner, the *Transcript* candidly admitted Proulx represented a group "to which it is necessary to cater a considerable extent on account of the strong vote which that class controls."[45] Mederic LaPorte, in the 1890s, and William Beaudro, a decade later, were aldermen with ambitions to become mayor and challenge the Yankee elite that controlled the Republican machine. The party quashed the ambitions of both and then gave them appointive positions in an effort to restore harmony and soothe French-Canadian feelings. LaPorte was perhaps the most powerful Republican politician of the period and proved to be a difficult man for the party leaders to control. As a leader of the liquor ring, LaPorte had built a power base that was not confined to the French-Canadian community. He twice unsuccessfully sought the mayoral nomination and was consoled on each occasion with a visible appointed position, in an effort by the GOP to retain the loyalty of French-Canadian voters.[46]

Paralleling the development of the practice of appointing French Canadians to certain municipal positions, party leaders began to guarantee them a certain number of elected positions on the city council. In discussing the possible successor to a French-Canadian common councilor in 1888, the *Transcript* announced that he should be French Canadian too, inasmuch as it was generally agreed that "the French residents are supposed to have at least one representative in the council."[47] Both parties usually accepted this axiom, and especially before the abolition of the common council in 1896, the slates in the French-Canadian wards generally included one or more French-Canadian candidates for the council. Noting in 1895 that the Democratic ticket in Ward Four, put together by Alderman Peter O'Shea, contained a French Canadian, the *Transcript* commented that "it is no more than right that the French should have a representative in the council. O'Shea has always brought a Frenchman with him when elected. P O' is a hustler always."[48]

By the early 1890s both parties in effect acknowledged that the alderman's seat in Ward Two should go to a French Canadian, and rarely did either nominate a candidate who was not French Canadian. Until the dismantling of the Democratic ring in the late 1890s, and because of the size of the Irish Democratic vote, the Republican party needed the French-Canadian vote more than did their opponents. The large Irish vote, plus the constant warfare on liquor-related issues between Irish politicians, caused the Democratic leaders to ignore the political sensibilities of the French Canadians and allowed the GOP to make inroads. This was especially true among those French Canadians who became voters in the late 1880s and after, who had less allegiance to the Democratic party and had repeatedly witnessed the cavalier manner with which the Democrats treated the French-Canadian community. The Republicans took full advantage of this situation and included many more French Canadians on their tickets than did the Democrats. As was the case with their patronage appointments, the GOP French-Canadian nominees were given visibility and prestige, but usually had little chance of achieving election or power. On eight occasions between 1889 and 1910, a French Canadian was on the Republican slate for either city clerk, state representative, or state senate. Of these, only one was successful, a 1905 candidate for state representative.[49]

In spite of their client status within the Republican party, more French Canadians gravitated to the GOP because the Republicans made more promises and offered more opportunities than did the Democrats. Even the brief flurry of American Protective Association activity within the Republican party between 1893 and 1895 did not deter the French Canadians. When the Republicans began to move against the Irish machine in the late 1890s, they emphasized their support of the French-Canadian community. For example, in 1900, when a Democratic circular, printed in French, attacked the Republicans for doing nothing for the French Canadians, the *Transcript* responded with a list of fourteen Republican French Canadians who held elective or appointive office in the city. In the first decade of the twentieth century, the *Transcript* continually emphasized the support the GOP received from leading French Canadians, and ridiculed Democratic professions of concern for the French Canadians.[50]

The Democrats unwittingly abetted the Republicans by making a series of political blunders which further alienated the French-Canadian community. During the 1894 campaign in which liquor was the overriding issue, ring boss Connors offended many French-Canadian Democrats by claiming that he could buy all the French-Canadian votes in Ward Four with $25 or the promise of a license. In 1899

Democratic leader John Sheehan published an article in his newspaper, *The Free Press*, indicating that his party would win even if the entire French-Canadian vote went Republican. The failure of the Democrats to nominate any French Canadians on their city-wide slate in 1896 further eroded their support. Only after 1906, when the liquor interests in the party had been repudiated, did the Democrats again actively solicit the French-Canadian vote through nominations and appointments to party positions, a practice common in the Republican party for nearly two decades. The Democratic advertisements acknowledged the Republican preference of French Canadians, but urged them to believe that the Democratic party now had their best interests at heart. For the most part Democratic appeals went unheeded, and in city elections, most French Canadians favored the Republicans.[51]

The differing treatment of French Canadians by the two political parties influenced their vote. In general, Republicans proved more accommodating, primarily because they needed their vote if they were to have any chance of unseating the Irish. Although the French Canadians could only marginally influence GOP policy, their political sensibilities were handled carefully and they were given visible and prestigious positions within the party and in Republican city administrations. On the other hand, cultural and ethnic differences between the Irish and French Canadians led the Irish-controlled Democratic party to alienate the French-Canadian voters by only reluctantly appointing or nominating French Canadians and failing to support those who did run as Democrats.

French Canadians had some leverage and bargaining power because of the political balance in Holyoke, but before 1910 they were seldom in a position to control events. Their most conspicuous political failure was the inability of their leaders to unify French Canadians and effectively use their power. Repeated attempts were made to elect French-Canadian candidates, regardless of party, but the efforts usually failed because of political differences, personal feuds, or overzealousness.

In the 1880s and 1890s, French-Canadian political clubs were created in those wards with a large French-Canadian population. These groups were independent of one another and usually nonpartisan. The major purpose of these clubs was to unite French-Canadian voters behind the same candidates and then attempt to persuade one of the political parties to include them on their slate. Until the common council was abolished in 1896, there was a reasonable likelihood that one or more of the three nominees for the council would be French Canadian. However, the process of candidate selection clearly shows that French-Canadian wishes were at the mercy of party leaders. It was not uncommon for the French-Canadian caucus to result in more disunity than harmony. In 1893, for example, the Ward Two French Independent Club was torn apart by disagreements over a choice for alderman. The French-Canadian position in ward politics was weakened further by disputes within the ward, especially within the Democratic party. Feuding Irish politicians, each seeking the ward's alderman's chair, would present separate slates for the common council to the ward caucus. Each ticket would usually include at least one French Canadian for ethnic balance, a practice which further split French-Canadian influence.[52]

In the case of Pierre Bonvouloir, French-Canadian ethnic pride outweighed political affiliation, and he enjoyed near-unanimous support from the French-Canadian community during his long political career. However, other French-Canadian aspirants were not as fortunate. The Republican machine, which had won the city election in 1898, moved to strengthen its support among French Canadians by nominating Daniel Proulx for the state senate the following year. Proulx was an attractive candidate with excellent prospects for election, and received the full support of the Republican party. The *Transcript* called his nomination "both wise and strong. It will give the French people a chance for legislative representation. They have never gotten so very much politically from either party. This year all French voters ought to be Republican for Senator at least."[53] In spite of the impressive support from Republican and French-Canadian leaders, Proulx lost. Some 500 French-Canadian voters, approximately the margin of Proulx's defeat, did not cast ballots in the election, causing the Holyoke French-Canadian newspaper to conclude that the French Canadians had made themselves a laughing stock and had diminished the value of their vote.[54]

If apathy was an ingredient in Proulx's defeat, overzealous support could also prove fatal. In 1906 John Goddu, a one-term state representative, was selected to challenge the same Irish Democratic state senator who had beaten Proulx seven years earlier. *La Justice* destroyed any hope of victory for Goddu when the newspaper asked Democratic French Canadians, "Why should you deliberately propose to sacrifice the only chance we have to send one of our own to the Senate?"[55] The French-Canadian community's reaction to this remark indicates the degree to which they had become politically independent. Many expressed their outrage at *La Justice*'s statement, and reportedly hundreds decided to vote Democratic in protest.[56] A similar incident occurred two years later when *La Verdette*, a short-lived rival to *La Justice*, supported a French-Canadian candidate by publishing remarks that ridiculed the Irish. French-Canadian politicians quickly disassociated themselves from the *La Verdette* statement, but their candidate, the first

French-Canadian chairman of the school committee, was not reelected.[57]

In the 1890s, the French-Canadian vote shifted toward the Republican camp in city-wide elections. But in races between two French Canadians the results were not so predictable. Between 1899 and 1910, the heavily French-Canadian Precinct 2A supported the Republican candidate for mayor in every election except one. In the same twelve-year period, the ward was represented by Democratic aldermen for ten of those years. Whereas most of the ward's voters perceived that French-Canadian interests would be better advanced by the city's Republicans, in ward politics, personalities, patronage, and effectiveness in office overcame partisan considerations.[58]

Prior to 1910, French Canadians in Holyoke increased their political influence but were generally unable either to exhibit power independent of the two major political parties, or to achieve dominance within one. Throughout this period, community leaders could not politically unite the French-Canadians and use their vote to gain more patronage. Local political circumstances permitted Republicans to be more accommodating to the French Canadians than were the Democrats, as Republicans attempted to increase their power base and oust the entrenched Irish machine. The GOP offered more than political accommodation. The French Canadians had been predominately Democratic in the 1870s and 1880s, and had followed the political lead of their coreligionists, the Irish. The growth and changes that had become evident in the French-Canadian community by the mid 1880s also changed their perceptions of the two political parties, particularly in local affairs. The Republicans were able to convince the French Canadians that they were the party of integrity and stability, without raising the specter of anti-Catholicism and anti-immigration which existed within some elements of the party. At the same time, the Democrats made the decision easier for the French Canadians by their administration of the liquor ring and their apparent lack of concern with French-Canadian political feelings. By 1900 the second generation had become politically active. Although less susceptible to overt ethnic flattery, they were still unable to make significant inroads into the political power structure. As a result, they continued to take what they could from the Republicans.

Table 1   Estimated Number of French-Canadian Voters in Holyoke, 1885–1910

	Number French-Canadian Voters	Total Voters in City	French-Canadian Voters as a Percentage of Total Voters
1885	258	4046	6.4
1887	500	NA	NA
1892	600+	4843	12.4
1895	800	6597	12.1
1898	1200	6687	18.0
1910	2100	9810	21.6

SOURCE: Derived from *Holyoke Transcript*, Sept. 16, 1887, Dec. 12, 1898; *Springfield Republican*, Sept. 18, 1892; Mass. Labor Bureau: *Annual Report* (1888), p. 155; U.S. Bureau of the Census, *1910*, vol. 2, p. 892; Massachusetts Census, *1895*, 1, p. 237; Massachusetts, Secretary of the Commonwealth, *Number of Assessed Polls, Registered Voters and Persons who Voted in Each Voting Precinct at the State, City, and Town Election,* 1893, p. 25, 1899, p. 13.

Table 2   Vote for Mayor and Liquor Referendum in City of Holyoke and Ward Two, Precincts A and B, 1898

	Mayor		Liquor	
	Chapin(R)	Sheehan(D)	Yes	No
City Total	2949	2584	2785	2716
Precinct 2A	201	229	275	137
Precinct 2B	149	207	234	124

SOURCE: Holyoke, *Election Register*, City Clerk's Office, 1898.

Table 3 Republican Mayoral Vote, Precinct 2A, Holyoke, 1896–1910 (in percentage)

1896	34.8	1904	36.4[a]
1897	24.4	1905	65.0
1898	46.8	1906	49.7
1899	50.2	1907	60.9
1900	62.9	1908	56.6
1901	63.7	1909	63.4
1902	51.3	1910	64.3
1903	57.3		

SOURCE: Holyoke, *Election Register*, City Clerk's Office, 1896–1910.

[a]Three-way race.

Table 4 Property Taxes of French Canadians in Wards One, Two, and Four, Holyoke, 1875–1900

	1875			1880			1885		
Ward	1	2	4	1	2	4	1	2	4
Tax Amount									
$100–200	0	1	4	0	2	4	0	8	5
200–500	1	2	1	0	3	2	1	4	5
500–1000	0	0	1	0	0	0	0	0	1

	1890			1895			1900		
Ward	1	2	4	1	2	4	1	2	4
Tax Amount									
$100–200	5	14	5	12	26	5	14	43	5
200–500	1	6	5	2	5	1	6	21	1
500–1000	0	1	1	0	0	1	1	1	0

SOURCE: Based on lists of major Holyoke tax payers published in the *Transcript* and *Republican*, 1875–1900. Figures are not available by ward after 1900.

Notes

1. Ralph D. Vicero, "Immigration of French Canadians to New England, 1840–1900: A Geographical Analysis" (Ph.D. diss., University of Wisconsin, 1968), passim.

2. Massachusetts, Bureau of the Statistics of Labor, *Annual Report* (1881), pp. 469–70.

3. Ibid.

4. Quoted in Harold F. Wilson, *The Hill Country of Northern New England: Its Social and Economic History, 1790–1930* (New York: Columbia University Press, 1936), p. 162.

5. Henry Loomis Nelson, "French Canadians in New England," *Harper's New Monthly Magazine* 87 (July 1893): 183; Jacques Ducharme, *Shadows of the Trees* (New York: Harper Bros., 1943), p. 168; Letter from Jacques Ducharme to Peter Haebler, Nov. 4, 1974.

6. Duane Lockard, *New England State Politics* (Princeton, N.J.: Princeton University Press, 1959), pp. 311–13; Daniel B. Walker, "The Presidential Politics of the Franco-Americans," *Canadian Journal of Economics and Political Science* 28 (August 1963): 353–56.

7. Ronald A. Petrin, "Culture, Community and Politics: French Canadians in Massachusetts, 1885–1915" (Paper delivered at the Third Annual Conference of the French Institute, Assumption College, Worcester, Massachusetts, March 1982: The Little Canadas of New England).

8. Constance McLaughlin Green, *Holyoke, Massachusetts: A Case History of the Industrial Revolution in America*, rev. ed. (Hamden, Conn.: Archon Books, 1968), passim; Peter Haebler, "Habitants in Holyoke: The Development of the French-Canadian Community in a Massachusetts City, 1865–1910" (Ph.D. diss., University of New Hampshire, 1976), passim.

9. See, for example, Massachusetts Labor Bureau, *Annual Report* (1882), pp. 1–92.

10. Samuel P. Hays, "The Changing Political Structure of the City in Industrial America," *Journal of Urban History* 1 (November 1974): 10–14.

11. *Holyoke Transcript*, March 13, 1873.

12. Paul Kleppner, *The Cross of Culture: A Social Analysis of Midwestern Politics, 1850–1900* (New York: The Free Press, 1970). Kleppner maintains that religious differences (ritualism versus pietism) were the central elements in determining midwestern political attitudes. More important, in Kleppner's view political affiliations were an extension of religious beliefs. The ritualists and pietists had differing concepts of public morality and this was reflected by their voting habits. For example, ritualistic Catholics and German Lutherans more often identified themselves with the Democratic party, whereas pietists—Norwegians,

Welsh, and native Baptists and Methodists—were usually Republican. During the depression of the 1890s, Kleppner contends that there was a shift in the traditional basis of political alignments. The Bryan campaign of 1896 appealed to pietistic values and changed the nature of the party's support. At the same time, the Republicans sublimated divisive cultural differences to promote themselves as the party of "prosperity."

Kleppner's approach is innovative, but it is difficult to apply to Holyoke. The two largest ethnic groups in the city, the Irish and French Canadians, constituted 60 to 70 percent of the total population during the period, and both were Roman Catholic, i.e., ritualistic. Yet the Irish remained loyal to the Democrats whereas the French Canadians increasingly voted Republican in local elections, particularly after 1898. If the ritualistic versus pietistic model does not hold true for Holyoke, social and cultural differences between the Irish and French Canadians help explain the nature of the political alignments in Holyoke.

13. *Transcript*, Nov. 17, 1893.

14. Haebler, "Habitants," p. 263, table 38.

15. U.S., Bureau of the Census, 1910. vol. 2, p. 892.

16. Holyoke, *Municipal Register*, 1886–1910; Franco-American Centennial Committee, "The Franco-Americans Honor Holyoke's Historic Hundredth," Holyoke, 1973, pp. 38–39.

17. Holyoke, *Municipal Register*, 1886–1910.

18. *Springfield Republican*, Feb. 21, 1892.

19. Green, *Holyoke*, pp. 263–65.

20. *Transcript*, Dec. 8 and 11, 1899.

21. Holyoke, *Election Register*, City Clerk's Office, 1886–1910.

22. *Transcript*, June 14, 1889.

23. Ibid., April 2, 1892.

24. Ibid., Nov. 23 and 24, 1891, March 16, 1892, April 1, 2, and 4, 1892; *Republican*, April 3, 1892, Dec. 4, 1892.

25. *Transcript*, March 20, 1893, April 1, 3, and 5, 1893; *Republican*, April 1, 2, and 4, 1893.

26. After 1889, first-class licenses cost from $1,000 to $1,500 per year and were an important source of city revenue.

27. Massachusetts, *Acts and Resolves of the General Court*, 1888, chap. 386; Green, *Holyoke*, pp. 253–55; *Republican*, May 3 and 29, 1887, July 28, 1887, Feb. 12, 1888; *Transcript*, June 12, 1888, April 24, 1889, May 4 and 15, 1889.

28. Massachusetts, *Acts*, 1894, chap. 428; *Republican*, Dec. 6, 1893, Jan. 5, 1894, March 7 and 20, 1894, April 2 and 4, 1894, June 5, 1894, July 3, 1894; *Transcript*, Jan. 15, 1894, March 30, 1894, May 1, 1894, July 2, 1894.

29. *Transcript*, Jan. 29, 1895, Feb. 13, 1895, May 10, 1895; *Republican*, Feb. 9 and 16, 1896.

30. The irony of the Keough case was compounded for the French Canadians by the nature of his appointment. In 1892 Keough and Daniel Proulx both sought the position of tax collector. After a long and confusing struggle involving a questionable ballot taken by the board of aldermen, the aldermen, largely through the adroit political maneuvers of Alderman Mederic LaPorte, overrode a ruling by the mayor, and named Proulx tax collector. Keough brought suit and the Massachusetts Supreme Judicial Court eventually declared him the tax collector. For details see Massachusetts, Supreme Judicial Court at Springfield, *Petition of James Keough for a Writ of Mandamus* v. *the Board of Aldermen of the City of Holyoke and Daniel Proulx*, case no. 95, filed Feb. 20, 1892.

31. *Transcript*, July 16, 1895; *Republican*, Jan. 24, 1895, Oct. 31, 1897, May 23, 1898, August 14, 1898.

32. Green, *Holyoke*, pp. 268–77.

33. Holyoke, *Election Register*, 1886–1896.

34. Ibid., 1886–1900. The ethnic breakdowns of each ward are based on information derived from Holyoke, *Assessors Field Books*, 1880–1900.

35. Holyoke, *Election Register*, 1885–1898.

36. Ibid., 1886–1910.

37. Ibid., 1898–1910.

38. *Transcript*, Dec. 4 and 8, 1886; *Republican*, Dec. 5, 8, 9, and 16, 1886. An interesting sidelight to the race was that in three non-French-Canadian wards a total of 79 voters, more than Bonvouloir's margin of victory, cast their ballots for "Peter" Bonvouloir, whereas the remainder of his votes were for "Pierre." A recount gave a majority of the "Peter" ballots to Bonvouloir, making his final margin of victory 43 votes.

39. *Transcript*, Nov. 16, 18, 20, and 25, 1889; *Republican*, Nov. 24, 1889.

40. *Transcript*, Nov. 30, 1889.

41. Ibid., Dec. 4, 1889.

42. Ibid., Dec. 6, 1889; *Republican*, Dec. 1, 4, and 8, 1889.

43. *Transcript*, Dec. 6, 1901.

44. Ibid., Dec. 1, 1890, Nov. 11, 1891, Dec. 1 and 3, 1891, Nov. 12, 1895, Oct. 5, 1898; *Republican*, Nov. 16, 1890, Dec. 3, 1890, Nov. 22, 1891, Dec. 3, 1891, Dec. 7, 1892, Oct. 10 and 21, 1898.

45. *Transcript*, May 31, 1899.

46. Ibid., Oct. 6, 1893, Nov. 25, 1893, Nov. 27, 1895, August 17, 1897, Oct. 5, 1897, Nov. 10, 1897, Jan. 12 and 13, 1898, Nov. 16, 1904, July 12 and 19, 1907, July 1, 1908, August 1, 1908, Feb. 24, 1910, March 4 and 9, 1910; *La Justice*, March 3 and 10, 1910; *Republican*, May 16, 1894, Jan. 16, 1896, Oct. 19, 1896, Nov. 15, 1896, Jan. 29, 1897, Feb. 17, 1897, Oct. 22 and 23, 1897, Dec. 15, 1897, Jan. 17, 1898, Sept. 27, 1898; Holyoke, *Municipal Register*, 1886–1910; "Holyoke's Historic Hundredth," pp. 42–43.

47. *Transcript*, August 1, 1888.

48. Ibid., Nov. 2, 1895.

49. Ibid., Oct. 2, 1889, Oct. 19, 1892; Holyoke, *Election Register*, 1889–1910.

50. *Transcript*, Nov. 17, 1893, Oct. 22, 1894, Nov. 3, 1894, Oct. 12, 1895, Nov. 20 and 30, 1903, Dec. 3, 1903, Dec. 5, 1908, Dec. 4, 1909; *Republican*, Sept. 2 and 23, 1894, Sept. 26 and 29, 1895.

51. *Transcript*, Dec. 4, 1894, Oct. 3, 1907, Jan. 12, 1909, Oct. 3, 1909; *Republican*, Dec. 3, 1896; *La Justice*, August 19, 1909, Nov. 3, 1910.

52. *Transcript*, Nov. 23, 1886, Nov. 21, 23, and 25, 1887, Dec. 1, 2, and 5, 1887, Sept. 5, 1891, Nov. 5, 1891, Nov. 5, 1895, Dec. 1, 1900, Dec. 4, 1902; *Republican*, Nov. 19, 1887, Dec. 1, 1887, Nov. 17 and 21, 1893.

53. *Transcript*, Oct. 30, 1899.

54. *La Presse*, Nov. 17, 1899.

55. *Holyoke Evening Telegram*, Nov. 3, 1906.

56. Ibid.

57. *Transcript*, Nov. 25, 26, and 28, 1908.

58. Holyoke, *Election Register*, 1898–1910.

The Immigrant Response to Industrialism in New Bedford, 1865–1900

THOMAS A. McMULLIN

Although industrialization transformed many American cities in the latter half of the nineteenth century, few urban centers experienced as dramatic a change as New Bedford, Massachusetts. On the eve of the Civil War, the city was still a mercantile seaport, dominated by the whaling trade. In the years after the war, the fine goods cotton textile industry came to dominate the economic life of New Bedford. By the turn of the century New Bedford, with forty-two textile mills, was one of the two major American centers of cotton textile production.[1]

The large majority of men and women who came to work in the textile mills were immigrants; throughout the entire period, over three-fourths of the adult mill workers were foreign-born.[2] These workers responded to their new environment in a variety of ways, but one of the most persistent themes of their experience was resistance to aspects of the industrial system they found oppressive. In a long series of strikes, textile operatives fought particularly against speedups and wage cutbacks. An examination of these conflicts will suggest the importance of ethnic traditions, the attitudes of the larger community toward worker grievances, and the nature of the employing industry in shaping the immigrant response to industrialism.

Differences between operatives and millowners became

apparent as early as 1867. During the previous year the national movement among labor reformers for the eight-hour day had gained considerable momentum. Yet, for cotton textile operatives such as those at the city's Wamsutta Mills—who worked a minimum of eleven hours a day—an eight-hour day remained an unrealistic dream. The reform movement's support for shorter hours, however, gave the textile workers the hope that they could reduce their workday to ten hours. When nearby Fall River textile workers—the most aggressive in the industry—had struck in late 1866 and won a ten-hour day, New Bedford workers were further encouraged.[3]

On January 1, 1867, the agent of the mills, Thomas Bennett, placed the Wamsutta Mills on a ten-hour day. Bennett did this without any direct pressure from the workers, having made this decision on the assumption that his competitors in other textile centers would follow with a shortened workday. This did not happen, and on January 28, the agent announced that the factory would return to a schedule of eleven hours. The mill employees were furious and called a meeting, threatening to strike. Bowing to the pressure, Bennett consented to extend the trial period of the ten-hour day for one month, but insisted on reducing the pay of unskilled day hands by one-eleventh. This agreement proved acceptable to the skilled weavers and spinners who had organized the protest meeting, in that they were paid by the piece. The day laborers resented the decision, however, and divisions within the factory disrupted production for two weeks until February 16, when a frustrated Bennett took out his wrath on the committee of skilled workers who had arranged the one-month extension of the ten-hour day. He discharged five of the eight committee members, causing a worker walkout. Five hundred men and 100 women met two days later in the Eight-Hour League Hall to organize their strike. The operatives voted to strike until Bennett reinstated the five committeemen, continued the ten-hour day without any reduction in pay for the day hands, and dismissed two mill operatives hostile to the workers' committee.[4]

The Wamsutta strike became the decisive battle of the ten-hour movement among New England cotton textile operatives, gaining support from workers in other cities. For two and one-half weeks the strikers held out, until on March 6, the workers slowly began to return to the mill. The Wamsutta management rehired none of the strike committee members, and the failure of the New Bedford strike ended for the rest of the decade the movement to curtail the working hours of Massachusetts textile operatives.[5]

Although the New Bedford textile workers had failed in the 1867 strike, they were still willing to oppose unfavorable changes in working conditions and wages. The major reason for this tradition of opposition was suggested in a letter written to the New Bedford *Evening Standard*, which blamed the strike on English "bullies."[6] The largest ethnic group among the immigrant operatives in the 1860s and 1870s were English textile workers from the mills of Lancashire, who had brought to this country long experience in the urban industrial system and a strong tradition of craft unionism. Along with the "Lancashire Irish"—Celts who had spent as much as a generation or two in the textile mills of Great Britain before emigrating to New Bedford—these English workers came from industrial areas "where a strike was as natural as a day's rest on Sunday."[7]

Establishing another precedent for New Bedford's labor history, the 1867 strike elicited widespread support from the community at large. One of the city's two newspapers, the *Daily Mercury*, endorsed the ten-hour day, and the city's representative to the state legislature fought for a state law restricting minors to ten hours of daily labor. The strikers also received counsel and assistance from a number of New Bedford's middle-class reformers.[8]

The organization developed by the workers during the 1867 conflict did not survive the strike, and for the next ten years the New Bedford textile operatives remained relatively quiescent. Some of the English operatives at the Wamsutta Mills in the early 1870s turned to cooperation as a method of improving their condition. In 1871 the textile workers opened a cooperative store, but by 1876 the more permanent New Bedford Industrial Cooperative Association had begun operation. The mill workers imported England's Rochdale plan of cooperation, in which goods were sold at retail prices, with profits distributed annually to the customer. This cooperative also served as a convenient method of accumulating savings that paid interest to workers who bought shares. In addition, the cooperative gave credit to operatives. In its early years the association provided "for mutual aid in both a pecuniary and social sense."[9] Its annual meetings took the form of "old-fashioned English tea meetings," complete with dinner, entertainment, and the singing of "God Save the Queen." In 1877, although only seventy families owned shares in the cooperative, 500 people attended the tea meeting. The cooperative would continue to serve textile operatives through the rest of the century.[10]

Despite the hopes of some cooperative supporters that the movement would turn to the production of goods, the cooperative in New Bedford, as elsewhere, remained essentially a means by which groceries and other goods could be distributed to workers at reduced prices. The more traditional techniques of the strike and the union were the methods New Bedford workers would use to challenge the vicissitudes of industrialism.

In February 1877, almost ten years after their first strike, the Wamsutta workers again became involved in a conflict with mill management. The corporation announced the third cutback in pay in three years, and the operatives were also disturbed by what they claimed was the constant speedup in the mill's work. Those mill employees who had worked in England or corresponded with relatives there knew that although pay in America was better, textile operatives in the old country worked three and one-half hours a week less than the workers in New England. Weavers had to tend as many as eight looms in Massachusetts, whereas the English limit was four; and spinners had to cope with the constantly increasing speed of the mule frame machines with only one assistant, as against two in Lancashire.[11] The city's operatives not only compared their conditions to those in England, but also to those of an earlier period in New Bedford. In 1877, a spokesman for the workers recalled the days before mill agent Thomas Bennett's retirement in 1874. The mill had then been half the size, and despite longer hours, relations with management had been better. Indeed, in 1874, the 1,248 operatives of the mill had signed a testimonial statement honoring the retiring agent and had presented him with a gift.[12]

On February 5, 1877, after numerous meetings, over 2,000 operatives signed notices that they were leaving work. Only thirty-two operatives refused to give their notice. Twenty-six of these workers were French Canadians, emphasizing the emergence of ethnic divisions as a new and lasting problem for labor organization in the city. The French Canadians had first arrived in small numbers during the Civil War to replace departing soldiers, but their numbers increased throughout the period, and by the end of the century they comprised the largest ethnic group in the city's mills.[13]

Ethnic divisions were temporarily forgotten on February 8, when the corporation announced it would rescind the pay cut. But that decision was not enough. The operatives decided that "their united and determined action had brought about this partial concession of their demands."[14] The workers still hoped to gain back previous cutbacks, deal with the problem of speedups, and raise the pay in the new Number Five mill, where the pay rates were lower than in the older mills. On February 17, the operatives decided by a two-thirds vote to strike until the management met all their demands.[15]

As in the 1867 conflict, the textile workers received support from the larger community. William Henry Johnson, an ex-slave who had become an attorney and leader in the city's black community, continued the assistance he had given the strikers in 1867, serving in the new strike as legal advisor to the operatives. Daniel Ricketson, a member of one of the city's oldest and wealthiest families, chaired a number of the strikers' meetings. Storekeepers and businessmen in the North End, where the mill was located, offered financial aid to the strike committee. The two newspapers, the *Evening Standard* and the *Daily Mercury*, established a precedent for later strikes by attempting to remain impartial in their news stories, and by avoiding the strike issues on their editorial page.[16]

Although the strikers did not face opposition from the larger New Bedford community, they did have to deal with the reappearance of internal ethnic divisions which had appeared at the beginning of the conflict. Strike leaders admitted that French-Canadian operatives had always been the least enthusiastic about the strike, yet most of the emergency relief supplied by the strike committee went to French workers and their families. This became a source of dissension when, unlike some other textile workers' groups, French mill employees in other cities refused to aid the strike committee. [17]

As the strike wore on into its third month, the tensions increased between the English-speaking workers and the French Canadians. One local newspaper reported that the French-Canadian operatives would go into the mills cheerfully. The strike committee denied any ethnic divisions, one of its spokesmen claiming it was "a favorite game of capitalists to set different nationalities among the help to opposing each other." [18] The strike leaders were also careful to have French translators at their meetings, but their efforts were to no avail. On April 30, the day the corporation opened the mill, 400 operatives appeared for work. The president of the strike committee claimed that the majority of those who had gone to work were French, blaming their return on a statement delivered by the pastor of the city's French-Catholic church. The priest had advised those willing to work to go into the mills, and recommended that those who did not care to work should remain home and attend to their own affairs. [19]

The ethnic division in New Bedford's working class went much deeper than the statement of a local pastor. The French Canadians came to the factories of New Bedford from a cultural background far different from that of the Lancashire natives. Most were farmers fleeing an overcrowded rural countryside, with little experience in urban or industrial ways. A minority in their own land, the French Canadians brought to New England the belief that only through ethnic and religious solidarity could they preserve their French cultural island in the English-speaking ocean of North America. For the French-Canadian immigrant, the ethnic parish, not the labor organization or the larger socioeconomic class, was the key to survival in an alien environment. [20]

Another factor weakening the class consciousness and militancy of the French-Canadian workers was their mobility. Many stayed only a short time in the mills; their goal was simply to obtain enough money either to buy some additional land in Canada or to pay off a mortgage there. The proximity of their native land also made it possible for them to return home to friends and family during hard times and strikes. Consequently, although the French Canadians could be mobilized in a city like New Bedford with its large contingent of English and "Lancashire Irish" workers, ethnic differences would remain a drag on working-class consciousness and activism.

In the 1880s, the New Bedford cotton industry underwent significant expansion, with new corporations adding new mills and thousands of workers. A massive increase in the number of confrontations between the operatives and management accompanied this rapid growth of the industry. There were at least thirty-one strikes in New Bedford mills between 1883 and 1893, of which only seven were clearly successful. Rarely did these strikes extend beyond the operatives of single crafts working in individual factories. None involved all of the workers in a mill. This particularistic response of the workers to industrial conditions was the result of the further development of the craft consciousness that the English workers had brought from Lancashire. The craft unions of the various trades such as the spinners, weavers, cardroom employees, and loomfixers developed on a permanent basis during this period. Of the thirty-one conflicts in the 1883–1893 period, the weavers struck twelve times, the spinners nine, and assorted groups such as the loomfixers, cardroom employees, backboys, and speeder tenders organized ten strikes. Of the twenty-three strikes for which causes could be clearly ascertained, wage cuts and demands for increased pay were responsible for thirteen.

Weavers or spinners, paid by the piece, struck five times against what they considered inferior supplies such as yarn or roving. Other strikes occurred over disputes concerning overtime, speedups, and the imposition of fines on weavers for imperfect work.[21]

The increasing restrictiveness of industrial discipline led workers on several occasions to leave their jobs in walkouts that could not really be called strikes. In 1886 young women workers led the other operatives out of the Acushnet and Potomska Mills to watch the Odd Fellows' procession. The mill management warned that a recurrence of this kind of walkout would lead them to close the mills for an indefinite time. In 1890 a number of workers did not return to the afternoon shift at the Potomska Mills, choosing instead to watch a military parade. These employees fared worse than their predecessors, and most were fired. In 1891 French-Canadian workers, who celebrated New Year's Day more intensely than the native population, took the day off and went to the mill gates to persuade others to join them. Although the French Canadians might rebel against the industrial order on an occasion such as New Year's Day, the more serious walkouts—the strikes—witnessed a continuation of the tensions between the English and Irish operatives and the *Quebecois* that had appeared in 1877. On several occasions, the English-speaking immigrant workers blamed the French for the failure of strikes in the decade from 1883 to 1893.[22]

As a result of both the growing power of the city's craft unions and the severe dislocations in the American economy during the 1890s, New Bedford's textile workers moved away from the isolated craft strikes to unified job actions involving all of the city's textile workers. The first of these followed the "hard times" of 1893–94. Beginning in the summer of 1893, New Bedford mill management began to reduce hours, close down mills, and reduce wages. By the summer of 1894, wages had been reduced over 25 percent for many workers. In addition the weavers, the largest group of mill employees, believed that management was trying to defraud them by lengthening cuts, changing the type of material, and by utilizing other speedup techniques possible under the complicated piece-rate system of pay. The failure of the New Bedford manufacturers to follow the new state "particulars laws," confirmed for the weavers their worst fears. This legislation required the millowners to post in each factory the basis for computing pay rates, giving such information as the length, weight, and price of each cut. Under these pressures, all of New Bedford's textile operatives struck on August 20.[23]

Financial support soon came from textile workers elsewhere, in that the national unions had decided for the first time to make their stand on a wage cut at New Bedford rather than at nearby Fall River. One reason for this decision was a new awareness of the importance of the textile industry at New Bedford, a city that would soon be America's second most important center of cotton textile production. The strike also drew considerable public sympathy within the city. The *Evening Standard*, the city's largest newspaper, reported that "public sentiment is unanimously in sympathy with the operatives. People who generally have condemned strikes are emphatic in their opinion that the operatives deserve to win."[24]

The strikers were also aided by the fact that this strike occurred during the summer and fall, unlike the other major labor conflicts in the city in the period from 1865 to 1900, which took place during the winter. The workers could go clamming, fishing, and cranberry picking on Cape Cod. The pro-strike *Evening Journal* reported after five days of the conflict: "So far as the operatives are concerned, the strike has as yet been to most of them a pleasant vacation rather than a hardship."[25]

Nevertheless, as the strike dragged on for several weeks, the vacation façade began to disappear. This strike, as well as the other major ones of the period, occurred during a time of weak demand for cotton cloth. The failure of the mill management to cooperate fully with the State Board of Arbitration and Conciliation in 1894 suggested that the millowners were not totally unhappy with strikes such as this, viewing them as a way to cut down on unwanted inventory.[26]

By early October 1894, however, the market for cotton cloth had improved. After seven weeks of the strike, management and the spinners, the most powerful of the craft unions, agreed to a compromise cutdown on half the amounts announced on August 13. The other unions, including the reluctant weavers, had little choice but to follow.[27]

With a continuation of the improving market for cotton cloth in 1895, the New Bedford manufacturers restored pay rates to the level existing before the 1894 wage cut. Yet the period of prosperity was short-lived, and in December 1897, the New Bedford manufacturers announced a 10 percent cut in pay rates for the 9,000 cloth mill employees. This decision, along with the weavers' charges of increasing speed-ups and capricious fining for imperfect work, set the stage for a new strike early in 1898.[28]

On January 17 the workers, with the exception of those who worked in yarn mills, did not appear for work. As in earlier strikes, the operatives had widespread community support. Even the trade journal, the *American Wool and Cotton Reporter*, noted that "the sympathy of the people as a whole, including the city government itself, has been with the strikers. It is difficult to find, outside of a small coterie of mill agents and owners, any one in that community who does not express bitterness of feeling toward the manufacturers."[29] In terms of actual financial support for the strikers, labor leaders noted that those elements in the community that had close economic ties to the workers offered the most aid. Retail merchants, particularly liquor dealers, were most generous in their assistance.[30]

The strike also gained considerable support from outside the city, for, as in 1894, the national unions had decided to make their stand on wage cutbacks at New Bedford. And until the sinking of the *Maine* diverted the public's attention, a number of newspapers, particularly those of Hearst and Pulitzer in New York, gave the strike detailed, sympathetic, and often sensational coverage.[31]

Despite extensive support for the strike in New Bedford and elsewhere, internal divisions and problems appeared within the workers' ranks as the strike dragged on. The strong craft orientation brought to this country by English labor leaders produced divisions. The spinners and other craft groups feared that the weavers might end their strike if the fines controversy was settled, an issue the nonweavers felt was extraneous to the main problem of the cutback. For their part, the weavers' antagonism to the spinners went back to the 1894 strike. The weavers believed that the spinners had been able to end that strike unilaterally without even consulting the weaker weavers' union.[32]

Divisions between union and nonunion operatives also weakened the strike effort. The weavers' union, representing the largest group of operatives, could give funds only to limited numbers of nonunion workers, and constantly had to face the fear that these strikers might return to work out of desperation. Closely tied to the problem of nonunion workers was the ethnic division in the operatives' ranks. The continued problem of ethnicity was apparent in a circular the Weavers' Protective Association published in English and French about four months before the strike. The circular began with a plea: "Shall we still continue to be a union of Englishmen and Frenchmen or a union of workers?", and concluded, "Again we earnestly appeal to you to join our ranks, to sink your national, religious, and political prejudices, to stand with us in the hour of trial, and advance upon our enemies, not as a hopeless, helpless mob, but as a class-conscious and organized army."[33]

The call was unheeded, for as the strike progressed it was evident that the majority of French Canadians were not in the unions, and they could not get full strike benefits. The *Quebecois* comprised the majority of the workers who were dependent on the meager funds provided by public relief during the strike. Ironically, the most severe criticism of the French failure to join the unions came from New Bedford's three French-Catholic priests and the editor of the city's French-language paper. Each spokesman stated that the suffering among the French operatives was the result of their not joining unions.[34] These statements appeared to have grown more out of an awareness of the desperate condition of the French-Canadian workers rather than out of support for unions and strikes.

Another divisive force during the 1898 strike was its escalation into an ideological battleground for the national leaders of the American Federation of Labor and the Socialist Labor Party. Both the AFL's Samuel Gompers and Socialist Labor leader Daniel De Leon spoke in New Bedford during the strike, expending much of their energy on vitriolic attacks against each other's organization. Moderate socialist leader Eugene V. Debs also appeared in the city to gain support for his group, the Social Democracy. None of these groups won the support of a majority of the workers, but the bitter conflict between "pure and simple" trade unionists and the Socialist Laborites weakened the workers' cause.[35]

The strike, strained by internal divisions, lingered on into April. The eight-week limit on public relief for strikers had cut off aid to many nonunionized workers, leaving them dependent on charity soup kitchens for existence. The impending war with Spain had taken the strike out of the news, and outside support had diminished considerably. The crucial break in the strike came when French priests, claiming that their parishioners were starving, met with the mill-owners and asked them to open the mills. On Sunday, April 3, the French-Canadian priests read a statement in their churches announcing that they understood the mills would open. "We do not wish to advise you what to do, but want you to think the situation over carefully. Your duty to God and to your country is that you must support your children, you must not starve yourselves, but act like wise men and women."[36] On Thursday, April 7, the corporations, with the backlog of cloth diminishing, announced that the mills would open the next Monday, April 11.

Within two days of the opening, over one-third of the workers had returned to work, but thousands still stayed out. For the first time in a New Bedford strike, violence threatened as thousands of strike supporters attempted to keep workers out of the mills. For the first few days, Mayor Charles Ashley, a member of the Knights of Labor and a popular figure among the textile operatives, took no action concerning the crowds. However, on the fifth day after the mills had opened, as hostility and confrontation increased, Ashley read the riot act, prohibiting large crowds and calling in the forty-one members of the Massachusetts State Police. A few days after the opening, the corporations had issued an ultimatum to the large number of operatives who lived in company housing to either return to work or move.

Private landlords, who like the corporations had not demanded rent during the strike, now also put pressure on their tenants. These final blows for all purposes ended the strike by April 25, although the spinners did not give in until May 23.[37]

Thus, the 1898 strike failed, as had almost all of its predecessors. Yet the New Bedford textile workers had developed a record of persistent resistance to the demands of industrial management that they found unacceptable. During numerous conflicts they closed ranks to fight management in an industry that was then and is now largely unorganized by labor.

This pattern of recalcitrance indicated the importance of the "cultural baggage" that immigrants brought to America. The mill workers who came to New Bedford from the industrial cities of Lancashire continued to dominate the textile workers' movement throughout the period, despite this group's declining percentage of the total mill labor force. These English workers brought with them an established urban working-class orientation and tradition of resistance to employers. This heritage was reinforced by other aspects of Lancashire culture. For example, many New Bedford textile workers had worshiped in England in chapels of the Primitive Methodist movement, a religious group that grew rapidly in New Bedford near the end of the century. Primitive Methodists, unlike their mainstream counterparts, did not have bishops, and they emphasized democratic lay control of the church. This tradition of opposition to authority and hierarchy meshed well with the labor protest movement, and Primitive Methodists played a disproportionately large role in the development of English trade unions. In New Bedford, Primitive Methodist ministers were former workingmen sympathetic to the labor cause, such as the first pastor, Nathaniel W. Matthews, who was a former collier and secretary of a Knights of Labor assembly.[38]

The attitudes of the larger New Bedford community toward the immigrant workers also influenced the factory workers' response to industrial conditions. Workers were emboldened by the fact that little antagonism and considerable support existed in the city for the operatives in their conflicts with management. New Bedford was not a large city in the late nineteenth century, and textile strikes were major events followed by the entire community. This extensive knowledge of the conflicts, aided by the attempts at impartiality during strikes by the city's two newspapers, encouraged sympathy.[39] The community was also aware of the workers' economic and political importance in an industry that dominated the city's economy. Although native New Bedfordites did have fears about the impact of immigration, their anxieties were muted by the lack of immigrant labor violence and radicalism, as well as the small number of "new" immigrants. Finally, the heritage of New Bedford's past may have played a role in the attitudes toward immigrant strikers. The city had been founded and developed by Quakers, who had established a tradition of liberalism. Before the Civil War, New Bedford was a haven for runaway slaves such as Frederick Douglass, who wrote: "I could have landed in no part of the United States where I should have found a more striking and gratifying contrast, not only to life generally in the South, but in the condition of the Negro people there, than in New Bedford."[40] The same liberalism of some New Bedfordites that made the city a refuge for runaway slaves before the Civil War appeared to play a role in creating a sympathetic attitude toward immigrant workers in the late nineteenth century.

Yet, despite their tradition of resistance and the support of the larger community, New Bedford textile workers rarely won their conflicts with management, let alone developed a persistent and pervasive class consciousness or ideological base. One cause of this lack of success was the nature of the cotton textile industry. In an era in which the general economy suffered from wide cyclical swings, the cotton textile industry, highly decentralized in ownership and location, was extremely sensitive to boom and bust periods.[41] Manufacturers were quick to reduce wages in hard times, and reluctant to end strikes that worked off unwanted inventories. Decentralization also created problems for worker solidarity, for during prolonged strikes, operatives could and did go elsewhere to seek work. Technological advances made employment of less skilled workers possible, slowly weakening the operatives' position. And millowners in New England were already holding the threat of southern competition over their workers' heads.

Although operatives of the different ethnic groups walked off the job together in the long series of strikes, ethnic divisions obviously weakened the workers' position. The differing response of French-Canadian and English immigrants to American industrial conditions remained a source of tension. At the turn of the century, the arrival of new immigrant groups of workers into the mills, such as the Portuguese and the Poles, would exacerbate these problems. And ironically, the craft tradition of the English, the ethnic group most oriented to labor activism, would continue to be a divisive force among New Bedford textile operatives in the twentieth century.

The experience of textile workers in New Bedford suggests that immigrants did not adjust to urban industrial conditions in a uniform manner.[42] This adaptation was a complex and contradictory process in which workers evinced both solidarity and conflict between ethnic groups, and both resistance and accommodation to mill management. Fitting neither contemporary stereotype of immigrant workers as docile drones or violent radicals, the actions of the New Bedford workers indicated the importance of cultural heritage, the attitudes of the receiving community, and the state of the employing industry in shaping the immigrants' response to the industrial system.

Notes

1. Massachusetts, Secretary of the Commonwealth, *Statistical Information Relating to Certain Branches of Industry in Massachusetts, 1865*, p. 100; *Massachusetts, Census of Massachusetts, 1905*, vol. 3, p. 102; Melvin T. Copeland, *The Cotton Manufacturing Industry of the United States* (Cambridge, Mass., 1912), pp. 28–30. For a detailed discussion of industrialization in New Bedford, see Thomas A. McMullin, "Industrialization and Social Change in a Nineteenth-Century Port City: New Bedford, Massachusetts, 1865–1900" (Ph.D. diss., University of Wisconsin, 1976).

2. In 1875, 26.4 percent of the New Bedford textile operatives were of English birth, 18.2 percent were Irish born, 14.4 percent were natives of Canada, and 5.5 percent were Scots. In 1900, the Census Bureau, using the category, "Persons having either both parents as specified or one parent born as specified and one parent native," found that 40.8 percent of the city's textile workers were French Canadian, 24.1 percent English, 11.6 percent Irish, 1.7 percent Polish, and 18.9 percent "Other." A large percentage of the "Other" group in 1900 were Portuguese from the Azore Islands. Massachusetts Bureau of Statistics of Labor, *Ninth Annual Report, 1878*, pp. 216–17; United States, Bureau of the Census, Special Reports, *Occupations at the Twelfth Census*, pp. 625–27.

3. David Montgomery, *Beyond Equality: Labor and the Radical Republicans, 1862–1872* (New York, 1967), pp. 234, 277–78; Boston *Daily Evening Voice*, Oct. 31, Nov. 5, 8, Dec. 3, 1866.

4. New Bedford *Daily Mercury*, Feb. 6, 18, 19, 20, 21, 22, 1867; New Bedford *Evening Standard*, Feb. 16, 20, 1867; Montgomery, *Beyond Equality*, pp. 284–85.

5. New Bedford *Evening Standard*, March 12, 1867; New Bedford *Daily Mercury*, March 7, 12, 15, 1867; Montgomery, *Beyond Equality*, p. 290.

6. New Bedford *Evening Standard*, March 6, 1867.

7. An English textile worker in Fall River, Massachusetts, quoted in Massachusetts Bureau of Statistics of Labor, *Thirteenth Annual Report, 1882*,

p. 340. For labor activity in the English textile industry, see Sidney Webb and Beatrice Webb, *The History of Trade Unionism* (London, 1920), pp. 116–23, 307–13, 475–80. For the crucial role of English immigrants in the New England textile labor movement, see Rowland T. Berthoff, *British Immigrants in Industrial America, 1790–1950* (Cambridge, Mass., 1953), pp. 33, 95–98.

8. New Bedford *Daily Mercury*, Jan. 28, Feb. 6, 19, 21, 22, 25, 1867.

9. New Bedford *Daily Mercury*, Jan. 29, 1877. See also Edward Webster Bemis, "Cooperation in New England," in *History of Cooperation in the United States* (Baltimore, 1888), pp. 46, 63; New Bedford *Evening Standard*, Nov. 23, 1871.

10. New Bedford *Evening Standard*, August 24, 1877, July 23, 1879, July 14, 1887, May 26, 1888; New Bedford *Daily Mercury*, Feb. 26, April 5, 1877; Fall River *Labor Standard*, Feb. 28, 1880; Massachusetts Bureau of Statistics of Labor, *Eighth Annual Report, 1877*, pp. 98–101.

11. New York *Labor Standard*, April 21, 1877; New Bedford *Evening Standard*, Feb. 5, 1877; Berthoff, *British Immigrants*, pp. 34–35. For the opposition of American industrial workers elsewhere to increases in industrial discipline, see Herbert Gutman, "Work, Culture, and Society in Industrializing America, 1815–1919," *American Historical Review* 78 (June 1973): 531–88.

12. William W. Arnold to Thomas W. Bennett, Jr., April 18, 1874, Thomas W. Bennett Jr. Papers, Old Dartmouth Historical Society, New Bedford, Massachusetts; New Bedford *Daily Mercury*, March 5, 1877.

13. New Bedford *Daily Mercury*, Feb. 2, 5, 8, 1877; New Bedford *Evening Standard*, Jan. 23, 26, 27, Feb. 8, 1877; New York *Labor Standard*, Feb. 17, March 31, 1877.

14. Quote from New Bedford *Daily Mercury*, Feb. 10, 1877; See also New Bedford *Evening Standard*, Feb. 9, 12, 1877.

15. New Bedford *Evening Standard*, Feb. 17, 1877; New Bedford *Daily Mercury*, Feb. 11, 15, 1877.

16. New Bedford *Evening Standard*, Feb. 5, 21, April 25, 1877; New Bedford *Daily Mercury*, Jan. 21, March 5, April 25, 1877. For Johnson's life, see New Bedford *Daily Mercury*, June 12, 1897. For Ricketson, see *Dictionary of American Biography*, ed. Dumas Malone, vol. 15 (New York, 1935), pp. 586–87.

17. New Bedford *Daily Mercury*, Feb. 26, 27, March 20, April 30, 1877; New Bedford *Evening Standard*, Feb. 5, 23, 28, March 20, 21, 1877.

18. New Bedford *Evening Standard*, April 25, 1877; New Bedford *Daily Mercury*, April 23, 24, 1877.

19. New Bedford *Evening Standard*, April 30, 1877; New Bedford *Daily Mercury*, May 1, 1877. For the desire of textile manufacturers to hire the more "docile" French-Canadian workers, see Massachusetts Bureau of Statistics of Labor, *Thirteenth Annual Report, 1882*, p. 64.

20. Iris S. Podea, "Quebec to 'Little Canada': The Coming of the French Canadians to New England in the Nineteenth Century," *New England Quarterly* 23 (September 1950): 366–67; Egbert C. Smyth, "The French Canadians in New England," *Proceedings of the American Antiquarian Society* 7 (October 1891): 318; Everett C. Hughes, *French Canada in Transition* (Chicago, 1943), passim.

21. I have arrived at the number of strikes through an examination of the New Bedford newspapers for the period.

22. New Bedford *Evening Standard*, April 27, 28, 1885, Jan. 25, April 27, 1886, Oct. 13, 14, 1890, Jan. 1, 1891.

23. New Bedford *Evening Standard*, July 31, August 3, 4, 23, Sept. 9, 11, 1893, Jan. 6, 15, Feb. 28, August 1, 6, 16, 17, 18, 20, 1894; New Bedford *Daily Mercury*, August 6, 9, 17, 1894; New Bedford *Evening Journal*, August 13, 16, 1894. For the "particulars law," see Massachusetts, *Acts and Resolves of the General Court, 1894, Chapter 534.*

24. New Bedford *Evening Standard*, August 18, 1894. For a report of public support, see also New Bedford *Evening Journal*, August 22, 1894.

25. New Bedford *Evening Journal*, August 25, 1894.

26. New Bedford *Evening Journal*, August 23, 1894; New Bedford *Evening Standard*, August 24, 28, 1894. The Board of Arbitration and Conciliation was created in 1886. Its findings were only advisory and did not have to be followed by either party. Massachusetts, *Acts and Resolves of the General Court, 1886, Chapter 263.*

27. New Bedford *Evening Journal*, Oct. 9, 11, 1894; New Bedford *Evening Standard*, Oct. 10, 1894.

28. New Bedford *Evening Standard*, April 16, 1895, Nov. 2, 1896, July 14, 1897, August 25, 28, 1897, Dec. 8, 31, 1897, Feb. 16, 1898.

29. Reprinted in New Bedford *Evening Standard*, March 3, 1898.

30. New Bedford *Evening Standard*, Feb. 14, 1898.

31. For national newspaper coverage of the strike, see "Scrapbook of Clippings concerning the 1898 Textile Strike at New Bedford," Widener Library, Harvard University.

32. New Bedford *Morning Mercury*, March 9, 10, 12, 1898; New Bedford *Evening Standard*, Feb. 18, 19, 28, March 9, 10, 12, 1898.

33. New Bedford *Evening Standard*, Sept. 3, 1897; New Bedford *Morning Mercury*, Feb. 3, 1898.

34. Article from *L'Echo du Soir*, the city's French newspaper, reprinted in New Bedford *Evening Standard*, Jan. 29, 1898. See also New Bedford *Evening Standard*, Jan. 15, Feb. 15, 1898.

35. New Bedford *Evening Standard*, Feb. 10, 11, 12, March 4, 5, 7, 11, 12, 14, 17, 23, 1898. See also New Bedford *Morning Mercury*, Feb. 10, 11, 1898. For Gomper's interpretation of the New Bedford conflict, see *Report of the Proceedings of the Eighteenth Annual Convention of the American Federa-*

tion of Labor Held at Kansas City, Missouri, December 12th to 20th Inclusive, 1898, p. 18. See also *American Federationist* 4 (February 1898): 275–76. For De Leon's position, see Daniel De Leon, *What Means This Strike* (New York, 1943); *People*, Feb. 6, 13, 27, March 13, 17, April 3, 1898.

36. New Bedford *Evening Standard*, April 5, 11, 12, 13, 15, 18, 19, 21, 25, May 23, 31, 1898; New Bedford *Morning Mercury*, April 7, 11, 12, 13, 15, 16, 19, 1898.

37. New Bedford *Evening Standard*, April 5, 11, 12, 13, 15, 18, 19, 21, 25, May 23, 31, 1898; New Bedford *Morning Mercury*, April 7, 11, 12, 13, 15, 16, 19, 1898.

38. Robert F. Wearmouth, *Methodism and the Working-Class Movement of England, 1800–1850* (London, 1937), pp. 16, 208, 229; New Bedford *Evening Standard*, April 18, May 25, 1888, Feb. 4, 1892; New Bedford *Sunday Standard*, Oct. 10, 1909; John H. Acornley, *A History of the Primitive Methodist Church in the United States from its Origins and the Landing of the First Missionaries in 1829 to the Present Time* (Fall River, Mass., 1909), pp. 257, 258. See also miscellaneous pamphlets and newspaper clippings on Primitive Methodism in possession of South Primitive Methodist Church, New Bedford.

39. For the impact of size on worker-community relations, see Herbert Gutman, "Class, Status, and Community Power in Nineteenth-Century American Industrial Cities—Paterson, New Jersey: A Case Study," in Frederick C. Jaher, ed., *The Age of Industrialism in America: Essays in Social Structure and Cultural Values* (New York, 1968), pp. 263–87. See also Melvyn Dubofsky, *Industrialism and the American Worker, 1865–1920* (Arlington Heights, Ill.: 1975), pp. 31–32. For the importance of community support for striking workers in other industrial cities, see John T. Cumbler, *Working-Class Community in Industrial America: Work, Leisure and Struggle in Two Industrial Cities, 1880–1930* (Westport, Conn., 1979), pp. 76, 80–81, 83–84; and Daniel J. Walkowitz, *Worker City, Company Town: Iron and Cotton-Worker Protest in Troy and Cohoes, New York, 1855–84* (Urbana, Ill., 1978), pp. 221, 226. The community support for workers in New Bedford did not arise from an antagonism to outside control of industry, as the large majority (88.6 percent) of officers and directors of the textile corporations between 1865 and 1896 were local residents.

40. Frederick Douglass, *Life and Times of Frederick Douglass* (New York, 1941), p. 231.

41. Herbert J. Lahne, *The Cotton Mill Worker* (New York, 1944), p. 13.

42. For a discussion of the complexity of the American workers' response to industrialism, see Daniel T. Rogers, "Tradition, Modernity, and the American Industrial Worker: Reflections and Critique," *Journal of Interdisciplinary History* 7 (Spring 1977): 655–81.

THREE

Social Change and
Social Mobility

Introduction

In addition to affecting politics and working-class consciousness, the industrial revolution in Massachusetts had serious social consequences. Social relationships predicated upon the traditions of farm life were transformed by new demographic patterns. Uprooted from farm and village, the migrant to the city was forced to reinvent the fabric of familial and social ties. High population densities marked by residential transience generated a sense of isolation and anonymity among newcomers. Total worker dependence upon the unpredictable price system, coupled with unsatisfying and routinized jobs, served to increase feelings of insecurity amid the strange urban environment. The far-reaching move to the city challenged the traditional moral order and seemed to portend the coming of a major social upheaval.

So devastating was the urbanization process thought to be that urban ecologists and sociologists, such as Robert Park and Ernest Burgess, believed that the city weakened the "intimate relationships of the primary group," thus vitiating the conditions necessary for social control. Others, among them Herbert Gans and Jane Jacobs, countered this antiurban bias by illuminating the urban forms of voluntary associations that provided intimacy and even unity among divergent groups.[1] In the essay by Alex Keyssar on social change in Massachusetts, the general attributes of urbanization are considered as forces affecting both social cohesion and social fragmentation. After an accounting of how the industrial revolution inspired social change, Keyssar states that "the sources of social cohesion proved to be stronger than the sources of division, and the boundaries between classes and ethnic groups eventually softened rather than hardened."

A major impetus in the migration to the city was the desire for economic betterment. In many instances, the call to the cities was encouraged by those who had already made the arduous journey. One French-Canadian worker in Springfield wrote to a friend: "The pay is good Basile. We work from sunrise to sunset, but on Sunday the mills are closed and it is like a church holy day. The work is not hard. Some of the children are working and we make more money than we can spend. Let me know what you decide, and if you want to come I will speak to the foreman."[2] There seems little doubt that harsh as the conditions of urban life were, one must agree with historian Stephan Thernstrom that "Lowell was a damn sight better than County Cork."[3] Bringing with them low expectations, the migrants saw visible improvement in their new lives.

The controversy over the reality of social mobility in American society is not one to be answered here. That room at the top was limited seems apparent, but that there was impressive social mobility for lower and middle classes, also is generally conceded. In his analysis of social mobility in nineteenth-century Boston, Thernstrom maintained: "The common move was not from rags to riches but from rags to respectability."[4] Fluidity of status, however, was affected by important gradations of class—whether you were native-born, a British-American Protestant migrant, an Irish-born Catholic, and if you were first or second generation. First-generation men who started out in menial jobs certainly advanced on the occupational ladder, but usually not to white-collar ranks unless they were Yankees. Irishmen of the second generation fared worse than other second-generation immigrants such as the British, Germans, and Russian Jews.[5] Although at the low end of occupational achievement, some Irish found success in politics.

Irish political ascendancy in Boston and the state was long in coming, and not without fierce struggles and countless compromises with Yankees.[6] After a long and eventful political career, James Michael Curley recalled the difficulty of making it in Boston: "Even as a boy, I knew I belonged to an Irish-Catholic minority who were despised socially and discriminated against politically. . . . [Therefore] I chose politics because industrial conditions were deplorable and prospects of ever getting anywhere seemed remote."[7] Assimilation and total acceptance for an Irish Catholic was difficult but not impossible. Some few Brahmins, like Thomas Wentworth Higginson, George Frisbee Hoar, Charles W. Eliot, and the Reverend Edward Everett Hale, were articulate defenders of Irish efforts at Americanization, and staunch opponents of immigration restriction.[8] One of their protégés, a first-generation Irish Catholic, John Boyle O'Reilly, was to do much to promote Irish acceptance into the mainstream of Boston social life. A Brahmin friend of O'Reilly, Boston lawyer and novelist Frederick Stimson, remembered him as "an American patriot" who "was first (one sometimes fears the last) to bring the Puritan Yankee into sympathy with the Irish Catholic."[9] The essay by Francis R. Walsh focuses on the unique contribution of John Boyle O'Reilly, contending that his career "encapsulates the events, the sense of success and loss that made up that era."

The urbanization of society, with its pronounced impact upon social mobility, also altered patterns of play and recreation. Rural sports, largely participatory village games of competition in strength, or animal contests, gave way to the more regimented, rule-oriented spectator sports of the city. Commercialization and the rise of professional athletics engendered not only a new business venture, but aided the process of assimilation and social mobility. Both the competitiveness and cooperation of professional baseball teams taught spectators to appreciate "baseball's demonstrations of efficiency and excellence—qualities many of them took as keys to success in industrial America."[10] Rooting for the home team created new loyalties for the uprooted, and provided immigrants with an instrument for easy acceptance into the community.

The move from baseball as an amateur sport run by gentlemen sportsmen, to a professional sport where "winning became the dominant motive" was heralded by the creation of the first professional, albeit short-lived, major league in 1871, the National Association of Professional Baseball Players. The league's major winning team was the Boston Redstockings. With the best and highest-paid players, and a prodigy named Albert Goodwill Spalding (later to become a sporting goods magnate), the Boston Redstockings won four consecutive championships. "All Boston took half a holiday" to see them beat their rivals, the Philadelphia Athletics, in the first game of the '72 season.[11] The nineteenth century witnessed the change from sports as amateur recreation to sports as an important aspect of American competitiveness and the drive to excel.

The confusion between winning and enjoying sports was to intrude even into that bastion of Brahmin culture, Harvard University. The essay by Ronald A. Smith examines the changes and turmoil that took place in college athletics at Harvard between 1869 and 1909. Whether a Harvard education was to breed the well-rounded gentleman, or was to promote excellence—either in scholarship or sports—became the question of the day. Smith argues that "a more open society will produce excellence and winning based upon performance," and that Harvard "gave in to the demands of American society" on that score. A student of the class of 1876 wrote that "books were giving way to sports already."[12] George Santayana recalled amusingly: "Old Harvard men will remember the sweet sadness of Prof. [Charles Eliot] Norton. He would tell his classes, shaking his head with a slight sigh, that the Greeks did not play football."[13]

Indeed, in the Gilded Age, during the long reign of President Charles W. Eliot (1869–1909), Harvard was transformed because of the modernization of American society and the need to respond to the social changes wrought by industrialization. A far-sighted President Eliot saw to it that Harvard would become a major research institution that would attract the brightest scholars, and that the undergraduate curriculum would be revised to accommodate the requirements of the new age. A free-elective system, the creation of discipline-oriented departments, higher salaries for faculty, with paid sabbaticals and pensions, all were part of the President's plan to upgrade intellectual standards. Equally important was Eliot's attempt to devise a "meritocratic" university, by easing class-dominated admission policies and by recruiting talented students from all classes and races. Although it never eliminated its primary recruitment from a nucleus of fashionable families, Harvard became "more socially heterogeneous than any other university" in the Ivy League.[14] The alterations at Harvard University were just one example of the substantial social changes derived from the new industrial society, affecting elites as well as all other classes of society in Massachusetts.

Jack Tager

Notes

1. Robert E. Park, "The City: Suggestions for the Investigation of Human Behavior in the Urban Environment," in *The City*, ed. Robert E. Park, Ernest Burgess, Roderick McKenzie (Chicago, 1925); Ernest Burgess, "The Growth of the City: An Introduction to a Research Project," *Publications of the American Sociological Society* 18 (1923): 85–97; Herbert J. Gans, "Urbanism and Suburbanism as Ways of Life: A Re-evaluation of Definitions," in *Human Behavior and Social Processes*, ed. Arnold Rose (Boston, 1962), pp. 625–48; Jane Jacobs, *The Death and Life of Great American Cities*, Vintage ed. (New York, 1961).

2. *Springfield's Ethnic Heritage: The French and French-Canadian Community* (Springfield, Mass., 1976), p. 9. A study of the conflicts of industrialization in a rural context is that of Jonathan Prude, *The Coming of Industrial Order* (New York, 1983).

3. Stephan Thernstrom, "Urbanization, Migration and Social Mobility in Late Nineteenth-Century America," in *American Urban History*, ed. Alexander Callow, 2d ed. (New York, 1973), p. 401.

4. Stephan Thernstrom, *The Other Bostonians: Poverty and Progress in the American Metropolis, 1880–1970* (Cambridge, Mass., 1973), p. 73.

5. Ibid., pp. 121, 133, 134; also, Thernstrom, "Immigrants and WASPs: Ethnic Differences in Occupational Mobility in Boston, 1890–1940," in *Nineteenth-Century Cities*, ed. Stephan Thernstrom and Richard Sennett (New Haven, 1969), pp. 130–31, 141. The evidence is also clear that black migrants to Boston between 1865 and 1900 fared worse than all other groups, lacking any sort of social mobility. Beginning at a level equal with first-generation Irishmen, as far as education and menial labor jobs, blacks were constantly denied access to positions in the factory system that would improve their status. This was one instance when employers chose not to hire available cheaper labor because of discrimination and fear of worker unrest. Elizabeth Pleck wrote that "black economic progress did not fit the mold of even the most limited example of nineteenth-century immigrant advance, that of Irish Bostonians." Elizabeth H. Pleck, *Black Migration and Poverty: Boston 1865–1900* (New York, 1979), pp. 7–8.

6. Peter Eisinger, "Ethnic Political Transition in Boston, 1884–1933: Some Lessons for Contemporary Cities," *Political Science Quarterly* 93 (1978): 237.

7. James Michael Curley, *I'd Do It Again: A Record of All My Uproarious Years* (Englewood Cliffs, N.J., 1957), pp. 32, 46.

8. See Barbara M. Solomon, *Ancestors and Immigrants* (Cambridge, Mass., 1956).

9. Frederick J. Stimson, *My United States* (New York, 1931), p. 116.

10. Gunther Barth, *City People: The Rise of Modern City Culture in Nineteenth-Century America* (New York, 1982), pp. 167, 180.
11. David Quentin Voigt, "The Boston Redstockings: The Birth of Major League Baseball," *New England Quarterly* 43 (December 1970): 533, 542.
12. Stimson, *My United States*, p. 48.
13. George Santayana, *The Genteel Tradition at Bay* (New York, 1931), p. 3.
14. Seymour Martin Lipset and David Riesman, *Education and Politics at Harvard* (New York, 1975), pp. 125, 92–96, 105–6.

Social Change in Massachusetts in the Gilded Age

ALEXANDER KEYSSAR

The literature of social criticism in late nineteenth-century America—and in late nineteenth-century Massachusetts—was filled with intimations of impending crisis. Barely had the guns of the Civil War been silenced when voices were raised throughout the northern states proclaiming the imminence of a new set of dangers to the Republic: the dangers of industrialization that was too rapid, of inequalities that were too drastic, of mounting class conflict and deepening ethnic antagonisms. Henry K. Oliver (the first, and unfairly eclipsed, chief of the Massachusetts Bureau of Statistics of Labor) and Wendell Phillips sounded these themes in the late 1860s and early 1870s, and they were repeated, with increasing frequency and urgency, throughout the Gilded Age. By the late 1880s and early 1890s, American society seemed—to some sober-minded contemporaries at least—to be spiraling out of control, to be losing its cohesion, to be standing on the brink of dramatic, if not revolutionary, change. The center was not holding, and could not hold, in a nation dominated by the "trusts," and increasingly populated by the foreign-born poor. The most well-known literary presentation of this apocalyptic vision was Edward Bellamy's best-selling utopian novel, *Looking Backward*, published in 1888. And Bellamy was not alone in his apprehensions or in his leap into utopian (or anti-utopian) visions. Many of his sentiments, if not his prescriptions, were shared by writers as diverse as Henry George, Ignatius Donnelly, and Boston's own William Dean Howells, the editor of the *Atlantic*. A crisis seemed to be at hand; the stresses on American society seemed to have reached the breaking point.[1]

But no great crisis materialized in late nineteenth- or early twentieth-century America. Neither in the United States as a whole, nor in Massachusetts did things fly apart or even fall apart. The economic storms of the late nineteenth century were weathered; the "trusts" retained much of their power, and immigrants kept coming; social reforms were instated at a very gradual and undramatic tempo. No apocalypse occurred, and the apocalyptic thinkers of the era either have been ignored by history (a common fate of false prophets) or—worse—have been relegated to the status of "data" for intellectual historians.

Contemporary historians of late nineteenth-century society also tend to discount the perceptions of writers like Bellamy and Oliver: with appropriate retrospective wisdom, they generally focus their attentions not on the fragmentation of that society but on the sources of its cohesion, not on crises but on continuities. The era is widely identified with the emergence of important modern institutions—national corporations and national trade unions, for example—and with the triumph of unifying, homogenizing forces in the society as a whole. And the historical record of Massachusetts (which is unusually rich and has been, perhaps, more carefully studied than that of any other state in the union) offers abundant evidence of the power and breadth of those unifying forces. The Gilded Age witnessed social changes that served to produce common values and common cores of experience for many of the diverse peoples of the Commonwealth.

A key ingredient in such changes, of course, was economic growth. Despite the downturns in the business cycle that appeared with troubling regularity every decade, the economy of Massachusetts grew very rapidly during the late nineteenth century. The manufacturing industries that had become so prominent in the state prior to the Civil War (shoes and textiles primarily) continued to expand and dominate national markets. Relatively new industries (e.g., rubber and electrical machinery manufacturing) appeared and flourished, and the commercial and transportation sectors were enlarged to accommodate the growth of manufactures. Each decade saw visible increases in the size of the Commonwealth's labor force, in the number and size of firms, in the quantity of capital invested in the state's industries, and in production and wealth. This growth, moreover, was not confined to the state's large and famous manufacturing centers—Fall River, Lawrence, Lynn, Worcester, and Boston. The rhythms of industrial life became dominant in dozens of small cities and in scores of towns, from the Connecticut River Valley in the west to the edge of Cape Cod. While farms were being abandoned throughout the state, shoes were being manufactured in more than 100 different communities, textiles in more than fifty. Residents of Upton began to produce baseballs, and in 1880, Berkshire County boasted twelve firms that made foundry and machine-shop products. Throughout the Commonwealth, men, women, and children became familiar with the conditions and artifacts of industrial life that had, only decades earlier, seemed so foreign to them.[2]

The extension of industry was accompanied, although not quite matched, by the extension of urban living environments. Not only did a steadily rising proportion of the state's population move to the metropolitan area of Boston, but communities outside the capital became urban centers in their own right. By 1900, Springfield, Worcester, Fall River, Lowell, Lawrence, and New Bedford each had more than 50,000 inhabitants, and more than two dozen communities in the state had been incorporated as cities. This urbanizing trend was not new in late nineteenth-century Massachusetts, but at some point in the Gilded Age the typical resident of the Commonwealth became a city dweller rather than an inhabitant of a small town. He or she became accustomed to congested residential environments, to the sight of hundreds of strangers walking the streets, to time measured on the clock rather than by the sun, and—as the turn of the century neared—to paved streets, sewage systems, buildings of unprecedented height, and even elevators. (By 1897, there was even a subway in Boston.) Indeed, in a state as small and heavily populated as Massachusetts (in contrast, perhaps, to Illinois, Pennsylvania, and New York), the gulf between city and country narrowed almost to the vanishing point, and some experience of urban life—with its excitements and attendant difficulties—was accessible to virtually all residents.[3]

Other changes also tended to unite the people of the Commonwealth, to create bonds that transcended traditional boundaries of space and time. Technological improvements in transportation and communication allowed people in different communities to see one another and stay in touch; continuing development of railroads, steamships, highways, and the telephone linked the state's inhabitants, both economically and socially, to men and women elsewhere in the nation and even in Europe.

At the same time institutions and organizations emerged that established (or cemented) ties among individuals with common occupational identities and interests but who lived in different parts of the state or nation. National trade unions, of course, were one example of this phenomenon, and professional associations were another. Similarly, the expansion of both secondary and higher education helped define a more national (or at least regional) culture, thereby facilitating the rapid transmission of ideas and information to people in different locales. Men and women read the same books in homes throughout the state. New colleges and universities opened their doors to fortunate students. For the first time, women from throughout New England were able to attend college in Massachusetts: Smith, Wellesley, and Mount Holyoke were all creations of the Gilded Age.[4]

Two final sources of unification and homogenization require mention, if only briefly. The first was social mobility, both as an aspiration and as an experience. Although Horatio Alger-like advances were few and far between in the Bay State, there did exist considerable opportunity for working men and their children to make modest improvements in their economic circumstance and occupational standing. Richard Ely was certainly correct when he noted that it was more likely that a workingman on a railroad would be "killed by a stroke of lightning" than that he would become president of the company. But it was possible for an unskilled railway laborer to become a semi-skilled operative, and his sons even had a decent shot at becoming skilled workers. Mobility of this modest kind was indeed widespread enough to be an important shared experience for the mobile themselves, and a source of hope for those who remained near the bottom of the economic ladder. The second source of unification was something of a democratization of consumption. People throughout the metropolitan area of Boston could go into town and enter the new department stores (even if many of them could not afford to buy much), and men and women throughout the state increasingly had access to identical consumer items, like cigarettes, cigars, beer, soap, and ready-made clothing. The development of national markets, coupled with falling prices (this was, in fact, the last prolonged period of deflation in American history), made it possible for a resident of North Adams or Framingham to consume exactly the same goods as someone in Boston.[5]

Taken together, these changes in Massachusetts society both reflected and contributed to a decline in the salience of local and provincial boundaries, a decline that was a significant feature of postbellum American history. The Gilded Age was not an era of mass culture or centralized bureaucracies, but it did witness the opening of new avenues of interaction and interdependence and the extension of the rhythms, values, and material artifacts of industrial society. By the end of the nineteenth century, the people of Massachusetts—from town to city, from west to east, from New Hampshire to Connecticut—had a lot in common.

But there was another side to the story, a darker side perhaps, one that greatly contributed to the apprehensions of men like Edward Bellamy. Stated briefly, this "other side" was the development—or the intensification—of dramatic class and ethnic cleavages within Massachusetts society. Class distinctions and ethnic tensions were hardly new to Massachusetts in the Gilded Age, but during these years the distinctions and tensions became more powerful, the gulf between the middle class and the working class yawned wider. Indeed it seems likely that in many different respects, the distance at the end of the nineteenth century between working-class and middle-class Massachusetts society was greater than during any earlier or subsequent period.

At the heart of this shift was a significant increase in the size of the industrial working class in Massachusetts and an equally significant—and obviously related—increase in the number of immigrants (and their children). Between 1870 and 1900, the number of industrial workers at least doubled (precise figures are difficult to determine, and the category itself is obviously fuzzy at the edges), and most of the men and women who contributed to this increase were either immigrants or their children. In 1870, for example, there were less than 100,000 foreign-born employees in the state's manufacturing industries; by 1900, there were a quarter of a million. At the turn of the century, in fact, only one-quarter of the men and women who worked in manufacturing were native-born children of native-born parents. But these older residents of the Commonwealth were, not surprisingly, much better represented in occupations that offered higher status and more ample earnings: roughly two-thirds to three-quarters of all male doctors, lawyers, college teachers, bankers, and manufacturers were native-born sons of native parents; only one out of every six participants in "professional service" was an immigrant. (The two largest groups of "professional" immigrants were clergymen and electricians.) Class boundaries in Massachusetts were becoming increasingly congruent with ethnic boundaries.[6]

Several additional dimensions of this change warrant mention. The first is certainly well known: the sources of immigration to Massachusetts became increasingly diverse during this period, and the number of non-English-speaking migrants grew very rapidly. In 1870, there were only 12,000 immigrants from non-English-speaking countries at work in Massachusetts; by 1900, there were roughly 125,000. (Both figures are estimates based on census data that obscure as much as they reveal.) Second, it should be stressed that immigrants and their children constituted a large proportion of the working class throughout Massachusetts, not just in Boston and in the eastern textile centers. The manufacturing industries of Chicopee, North Adams, Webster, and Taunton—just to name a few locales—all had sizable foreign-born contingents. And finally, it must be noted that the blue-collar occupations often tended to be dominated by men and women from particular ethnic backgrounds: natives were often clustered in skilled trades (machinists, for example); day laborers were predominantly Irish and Italian; and the state's cotton mills had a heavily French-Canadian labor force. The workplaces of the state, in effect, tended to be class and ethnic enclaves rather than "melting pots."[7]

But what was important, finally, was not the mere fact that these class and ethnic boundaries existed and overlapped, but rather that they mattered—and mattered deeply. The differences between middle-class and working-class life were significant and growing; they were, in many respects, differences of kind or quality rather than simply differences in quantity. Most blue-collar workers, of course, were paid much less than were entrepreneurs and professionals, but income differentials only begin to tell the tale.

The experiences people had when at work, for example, depended greatly upon their class position—and men and women in the Gilded Age were usually at work for sixty or more hours a week. From the Civil War to the turn of the century, blue-collar workplaces became noticeably more unlike middle-class working environments. They became much larger and much noisier, and work itself generally became more tedious, routine, and enervating. Technological changes transformed many skilled jobs into semiskilled jobs, and operatives became increasingly subject to tight supervisory controls. None of these trends, of course, was entirely new, but the Gilded Age does seem to occupy a distinctive place in the history of work as a period when vast

numbers of blue-collar jobs were being de-skilled and routinized. But it was also a period when those changes were
not yet affecting middle-class and white-collar positions (as
they would in the twentieth century). The working rhythms
and environments of tailors and shoemakers were much
more like those of doctors and lawyers in 1820 than they
were in 1890; similarly, clerical workers (and perhaps even
some managerial personnel in large firms) have more in
common with factory operatives today than they had 100
years ago.[8]

Another difference between working-class and middle-
class workplaces was that blue-collar employees were far
more likely to be injured or killed while at work than were
their more advantaged fellow citizens. Safety regulations
in factories were utterly minimal, and accident rates were
astonishingly high. Working people also suffered from
more gradual workplace-related dangers to their health.
Twenty-five years of working sixty hours a week in a textile mill left a number of forty-year-old men in such ill
health that they were unemployable; for this reason, among
others, working-class old age had emphatically different
tones than did old age among the Commonwealth's middle-class residents.[9]

Long before they reached old age, moreover, the state's
blue-collar workers had to cope with one source of insecurity almost uniquely their own: unemployment. The
word itself first appeared in print in Massachusetts during
the Gilded Age, and industrial workers throughout this
period were exposed to chronically high levels of "involun-
tary idleness." White-collar employees, even those holding
quite unexalted jobs, were rarely laid off during this period,
but each year saw between 20 and 35 percent of the state's
working class experiencing some unemployment. The depressions that occurred in the 1870s, 1880s, and 1890s were,

of course, felt throughout Massachusetts society, but the harshest consequences of those depressions were reserved for the state's blue-collar workers.[10]

Outside of the state's workplaces and factories, middle-class and working-class residents of Massachusetts led increasingly separate, and almost segregated, lives. People from all walks of life were moving to cities in general, and to the Boston area in particular, but they were not moving to the same streets, districts, and neighborhoods. The social segmentation and fragmentation of cities became much more marked during this period: the old "walking city" with its mix of interspersed residences and workplaces gave way to more sharply differentiated social spaces. Ethnic neighborhoods were formed throughout Boston; the middle class retreated to its own more stately quarters and eventually—thanks to advances in transportation technology—to the suburbs. The crowded tenements and boardinghouses that were so characteristic of late nineteenth-century urban life were the sole domain of immigrant workers and their children.[11]

Other dimensions of social life also served to heighten the distance between working-class and middle-class citizens of the Bay State. Religion was one. During the Gilded Age, the working class was increasingly composed of Catholics and—to a much lesser extent—Jews, whereas the entrepreneurs and professionals were predominantly Protestant. This coincidence of religious and class boundaries meant both that employers and their employees tended not to meet in church on Sundays, and also that they did not feel the sense of community or kinship that common religious beliefs and affiliations have sometimes provided to men and women of diverse economic standing.[12]

It must be acknowledged, however, that feelings of "community" might have been difficult to sustain even in the presence of a common religious culture, inasmuch as the people of Massachusetts were relocating at an almost astonishing rate during the Gilded Age. One study concluded that the total number of persons who ever lived in Boston between 1880 and 1890 was three times as great as the largest number that ever lived there simultaneously. And the residents of the Commonwealth who were the most peripatetic and without roots were the immigrants and blue-collar workers. Successful members of the middle class were far more "persistent" demographically than were foreign-born laborers and factory operatives.[13]

Finally, it should be noted that the differences between middle-class and working-class life experiences extended even into the relatively private sphere of the family. There were, to be sure, important variations among ethnic groups, but on the whole, working-class families tended to be larger than their middle-class counterparts, and children in the working class tended to be viewed as economic assets rather than as extensions of a lineage. Working-class children left school early (often extremely early, inasmuch as truancy laws were largely unenforced) and went to work; their mothers only rarely sought employment outside of the home, but they often cared for boarders as a way of contributing to the household economy. Both privacy and education were sacrificed to compelling material need, and the roles of both women and children were defined by the class context in which they lived. (For middle-class women, this was a period of considerable activism—made possible, in part, by the leisure time that accrued to them as a result of the increased availability of foreign-born female domestic servants.) The measured tones and spaciousness of the middle-class household—so effectively described, in fact, in Howells's novels—were far removed from the concerns and preoccupations of the working-class family.[14]

Thus, in many different respects, during the Gilded Age Massachusetts was becoming the home not of a society, but of two societies that were becoming increasingly alien to one another. Records of the period (written primarily by members of the middle class) were riddled with this sense of unfamiliarity and distance, with the apprehensions and fears that accompanied the growing cleavage between immigrant workers and middle-class natives. The working class looms both strange and somehow menacing in the pages of the Boston *Transcript,* in the novels of Howells and James, in *The Education of Henry Adams,* and in the proclamations of Boston's Brahmin advocates of immigration restriction. One of the most well-known books of the era was a description of life among the urban poor in New York entitled *How the Other Half Lives;* the most remarkable fact about the book was that it had to be written. [15]

The distance between these two societies was vividly revealed on those occasions when individuals or even the polity itself made some effort to cross the divide. Native-born middle-class representatives of charity organizations, for example, tended to treat applicants for aid (who were usually from the working class and often foreign-born) with a remarkable mixture of sympathy and suspicion, concern and contempt. In 1895, a case investigator for the Wells Memorial Institute encountered a young Irish-American widow with two children whose husband had been killed in a fire. Her husband's coworkers had raised thirty-eight dollars to give to the widow, and the investigator noted, with undisguised disapproval and bewilderment, that "she spent this money for mourning clothes for herself and five masses for his soul." The widow, it was concluded, was "idle, incompetent, and incapable of self-direction." Even those most progressive of Gilded Age reformers, the settlement-house workers, had difficulty masking their sense of distance: the settlement houses themselves were created, in part, to bridge the gulf between the "two societies," but a well-known publication by Boston's settlement residents opened with two chapters about immigration entitled, "Before the Invasion" and "The Invading Host."[16]

Nowhere was the gap between working-class and middle-class life better illustrated than in the state's treatment of the "tramp evil," a problem that surfaced during the depression of the 1870s and that remained a source of acute concern throughout the late nineteenth century. Tramps were poor, homeless men who traveled from town to town in Massachusetts, riding the rails, finding shelter in police stations or cheap lodging houses, occasionally begging for food, and looking for work. There were, almost certainly, some malingerers among them, but most tramps were simply unemployed workers hunting for jobs: their numbers rose dramatically during depressions and dropped just as dramatically during prosperous years. But for the state's middle-class citizens, profoundly unfamiliar with the conditions of working-class life as they were, tramps inspired fear and loathing. As a result, tramping was made a crime in Massachusetts in 1880, and it remained a crime until well after the turn of the century. It had, in effect, become illegal for a jobless worker to leave his home town and look for work.[17]

In sum, this portrait of social change and social patterns in the Gilded Age suggests that the fears voiced by the era's most apocalyptic social critics may not have been misplaced. The engines of industrial growth had created great wealth, but they had also bred dramatic inequalities and social distance. Moreover, the trends evident in the Gilded Age pointed to a future in which deepening social divisions might well undermine the stability of the political order. A polity that contained two separate and unequal societies was unlikely to endure for very long; a society in which class and ethnic boundaries were congruent and salient was far from the democratic ideal; a Commonwealth in which the "haves" and "have-nots" had radically different life experiences and barely knew one another was more likely to witness violent upheaval than gradual reform.

In the end, of course, the center did hold. The political order endured, the sources of social cohesion proved stronger than the sources of division, and the boundaries between classes and ethnic groups eventually softened rather than hardened. But the fact that the apocalypse did not arrive ought not lead us to mask or minimize the severity of the strains placed upon Gilded Age society, to conclude that the trends were not ominous ones, to believe that a safe voyage for the good ship Massachusetts was foreordained. To do so would be not only to misread the historical record but also to underestimate the achievement of the men, women, and institutions that successfully met the challenge that the Gilded Age left in its wake.

Notes

1. Regarding the emergence of some of these issues, with particular reference to Massachusetts, see David Montgomery, *Beyond Equality: Labor and the Radical Republicans, 1862–1872* (New York, 1967). Henry Oliver's apprehensions were voiced frequently in the early annual reports (1869 to 1873) of the Massachusetts Bureau of Statistics of Labor. For earlier years, cf. Carl Siracusa, *A Mechanical People: Perceptions of the Industrial Order in Massachusetts 1810–1880* (Middletown, Conn., 1979).

2. This description is based upon a far more detailed account of the economic growth of Massachusetts that is presented in my own forthcoming Cambridge University Press book: Alexander Keyssar, *Out of Work: The First Century of Unemployment in Massachusetts*, chaps. 2 and 3. The richest sources of data regarding the economic development of

Massachusetts are: the state census surveys, conducted in 1875, 1885, and 1895; the annual reports of the Bureau of Statistics of Labor; and the annual reports on the statistics of manufactures. See, for examples, Massachusetts Bureau of Statistics of Labor, *Census of Massachusetts: 1885*, vol. 1, pt. 2 (Boston, 1888), and MBSL, *Eighteenth Annual Report* (Boston, 1887).

3. *Twelfth Census of the United States, Special Reports, Occupations* (Washington, D.C., 1904), pp. 494–99, 506–11, 560–63, 588–91, 598–603, 625–27, 732–39, 760–63. See also Arthur M. Schlesinger, *The Rise of the City* (New York, 1933).

4. For general discussions of these themes, see Robert H. Wiebe, *The Search for Order* (New York, 1967), chaps. 2–5; Lloyd Ulman, *The Rise of the National Trade Union* (Cambridge, Mass., 1955); Walter T. K. Nugent, *From Centennial to World War: American Society 1876–1917* (Indianapolis, 1977); Lois Banner, *Women in Modern America: A Brief History* (New York, 1974); Schlesinger, *Rise of the City*, chaps. 6 and 7.

5. Stephan Thernstrom, *The Other Bostonians* (Cambridge, Mass., 1973), chaps. 4–9; Daniel J. Boorstin, *The Americans: The Democratic Experience* (New York, 1973), bk. 1, pt. 2.

6. *Ninth Census of the United States*, vol. 1 (Washington, D.C., 1872), pp. 739–40; *Twelfth U.S. Census, Occupations*, pp. 300–307.

7. *Ninth U.S. Census*, pp. 739–40; *Census of Massachusetts: 1885*, vol. 1, pt. 2, pp. 42–47, 612–21; *Twelfth U.S. Census, Occupations*, pp. 300–307. See Jonathan A. Prude, *The Coming of Industrial Order* (New York, 1983).

8. For treatments of these themes, see Melvyn Dubofsky, *Industrialism and the American Worker, 1865–1920* (Arlington Heights, Ill., 1975), pp. 1–71; David Montgomery, *Workers' Control in America* (New York, 1979), pp. 9–47; Daniel T. Rodgers, *The Work Ethic in Industrial America, 1850–1920* (Chicago, 1978), pp. 1–93; Harry Braverman, *Labor and Monopoly Capital* (New York, 1974), pp. 45–123; Herbert Gutman, "Work, Culture, and Society in Industrializing America, 1815–1919," *American Historical Review* 78 (1973): 531–88. Cf. Alan Dawley, *Class and Community* (Cambridge, Mass., 1976).

9. Dubofsky, *Industrialism*, p. 19; David H. Fischer, *Growing Old in America* (New York, 1977), pp. 157–80. Both industrial accidents and the problems of old age were discussed periodically in reports of the Massachusetts Bureau of Statistics of Labor.

10. Keyssar, *Out of Work*, chaps. 2 and 3.

11. Sam B. Warner, Jr., *Streetcar Suburbs* (New York, 1976), esp. pp. 15–66, 153–68; Robert A. Woods, ed., *Americans in Process* (Boston and New York, 1903), pp. 1–146.

12. Cf. Jama Lazerow, "A Good Time Coming: Religion and the Emergence of Labor Activism in Antebellum New England" (Ph.D. diss., Brandeis University, 1982).

13. Thernstrom, *Other Bostonians*, pp. 9–44.

14. Tamara K. Hareven and Maris A. Vinovskis, "Patterns of Childbearing in Late Nineteenth-Century America: The Determinants of Marital Fertility in Five Massachusetts Towns in 1880," and John Modell, "Patterns of Consumption, Acculturation, and Family Income Strategies in Late Nineteenth-Century America," both in *Family and Population in Nineteenth-Century America*, ed. Tamara K. Hareven and Maris A. Vinovskis (Princeton, 1978); Michael Haines, *Fertility and Occupation* (New York, 1979), pp. 205–38; Banner, *Women*, pp. 2–102; Forest Chester Ensign, *Compulsory School Attendance and Child Labor* (Iowa City, 1921), pp. 48–86.

15. See, for example, the chapter entitled "Chicago" in Adams's *Education*, and, of course, Howells's *A Hazard of New Fortunes* and James's *The Princess Casamassima*. Regarding the movement for immigration restriction, see John Higham, *Strangers in the Land* (New Brunswick, 1955) and Barbara M. Solomon, *Ancestors and Immigrants* (Cambridge, Mass., 1956).

16. *Report of the Massachusetts Board to Investigate the Subject of the Unemployed, House Document no. 50*, pt. 5, app. A (Boston, 1895); Woods, *Americans in Process*.

17. Keyssar, *Out of Work*, chap. 5.

John Boyle O'Reilly, the Boston *Pilot*, and Irish-American Assimilation, 1870–1890

FRANCIS R. WALSH

Like any period in American history, the Gilded Age is subject to a number of different interpretations. Books, articles, and course titles tell us that it was an age of excess, that it marked the emergence of a national economy, that it coincided with a search for order, and that it witnessed the decline of laissez faire. Whichever of these topics one wishes to pursue, there is general agreement that whatever progress was made during those years, it was achieved at enormous social, economic, and psychological cost.

One can approach the topic of Massachusetts in the Gilded Age in any number of ways. Perhaps more than in any other state, this subject is complicated by the fact that in addition to coping with all of the other problems of the day, Massachusetts, especially Boston, had to do so while experiencing a major shift of political power from Yankee to Irish hands.[1]

With this transition in mind, I will examine this period by focusing on the experience of one man, John Boyle O'Reilly, whose career as writer, editor, and activist touched on all of the events that made up the Gilded Age. I recognize that it takes a certain amount of temerity to view a particular period through the life—and a relatively short life at that—of one human being. I can offer two points in my defense. One is that in the words of David Potter, a microcosm is just as cosmic as a macrocosm. The other, perhaps more persuasive, is that by focusing on one individual, we can better understand the complex, and often contradictory, forces at work during those years. Certainly, O'Reilly's career encapsulates the events, the sense of success and loss that made up that era.

The general outline of John Boyle O'Reilly's life is well known. Born June 28, 1844, in Dowth Castle, Ireland, he joined the British Cavalry as a young man in order to convert Irish soldiers to the Fenian cause. Arrested for treason, he was sentenced to twenty years imprisonment in Australia. After one year in custody, he made a daring escape and reached America several months later. Soon after his arrival in Boston, he joined the staff of the Boston *Pilot*, the most influential Irish-American newspaper of the nineteenth century. He became editor-in-chief and co-owner of the paper in 1876. The author of two novels, a book on sports, and a steady stream of poetry, he became a leading figure in Boston's literary circles. A friend of Oliver Wendell Holmes, Emerson, Whittier, Wendell Phillips and others, he moved more easily between the two worlds of Boston—Irish and Yankee—than any other individual in his time. An advocate of sport and the outdoor life, he refereed at college athletic games, boxed with John L. Sullivan, and canoed the rivers of the East Coast. A colorful figure, he was probably the best-known Irish-American of his day. [2]

When O'Reilly first arrived in America on November 23, 1869, he was met by a local Fenian delegation. Expecting to see an older man, the welcoming committee thought O'Reilly was an imposter and it took a good deal of time to convince them that he was, indeed, the escapee from Australia. Despite these difficulties, O'Reilly fared better with the Fenian delegation than at the hands of historians, who have never been able to agree on the true identity of the *Pilot* editor. Where one historian concentrated on O'Reilly's success in reconciling Catholics and Protestants in Boston, another saw behind his "occasional gestures to the 'melting pot' . . . an undercurrent of xenophobia, of racial and religious separatism." Similarly, while one writer praised O'Reilly's "steadfastness, his unwillingness to pander to the public," another saw him as functioning as a weather vane of Irish-American thinking.[3]

Thomas Brown and Arthur Mann, the two writers who have come closest to appreciating the complex nature of O'Reilly's career, saw him driven by different forces. Brown, who viewed O'Reilly as the most gifted leader of the Irish-American nationalist movement, regarded him as a man forced to steer a careful course with the Brahmins looking over one shoulder and the Irish looking over the other. Arthur Mann, who characterized O'Reilly as a radical among Catholics and a moderate among non-Catholics, believed that O'Reilly's career as a social reformer was limited by his loyalty to the Catholic church.[4]

Most of these writers have only looked at O'Reilly as part of a larger study of either American literature, Irish-American nationalism, assimilation, or social reform. In fact, in view of O'Reilly's significance, there has been surprisingly little of value written specifically about him.[5] What we are left with is a series of group snapshots, with O'Reilly often just a face in the crowd. And when the dilemmas of O'Reilly's life are considered at all, as in the Brown and Mann studies, they have been portrayed as two-dimensional: a conflict between Brahmin and Irish, or a choice between secular reform and his church. But O'Reilly's task was far more complicated than merely threading his way through two conflicting forces. It is by considering the variety of pressures active in his life that one gains a better appreciation of the complexity of this period.

As editor of the *Pilot*, O'Reilly had to carefully regulate the information supplied to his readers, prudently balancing stories of Irish-American oppression with articles on Irish-American success. He was keenly aware that a steady diet of "Irish-need-not-apply" stories could crush what little hope existed in the beleaguered Irish-American community. Moreover, there was more than one Irish-American community. The faction-ridden Irish-American nationalist movement alone provided enough contradictory positions to challenge the most adroit politician. In addition to all of his other concerns, O'Reilly had his own career to consider. It is clear from a reading of the few surviving O'Reilly letters that the *Pilot* editor was a man on the make, absorbed in furthering his own fortunes. Consequently, O'Reilly's career can best be understood in terms of a high-wire act, with the performer not only subject to shifting winds of high velocity, but also forced to perform in an arena filled with opposing factions, each ready to cry out when he but tilted in a different direction.

It is little wonder, therefore, that despite his commitment to a life of physical fitness, O'Reilly was tortured by sleepless nights and periods of nervous exhaustion. Part of his condition can be traced to his work schedule and his drive to succeed. O'Reilly was, if nothing else, a true believer in the concept of the self-made man. In a letter written to an aunt in Ireland, shortly after his arrival in Boston, he described his regimen which included four lectures a week—a course of action he was sure would make him a fortune. In an Irish version of "the talented tenth," he argued in editorials and in his private correspondence that the Irish people would be judged by "the actions of their representative men." With this in mind, he lectured a group of recently freed Fenians that honest, hard work for one year would assure them more respect, and Ireland more help, "than a life-time of worthless conspiracy." And to John Devoy, the ideologue of Irish-American nationalism, he wrote that no matter which faction Devoy joined, he had a "right, a duty, to make his means of living a primary consideration." Three months later, he again advised Devoy: "Work for yourself. It pays best in the end."[6]

Writers like Arthur Mann have made too much of the Catholic church's influence in limiting O'Reilly's commitment to reform. His own success made it difficult to believe that the American social and economic system was beyond saving. In view of this, what is surprising is not that O'Reilly was not a radical, but that he exhibited any radical traits at all. Certainly, during O'Reilly's association with the *Pilot*, the paper devoted more attention to working-class agitation than did any other journal not under labor's direct control. Under O'Reilly, the *Pilot*'s editorial position switched from one of opposition, to one of full support of the workers' right to organize and, if necessary, to strike. On more than one occasion, readers were informed that the interests of the laboring class and capital were antagonistic.[7]

The paper's sympathies with the labor movement are best illustrated by the *Pilot*'s treatment of the Railroad Strike of 1877. Most of the American press condemned the strikers' actions. The *New York Times*, for example, portrayed the strikers as "hoodlums, rabble, bummers, looters, blacklegs, thieves . . . and idiots." A survey of the *Pilot*'s coverage of the strike leaves one with the feeling that the *Times* and O'Reilly were describing two different events. To the *Pilot*, the conduct of the mob in Pittsburgh when it had the city under its control was a model of restraint and "one of the most remarkable events in history." On the other hand, O'Reilly had little sympathy for the new captains of industry: men like Andrew Carnegie, "the mock philanthropist," and "those colossal robbers," Gould and Vanderbilt.[8]

Like most reformers of his day, O'Reilly had no systematic solution to the problems of labor and industry. Although at times he favored national ownership of the telegraph system and the mines, and government arbitration of workers' grievances, he could also describe himself a few weeks before his death as a "believer in the least government for the people."[9] But to perceive these contradictions as stemming simply from his unwillingness to stray too far from Catholic social policy, is to ignore the fact that his confusion was common to most Americans who were trying to uphold traditional values in the changing world of the late nineteenth century.

Trying to chart a consistent course on social reform, however, was child's play when compared to the difficulties of trying to secure safe passage through the political minefield that was Irish-American nationalism. In fact, one could make a case that the leaders of this cause inflicted more damage on themselves than did the Crown during those years. It was impossible to take a strong position on any issue without alienating some faction. Consequently, in 1881, when O'Reilly argued for concentrating on the Home Rule issue at the expense of land reform, he was subjected to a blistering attack. Patrick Egan, a leader of the Land League, claimed that the *Pilot* editor's position would only be supported in Ireland by "worthless, rotten whigs and runegade [sic] politicians." The *Catholic Herald* devoted three columns to branding O'Reilly "a dangerous enemy to the cause of Ireland." On other occasions, the charges against O'Reilly ranged from being "a straddler," to making money from his speeches for the cause, to being, in fact, an English spy.[10]

Little wonder that O'Reilly poured out his frustrations to John Devoy in 1886. "I despise Egan's judgment," he wrote, "but I am sure he means well. I dislike Sullivan's intense planning and manipulating; but it is his natural

way—I have sincere affection and respect for John Byrne;
but I abominate his method. . . . I have a tender friendship
for Rossa, but I think he ought to be killed for a darned
fool."[11]

But although freeing his fellow nationals in Ireland remained a major interest, and concomitantly, a constant
source of irritation in his life, O'Reilly's major concern was
liberating those Irish who had come to America. So while
devoting extensive coverage to news of Ireland, he could at
the same time deplore his readers' preoccupation with Irish
politics. "There is not one Irish person in ten thousand," he
wrote, "who will ever return to live in Ireland. . . . Is it
right to tell these people . . . that they must live solely for
that country's politics, and that until she is free they must
not become good citizens of this country?"[12]

Good citizenship, in O'Reilly's eyes, should be rewarded
with a fair division of the spoils. In pursuit of this objective,
the *Pilot* editor regularly monitored the number of positions
on the city's payroll awarded to his readers. Not surprisingly, O'Reilly was rarely satisfied. In 1878, he complained:
"Out of the entire city, one-half of which is Irish, there are
only two inspectors and four sergeants of Irish birth or de-
scent, while out of seventy officers in the stations, there is
only one of Irish birth and he holds the lowest grade."[13]

Even more dangerous, according to O'Reilly, was the lack
of Irish-Catholic personnel in the public school systems of
the Commonwealth. In 1884, O'Reilly noted: "Half of the
people of Boston are Catholic, a majority of the children in
the public schools are Catholic. Yet only eight of the twenty-
four school committeemen are Catholic, while only two
hundred of the 1,341 teachers are Catholic." The editor concluded by reminding his readers that the city had yet to
experience its first Catholic school-master.[14]

O'Reilly's interest in education stemmed not only from

the employment opportunities it offered, but also from its power to shape the public's view of the Irish. A case in point was a geography lesson allegedly offered in one school which taught that Great Britain was "noted for its love of law and order, and fair dealings," whereas Ireland was famous for its "peat, potatoes, poverty, and political disturbances." "If the school superintendent is responsible for this," thundered O'Reilly, "then he is the most contemptible specimen of an American."[15]

But too much criticism of the establishment could be self-defeating, for it could result in reinforcing an existing sense of pessimism among the paper's readers. A pre-O'Reilly editorial in the *Pilot*, which had asserted that "the Irish come out of slavery, with many of the marks still visible upon them" including a "consciousness of lower classness," was still relevant in the O'Reilly period.[16]

A major part of O'Reilly's campaign to instill a collective sense of self-confidence in his constituency is reflected in the paper's constant effort to remind its readers of their growing power. The Massachusetts census reports which were regularly reproduced in the *Pilot* were a major source of encouragement, for as O'Reilly noted, "they should enable us to grin and bear many things which we are not able today to change, but the death of which we can foresee by a simple arithmetical exercise."[17]

The demographic handwriting was on the wall; each new set of statistics provided the appropriate commentary. The message was clear: Boston was becoming an Irish city. Nor was O'Reilly adverse to applying a little editorial heat to help the melting process along. As early as 1872, the *Pilot* began to forecast that the day was not far distant when the "last descendant of the Puritans would be exhibited in a glass case as a national curiosity." And, adding prophetic insult to historical injury, the paper added that it would not be surprised to see Plymouth Rock used as a cornerstone for a Catholic church.[18]

Change was in the air according to the *Pilot*; doors long closed were opening, and the Irish were moving in. One striking result, said O'Reilly, was the "position of the Irish in America. They are no longer laughed at." The *Pilot* editor foresaw the imminent departure of the stage Irishman, "Paddy . . . who laughed and jested at every turn of fortune, who loved a fight for its own sake, and whiskey. . . . In his place we have the common-sense Irishman."[19]

O'Reilly sought to encourage more of these common-sense Irishmen by using the *Pilot* as a social lever. Mindful of the debilitating effect that signs bearing the message, "Irish need not apply," had on the morale of his readers, he regularly called attention to successful Irish-Americans to demonstrate that opportunity did exist. In 1877, for example, the *Pilot* published a list, gleaned from the city's tax rolls, of over 200 Boston Irish who held property valued at more than $15,000. Moreover, the progress of the Irish was not just a local situation, but a national phenomenon: "The name of Charles O'Connor is at the head of the list of constitutional lawyers, as A. T. Stewart is at the head of American merchants, John Roach of American shipbuilders, or Stuart or Corchran of American bankers."[20]

From the pages of the *Pilot* flowed a steady stream of articles guaranteed to inflate the Celtic ego. In one piece, demonstrating Irish athletic prowess, O'Reilly asserted that "it is well known to scientists that the Irishman is a man of extraordinary compactness of intellectual and physical strength." And as proof of this point, he reminded his readers of "the notable fact that nearly all the people who reach one hundred years of age in this country are Irish." The claim was documented by a long list of Irish centenarians. Why, the very roots of the country were Irish and

Catholic rather than Anglo-Saxon and Protestant. According to O'Reilly, "The Irish is no bastard or corrupt stock but one of the great seminal races of the earth." With that in mind, his readers could not have been surprised to learn that an Irishman had helped row Columbus ashore on that memorable occasion.[21]

Despite this outpouring of Irish chauvinism, O'Reilly never lost sight of the ultimate goal: assimilation into the larger community. Although he regularly deplored the lack of Irish candidates on the state ticket, O'Reilly could also reject a suggestion from a letter to the editor that the Irish vote only for their own. "We dissent," he responded. "We have exposed and condemned just such views when they were held by native Americans . . . and we do not propose to support them among our own people."[22]

O'Reilly's occasional salute to nonpartisanship was more a reflection of his recognition of the need to convince the Yankee ascendancy of the good citizenship of his readers than any real refutation of bloc voting. However, it also reflected the fact that much of O'Reilly's public life was played out in Yankee circles where he jealously guarded his reputation for fair play.

O'Reilly had more intimate contact with the city's native-Americans than any other Irish-American of his day. In 1879 he was elected president of both the Boston Press Club and the literary Papyrus Club. In the following decade he became the state's poet laureate. In this capacity he was asked to compose poetry for the memorial to Wendell Phillips in 1884, and for the unveiling of the Crispus Attucks monument two years later. And in what would have been an unimaginable gesture twenty years earlier, O'Reilly was asked to write a commemorative verse for the dedication of that holy of Puritan holies, Plymouth Rock. The editor of one Boston newspaper, after expressing his initial surprise that O'Reilly had been chosen over Whittier and Holmes for this honor, admitted "that none of our native singers could possibly have done fuller justice to the Pilgrim character and achievements." He concluded by noting that O'Reilly was not only a great Irishman, but in what must have been his highest accolade, "a great Yankee."[23]

How important praise like this was to O'Reilly is revealed in a letter to the critic Edwin P. Whipple, thanking Whipple for being the first native-American to recognize his work. "You cannot know," he continued, "because you cannot be a foreigner . . . how delightful it is to be recognized." And in a revealing passage, O'Reilly went on to claim to be more a Brahmin than Whipple or his friends. "Truly," O'Reilly concluded, "if I were not the editor of the *Pilot* . . . you would never think me such a terrific Papist and paddy."[24]

His role as an honorary Yankee-Brahmin meant that O'Reilly was subject to complaints from his new friends when he or his paper went too far. Oliver Wendell Holmes, for example, demanded that O'Reilly repudiate the rumor "that the *Pilot* has been stirring up ill feeling against my friend Mr. Lowell and inciting the Irish to give him a hot reception at the pier on his arrival." Holmes added that he could not believe the story, of course.[25]

With all of these pulls and pushes added to a hectic work-load, it is little wonder that O'Reilly began to feel the strain. A significant number of his letters are filled with complaints of "overworking," of his time "mortgaged away into futurity," of being a "city pack horse," and "being chained to the wheel."[26]

Although contemporaries referred to his open, cheerful, and robust nature, his letters suggest a man troubled over the course of his life. Occasional letters refer to a desire to "escape and let the busy world go past." And to a friend who left the newspaper business for a position at the University of Notre Dame, "I wish I could go . . . and rest for a whole year and never read a newspaper or speak with a man who read one." In another letter in which he predicted better times for a friend, he referred to himself as a prophet. In support of his qualifications for that role, he declared, "Prophets are unhappy as a rule, and Lord knows I'm qualified that way." Again in a letter to another friend arranging a canoe trip, he wrote, "Let us have a couple of weeks to ourselves forgetting all the meanness and worries of the outer world."[27]

One might dismiss all of this as simply the occasional complaints that are a natural part of any life. But coupled with the fact that O'Reilly's nights were made miserable by continuous bouts with insomnia, a condition often connected with depression, these complaints suggest a deeper problem. In a letter to a friend, he described his problems with vertigo and his fears of another attack: "I cannot sleep more than thirty minutes at a time," he confessed, "and if this continues, I shall either break down or have to give up work altogether and go abroad."[28] To make matters worse, O'Reilly's wife never recovered from the birth of their first two children. Although she had two more children, she remained a semi-invalid for the rest of her life, suffering from what was diagnosed as "nervous exhaustion."

The events of the late 1880s no doubt contributed to his distress and must have made him question his success in balancing one interest group against another. One source of anguish was the resurgence of anti-Catholicism in Boston. In 1887, over the protests of the Irish, the British-American Association was allowed to use Faneuil Hall to celebrate Queen Victoria's jubilee. Earlier in his career, O'Reilly had championed the right of Irish-Protestants to march in New York, claiming they "had as much right . . . as Irish-Catholic organizations." In a bitter speech to his supporters after the Faneuil Hall decision had gone against them, a different O'Reilly cried, "I will never, so help me God—may my tongue cleave to my mouth if I ever speak a word for man or cause in Faneuil Hall again."[29]

Previous gains seemed about to be erased in the school battles of 1889. In 1888 a Catholic had served as chair of the Boston School Committee, but charges of Catholic interference in curriculum decisions led to an anti-Catholic backlash in the elections of the next three years. By 1890 Catholics held only two of the twenty-four positions on the school committee. The *Pilot*, which up to this point had never taken a strong position in favor of a separate school system, now urged the remaining two Catholics to resign from the committee, and called upon its readers to "multiply the parochial schools."[30] The failure of what he termed "respectable Protestants," with whom he had worked so closely, to protest the anti-Catholic propaganda was especially disheartening. In an editorial written two weeks before his death, he asked his Protestant friends: "Did they ever pause to think that we have no Catholic Committee of One Hundred . . . no store windows filled with prurient bigotry?" Fair-minded Protestantism, he warned, "may withdraw its skirts . . . but so long as not a single voice is raised in press or pulpit against such disgrace to Protestantism, it cannot hold itself faultless of the indecency which its silence condones."[31]

The *Pilot* editor was also experiencing difficulties in Catholic circles. When a Congress of Catholic Laymen was planned to coincide with the celebration of the centenary of the American hierarchy, O'Reilly was not chosen as a speaker. In fact, he was not even asked to sign the call for the congress, even though far less influential Catholic Bostonians had been asked to do so. He was appointed to a committee to plan future congresses, but resigned out of pique on July 14, 1890. Three years after his death, the snubbing of O'Reilly was still a major source of indignation among his friends.[32]

With all of these problems, the summer of 1890 was especially difficult. By August 9, he had experienced several sleepless nights. That evening his wife also complained of being unable to sleep and asked him to bring a doctor. Arriving at midnight, the doctor examined Mrs. O'Reilly and gave her something to help her. Two hours later, O'Reilly again appeared at the doctor's door and informed him that his wife had spilt part of her medicine. The doctor gave O'Reilly a single dose to carry his wife through the night. At three o'clock that morning, Mrs. O'Reilly woke and found her husband slumped in his chair. A doctor was called and found the *Pilot* editor dead at the age of forty-six. The mystery surrounding his death has never been satisfactorily resolved. The official version was heart failure, induced by an accidental overdose of his wife's medicine.[33]

His death brought tributes from all over the United States, Canada, Australia, Ireland, and Great Britain. Many felt that O'Reilly's contribution was summed up best by a native-Bostonian, his friend Thomas Wentworth Higginson. O'Reilly's mission, declared the former abolitionist, was "the reconciliation in this community between the Roman Catholic Irishman and the Protestant American. . . . Himself a liberated convict, he set us free."[34]

But a stanza from O'Reilly's poem, "The Cry of the Dreamer," published in 1886, may have best expressed his own mood in those last years:

> I am sick of the showy seeming
>   Of a life that is half a lie;
> Of the faces lined with scheming
>   In the throng that hurries by.
> From the sleepless thoughts' endeavor,
>   I would go where the children play;
> For a dreamer lives forever,
>   And a thinker dies in a day.[35]

Notes

1. See Peter Eisinger, "Ethnic Political Transition in Boston, 1884–1933;
   Some Lessons for Contemporary Cities," *Political Science Quarterly* 93
   (1978): 217–39; Barbara Miller Solomon, *Ancestors and Immigrants* (Chicago, 1956).
2. See *Memorial of John Boyle O'Reilly from the City of Boston* (Boston, 1891),
   passim.
3. Van Wyck Brooks, *New England Indian Summer* (New York, 1940),
   p. 311; Roger Lane, "James Jeffrey Roche and the Boston *Pilot*," *New
   England Quarterly* 33 (1960): 343; A. J. Reilly, "Poet, Patriot, and
   Fighter," *Columbia* 24 (August 1944): 44; Donna Merwick, *Boston Priests
   1848–1910* (Cambridge, Mass., 1973), p. 66.
4. Thomas N. Brown, *Irish-American Nationalism* (Philadelphia, 1966), pp.
   180–81; Arthur Mann, *Yankee Reformers in the Urban Age* (Cambridge,
   Mass., 1954), p. 43.
5. John Betts has focused on two aspects of O'Reilly's multifaceted career:
   Betts, "The Negro and the New England Conscience in the Days of
   John Boyle O'Reilly," *Journal of Negro History* 51 (1966): 246–61; for
   an appreciation of O'Reilly's athletic career, see Betts, "John Boyle
   O'Reilly and the American Paidea," *Eire Ireland* 2 (1967): 36–52. James
   Jeffrey Roche, *The Life of John Boyle O'Reilly* (New York, 1891), written
   by O'Reilly's successor as editor of the *Pilot*, contains a number of
   O'Reilly's letters. Francis G. McManamin, S. J., has written a useful,
   but uncritical, biography: *The American Years of John Boyle O'Reilly*
   (Ph.D. diss., Catholic University of America, 1959; reprint ed., New
   York: Arno Press, 1976).
6. O'Reilly to "My Own Dear Aunt," Boston, April 5, 1870, in Roche, *Life
   of O'Reilly*, pp. 105–6; *Pilot*, Oct. 22, 1870; O'Reilly to John Devoy,
   Boston, Feb. 13, May 26, 1871, *Devoy's Post-Bag, 1871–1928*, ed. William
   O'Brien and Desmond Ryan (Dublin, 1948), 1:30, 41.
7. For an evaluation of the *Pilot*'s labor policies, see Aaron Abell, *American
   Catholicism and Social Action: A Search for Social Justice, 1865–1900* (New
   York, 1960), p. 54; *Pilot*, Oct. 2, 1886.
8. *New York Times* article quoted in Foster Rhea Dulles, *Labor in America,
   A History* (New York, 1955), p. 121; *Pilot*, July 28, 1877, July 20, 1889,
   July 1, 1882.
9. *Pilot*, Dec. 29, Sept. 1, Dec. 15, 1883; July 26, 1890.
10. For internecine Irish quarrels, see Brown, *Irish-American Nationalism*;
    Victor A. Walsh, " 'A Fanatic Heart': The Case of Irish-American Na-
    tionalism in Pittsburgh during the Gilded Age," *Journal of Social History*
    15 (1982): 187–204; Michael F. Funchion, *Chicago's Irish Nationalists,
    1881–1890* (Ph.D. diss., Loyola University of Chicago, 1973; reprint ed.,
    New York: Arno Press, 1976). Patrick Egan to John Devoy, Feb. 17,

1882, in *Devoy's Post-Bag* (Dublin, 1953), 2:281; *Catholic Herald*, n.d., in O'Reilly Scrapbook, Irish Collection, Boston College; *New York News*, July 29, 1886; *Pilot*, May 15, 1886; O'Reilly to John Devoy, Boston, Dec. 4, 1874, in *Devoy's Post-Bag*, 1:86.

11. O'Reilly to Devoy, Boston, May 3, 1886, *Devoy's Post-Bag*, 1:281.
12. *Pilot*, Oct. 20, 1877.
13. *Pilot*, Nov. 2, 1878.
14. *Pilot*, Sept. 19, 1885.
15. *Pilot*, Nov. 25, 1882.
16. *Pilot*, July 19, 1845.
17. *Pilot*, June 2, 1877.
18. *Pilot*, April 27, 1872.
19. *Pilot*, Nov. 5, 1881.
20. *Pilot*, Feb. 17, 1877; June 17, 1883.
21. *Pilot*, Dec. 11, 1886; Jan. 10, 1874; Dec. 6, 1884; June 8, 1878.
22. *Pilot*, Jan. 21, 1876.
23. Title of Boston paper not given, August 16, 1889, O'Reilly Scrapbook.
24. O'Reilly to Edwin P. Whipple, Boston, March 20, 1878 (Ms. 219, Boston Public Library).
25. Oliver Wendell Holmes to O'Reilly, Oct. 14, 1882 (Houghton Library, Harvard University).
26. O'Reilly to Mr. Burrell, Boston, Jan. 24, 1888 (Ms. Am. 1662, Boston Public Library); O'Reilly to William Onahan, Boston, Feb. 4, 1878 (Ms. 9–1–a, Onahan Collection, University of Notre Dame Archives); O'Reilly to Charles Warren Stoddard, Boston, June 21, 1882, in Roche, *Life of O'Reilly*, pp. 291–92.
27. O'Reilly to Maurice Egan, Boston, July 26, 1888 (Ms. 10–3–g, Hudson Collection, University of Notre Dame Archives); O'Reilly to Charles Hurd, Boston, Jan. 27, 1876 (Ms. 684, Boston Public Library); O'Reilly to Ned Mosely, Boston, April 26, 1888 (Ms. Acc. 2537, Boston Public Library).
28. O'Reilly to John Devoy, Boston, May 3, 1886, in *Devoy's Post-Bag*, 1:281.
29. *Pilot*, July 23, 1870; July 27, 1871; Roche, *Life of O'Reilly*, pp. 307–8.
30. James W. Sanders, "Boston Catholics and the School Question, 1825–1907," in *From School to Magnet School*, ed. James W. Fraser, Henry L. Allen, and Sam Barnes (Boston, 1979), p. 69; *Pilot*, June 21, 28, 1890.
31. *Pilot*, July 26, 1890.
32. O'Reilly to Mr. T. B. Fitz, Boston, July 14, 1890, in Roche, *Life of O'Reilly*, pp. 350–51; Katherine E. Conway to William Onahan, Boston, June 2, 30, 1893 (Ms. 9–1–e, Onahan Collection, University of Notre Dame).
33. McManamin, *American Years*, pp. 298–99.
34. *Memorial of John Boyle O'Reilly*, pp. 39–40.
35. Reprinted in Roche, *Life of O'Reilly*, pp. 463–64.

Harvard's Response to Excellence and Winning in College Athletics, 1869–1909

RONALD A. SMITH

There is an aristocracy to which sons of Harvard have belonged, and let us hope, will ever aspire to belong—the aristocracy which excels in manly sports. . . . President Charles W. Eliot, Harvard Inaugural Address, October 19, 1869

Almost from their beginnings, well over a century ago, men's intercollegiate athletics in America have been characterized by excellence in performance and an intense effort to win. And almost from the start, this emphasis upon excellence and winning has been denigrated primarily on the basis that if superior performance is to take place in colleges, it should occur in the classroom, not on the playing field. The opposition generally perceives that highly competitive athletics are given too much emphasis. Opponents feel that college athletics have a win-at-all-cost philosophy; that we are spending too much time and money on those who need it the least; that a commercial spirit permeates college sport; and that college athletics are no longer true to the amateur spirit.

In England, the birthplace of nineteenth-century intercollegiate athletics, opposition to highlighting college sport began by the 1870s. Opponents called such overemphasis "athleticism." In the 1800s, England was generally a decade to a generation ahead of America in the development of intercollegiate sport. Where England led, America followed, and that was true until the last two decades of the nineteenth century. However, social conditions peculiar to the United States, but nonexistent in England, prompted a major difference in the two countries' attitude toward excellence and winning in sports. According to many writers of that period, American colleges developed an extreme form of athleticism after the 1880s.

By the early 1900s, contemporaries began to compare English and American college sports. "The English," wrote a knowledgeable American observer at the turn of the century, "seem to play more for the love of sport and less for a desire to beat somebody than their American cousins." An Englishman wrote at about the same time: "The winning of a game being the only end that an American player has in view, he subordinated every other consideration," something which, he noted, was not true of an athlete at Oxford University. John Muirhead, an upper-class British traveler to America, got closer to the heart of the issue. Muirhead questioned the emphasis upon winning in American college sport, believing that "the desire to win must be very strictly subordinated to the sense of honour and fair play."[1]

The strict desire to win, as opposed to a sense of honor and fair play, was also of concern to Endicott Peabody. Peabody was an American patrician by birth, educated in the English public school of Cheltenham and at Cambridge University. He returned to America where he founded and became headmaster of the elite Groton School for Boys in Massachusetts. With this background and a love of sports he wrote an article titled, "The Ideals of Sport in England and America." He believed that the aim of sport in England "is recreation; in America it is victory." He saw, but did not criticize, a lack of the drive for excellence in English sport. "In England," wrote Peabody, "there is not perfection by any means,—the millennium has not come, even in

England,—but they do have one idea which appeals to the sportsman—athletics exist for the purposes of recreation; they are great fun." In America, he concluded that "we take the most promising men and make them practically perfect in our teams, for particular events."[2]

Why, though, did these differences exist between the English attitude—sports for fun—and the American attitude—perfection and winning? Why was it natural for British college athletics to be recreative, whereas American sports were so competitively intense? I believe Peabody had a large part of the answer, but he never reached a conclusion. In describing English existence, Peabody observed that life there is "more settled and tradition rules." He regarded England as a better place to live than America. Nevertheless, he noted that America is a better place in which to work, for the "life of the ordinary man who is in earnest counts for a good deal more." In America the society is "plastic," he said, not unchangeable.[3] The plasticity of American society which Peabody described might be noted in sociological terms as social mobility, the ability to move up or down in social status. The American belief in social mobility, I believe, is a key to understanding the emphasis upon excellence and winning in American intercollegiate athletics for the past century.

Unlike England, America did not have a locked in, stratified society in the nineteenth century. To a great extent, performance rather than peerage determined a person's place in the social order. In a stratified society such as England's in the 1800s, an individual's status was determined more by birth than by capacity. Thus, performance was of less importance to someone who already knew his rank than to someone who was striving for status in a more open society like America.

Alexis de Tocqueville, the keen observer of America, said

it a century and a half ago: "The great advantage of the Americans is that they have arrived at a state of democracy without having to endure a democratic revolution, and that they were born equal instead of becoming so."[4] A belief in the concept that Americans were "born equal" or "born free," and would differ from England in terms of social stratification and thus in an emphasis on performance, can bring meaning to a discussion of excellence and winning in college athletics. In *The Liberal Tradition in America*, Louis Hartz agreed with de Tocqueville, stating that Americans have always had a liberal or Lockean tradition; that Americans arrived in a state of democracy without having to endure a democratic revolution.[5] Hartz's point is that unlike Europeans, Americans had no feudal system (no "ancien régime") to revolt against and none to return to. Never having had an established aristocratic class, American society would naturally differ from a society historically ruled by such an upper class. American institutions, American colleges, and the athletics developed therein, would reflect this difference.

As colleges in England were almost exclusively of and for the upper class, it followed that the athletics that developed would have upper-class mores. The class system in athletics meant a gentleman's class system. Said H. J. Wingham—born in Scotland, educated at Oxford, and residing in the United States early in the twentieth century—"A man born in a gentleman's society has certain duties. He must have catholic tastes, be a many sided man, do nothing for pecuniary gain, and must not specialize. In sports he must play many activities for it would be ridiculous to practice one sport for half a year. That would upset a balance of character. The gentleman's tradition must be upheld."[6] A gentleman's code of social behavior easily translates into a code of sportsmanship, which exists best where there is a rigid class structure. For example, in medieval times, only the upper class practiced the code of chivalry, for the code could be best exemplified by those who knew their high station in society and could afford to be magnanimous. The nobility of mind could easily be carried over to the nobility of sport in victory or defeat. If one does not have to continually prove oneself to maintain one's status in athletics or in anything else, the logical conclusion is that there will be less of a demand for excellence of performance. Thus, one would expect less emphasis upon winning in English college athletics, which is the ultimate criterion on which most athletic performances are judged.

In America there were, of course, gentlemen on college campuses in the nineteenth century when organized sport first appeared. But America had a strong tradition of egalitarianism which stemmed from colonial days and was expressed by Thomas Jefferson in the Declaration of Independence: "All men are created equal." This was not an equality of talent, but of opportunity. There was greater opportunity for advancement, for upward mobility in America than there was in the more stratified English society. Where opportunity exists there is likely to be a greater struggle, and performance is more likely to be judged on the individual's pursuit of excellence. In athletics that pursuit often means winning. In an open society that acknowledges excellence of performance, status through winning seems only natural. One can easily discriminate in athletics between excellence and mediocrity. One wins or one loses. In athletics winning or losing is the absolute most often used to judge excellence.

Let us test the theory that the more stratified a society is in terms of social mobility, the less it will emphasize excellence and winning. To conduct this test, we will turn to the institution which, though not aristocratic in British eyes, was the most elite and aristocratic American college in the nineteenth century: Harvard. Harvard was the first American college, and it was the largest and wealthiest American college for much of the nineteenth century. Harvard had the most prestigious graduates. Nurturing it was that most traditional upper class, the patricians of Boston—often referred to as the Boston Brahmins. Harvard and Yale were the first colleges to have intercollegiate athletics. And beginning in the mid-1800s, both were the principal leaders in athletics for over a half-century. This suggests the likelihood that Harvard would strive for excellence and winning based upon the American ethos for perfection and success, but that it, more than other American colleges, would apply certain gentlemanly restraints to its athletics. In the end, one might advance the idea that Harvard would either relax its standards or lose out in its efforts to strive for excellence and winning in athletics while attempting to uphold its ideals.

Intriguing questions crop up. What was Harvard's early attitude toward excellence and winning in athletics? What gentlemanly limitations did Harvard place on the desire for excellence and winning? How were these attitudes manifested in its play against its closest rival, Yale? How long could a college that reined in its desire for excellence and winning compete successfully with those who imposed fewer restrictions? How would Harvard attempt to resolve its dilemma?

The early Harvard model will cover the years 1869–1909, corresponding to the forty-year tenure of Charles W. Eliot as president of Harvard. Charles Eliot was only thirty-five years of age when elected president of America's most distinguished college. Only eleven years before, Eliot had rowed for the college crew; although he was not an undergraduate, he held a tutorship in mathematics. When he became president in 1869, he delivered one of the great college presidential inaugural addresses. In this speech—given less than a month before the first intercollegiate football contest between Princeton and Rutgers—Eliot uttered important words about college athletics. "There is an aristocracy," he said, "to which sons of Harvard have belonged, and, let us hope, will ever aspire to belong—the aristocracy which excels in manly sports, carries off the honors and prizes of the learned professions, and bears itself with distinction in all fields of intellectual labor and combat. . . ."[7] Here was a challenge to Harvard to be best in athletics, as well as in intellectual efforts. This was not, however, as some later college presidents contended, to be an unprincipled chase for athletic honors and distinctions. Rather, Eliot saw athletics as providing healthful and manly physical exercise in a variety of outdoor sports. His enthusiasm for striving for excellence was tempered by his traditional upper-class attitude, common to Harvard College, which indicated that there should be limits on athletic efforts.

When Eliot had himself participated on the Harvard crew a decade before, he wrote to his fiancée: "I had rather win than not, but it is mighty little matter whether we beat or are beaten—rowing is not my profession, neither is it my love,—it is recreation, fun, and health. I am going to remember your injunction, and take the best possible care of myself, and row just as hard as I comfortably can, and not a bit harder."[8] This was a true gentleman's statement. In an early presidential annual report, he gave reinforcement to his belief that Harvard men should be moderate in their sports. He attempted to "dissuade students from making athletic sports the main business, instead of one of the incidental pleasures, of their college life."[9] If this attitude were to penetrate athletics at Harvard, it was not unlikely to appeal to those who truly sought excellence and winning.

"Incidental pleasure," for which Eliot rowed in 1858, was not a logical means of achieving his inaugural goal of an "aristocracy which excels in manly sports." It might be aristocratic, but it would not likely achieve excellence.

Though Harvard was the most prestigious American college and boasted the largest student body, it was never able to dominate athletics. It generally lost to Yale and Princeton in baseball, and especially in the important sports of crew and football. This lack of athletic success probably can be attributed to the attitude that pervaded Harvard, an attitude akin to the aristocratic British attitude of participation imbued with a sense of enjoyment and fair play.

What evidence is there to indicate that Harvard attempted to play sport more in tune with British gentlemen, while at the same time competing with American colleges who emphasized first and foremost excellence and winning? The gentleman's attitude at Harvard was more apparent in its faculty, administration, and alumni than in its student body. Harvard students, almost from the beginning, took winning seriously. By the 1860s, less than a decade after the first contest, Harvard and Yale crews were contesting their annual match in a highly competitive manner with little claim to true sportsmanship. For instance a donnybrook occurred at Worcester, Massachusetts, in the 1860 regatta when police battled fans of the Harvard crew, winners of a disputed race; for three years thereafter, contests were cancelled by school authorities. Then, in 1864, during the Civil War, Yale hired the first professional college coach, and defeated Harvard for the first time. A reporter noted at the end of the match that "no friendly hands met at the close of the conflict."[10] After one more loss to Yale, Harvard students asked former crewman William Blaikie to help them. Blaikie went to England to study their rowing system and then introduced it to Harvard. A series

of Harvard victories resulted, one of which occurred the
year Charles Eliot became president. That year, the Harvard
crew accepted an invitation to row against the Oxford crew
in London, England. While the first Harvard crew was
meeting the English best, the second crew was taking on
Yale in the annual challenge race. Harvard's desire for excellence and winning came to fruition as it came from behind to defeat Yale by two lengths. One of the Yale oarsmen
was so angered by this bitter defeat that he drove his oar
through the bottom of his boat.[11]

The rivalry and desire to win continued in crew into the
1870s, and was intensified by the addition of baseball in the
1860s, and football in the 1870s. By the early 1880s the expansion and intensity of Harvard athletics was such that the
faculty decided to take action. Baseball was the culprit
which precipitated the movement to create a faculty athletic
committee to control intercollegiate athletics in a more gentlemanly manner. The Harvard baseball team had had a record high 44-game schedule in 1870 (26 of which were played
out of term time), but in 1882, of its schedule of 28 games,
19 were played outside of Cambridge and 11 were played
against professional teams. Prompted by the frequency of
away games and of play against professionals, the Harvard
faculty appointed a committee to study the problem. Out
of this grew a recommendation for a Standing Committee
on the Regulation of Athletic Sports. The Harvard faculty
thus desired to curb the perfection of "athletics practiced
in a competitive spirit in emulation of professional athletes
and players" and to return them to a more gentlemanly attitude of "athletics practiced for sport, social recreation, and
health."[12]

The dichotomy between athletics for excellence and winning and athletics for recreation and fun in the gentleman's
tradition continued throughout the period. One year after

its founding, the Harvard Athletic Committee sent a letter to Yale requesting a conference of leading colleges to discuss policy regarding joint faculty control of intercollegiate athletics. Though Yale at first declined, Harvard nevertheless decided to send invitations to thirteen institutions, of which eight—including Yale—attended. The conference met twice and adopted a series of resolutions aimed at preserving amateurism under faculty control. It also set regulations on eligibility, and agreed to play against only those schools which passed the resolutions. The resolves were then sent to twenty-one colleges with a letter stating that they would be enforced when five colleges adopted them. Only the Harvard and Princeton faculties passed the resolutions. (It might be noted that *students* at every college opposed them.) With only two of twenty-one colleges adopting the resolves, the first faculty-controlled conference proposal died prematurely.[13]

The Harvard faculty continued its drive to imbue college athletics with a sense of sportsmanship and constraint. In 1884, the athletic committee fired the baseball coach who had been chosen by the students. Also, it refused to explain why the crew could not hire a specific crew coach. Soon thereafter, the athletic committee asked the faculty to prohibit football because "the nature of the game puts a premium on unfair play, inasmuch as such play is easy, is profitable if it succeeds, is unlikely to be detected by the referee, and if detected is very lightly punished." The committee further said that football "is brutal, demoralizing to players and to spectators, and extremely dangerous."[14] The faculty agreed.

Though football was reinstated within a year, questions concerning the ethics of winning did not subside. In 1887, the Harvard Board of Overseers, a group of elders who oversee but do not set policy, were asked to submit findings on whether undue prominence was given to Harvard athletics. The overseers' committee concluded that "professional methods and professional standards gradually creep in until the honorable emulation of gentlemen becomes a dishonorable struggle for a prize." They charged that "disputes over races, charges of trickery, complaints against umpires and referees have constantly occurred." The committee reached the opinion, with one dissenter, that the Harvard faculty should prohibit all intercollegiate athletics for one year.[15]

President Eliot then appointed a committee of three knowledgeable faculty members to examine Harvard athletics. This committee did not propose abolition of athletics, but it did agree that "the passionate desire to win . . . leads men to strain the rules of sport and sometimes to break them, and to bring accusations of bad faith against opponents or referees." According to the committee, this "ungentlemanly behavior, . . . professional spirit, [and] excessive desire to win" were the most serious charges brought against intercollegiate athletics.[16]

Harvard did not drop competitive athletics, but it continued to attempt reforms that were generally rejected by its fellow institutions. In 1890 Harvard tried unsuccessfully to secure an agreement with Yale regarding the eligibility of freshmen teams. The same year Harvard withdrew from the Inter-Collegiate Foot Ball Association because of the objectionable practices (principally Princeton's) of recruiting players and of playing professionals. Harvard further tried to eliminate all games played outside of New England, and to have a "dual league" with Yale. This was stifled by Yale and by interested Harvard alumni from New York City who desired to have the annual Harvard-Yale football game played in their city.[17] By the mid-1890s, the faculty again voted to abolish football because of "unsportsmanlike and injury-producing elements of the game."[18] The faculty's desire never came to pass, for the Harvard Corporation upheld the unanimous opinion of the athletic committee that Harvard could indeed compete "in the spirit of gentlemen."[19]

Toward the end of the 1890s, a faculty conference was held at Brown University to discuss methods of eliminating objectionable features of intercollegiate athletics. Harvard was one of six schools represented. Yale was conspicuously absent. The conference report proposed twenty rules changes, primarily those promoted by Harvard, and exposed almost as many malpractices in athletics.[20] It spoke out once again for the need for gentlemanly restrictions in American college sports. "We should not seek perfection in our games," the report emphasized, "but, rather, good sport. The notion that a team is disgraced if beaten, or even scored against, is altogether silly. What we all want is a good, manly struggle between fairly equal teams, who scorn to take unfair advantage."[21] What Harvard and a few other faculty-controlled athletic institutions wanted was the English view of competitive sports, which was difficult to achieve in a nation that lacked the aristocratic notion of sport.

As Harvard led the nation's colleges in the struggle to reform athletics through faculty control and by promoting a semblance of gentlemanly behavior, it was plain that at the same time, Harvard was struggling to produce athletic excellence and to win, especially against its prime rival Yale. It was the Yale rivalry that tested Harvard's resolve to pursue athletics in the American tradition of excellence and winning, within the bounds of the British upper-class attitude of sportsmanship and gentlemanly reserve. William James, Jr., a Harvard student in 1903, aptly summed it up when he said that Harvard was caught between beating

Yale and preserving the ideals of athletics.[22] A captain of the Harvard crew in 1908 remarked to President Eliot that "it is a pity that Harvard could not find someone as her chief competitor with standards of sportsmanship more near her own."[23] The faculty, however, more than the students, were attempting to set the standards after the faculty athletic committee was formed in 1882. Until 1882, Harvard fared well against Yale in competition in the three major sports, crew, baseball, and football. From the beginning in 1852 until 1882, Harvard led Yale: 16 wins to 6 losses in crew; 21 wins to 15 losses in baseball. But Harvard trailed in the new sport of rugby-football, 1 win to 4 losses. After 1882, until the end of the Eliot era at Harvard, Yale dominated all three sports. From 1882 through 1909, Yale had 19 wins and 7 losses in crew; 37 wins and 32 losses in baseball; and 18 wins and 4 losses in football.[24]

Several incidents in the early 1900s tend to indicate why Harvard's attitude toward winning in a gentlemanly tradition led to dominance by Yale, which had less than two-thirds of Harvard's enrollment in the late 1800s and early 1900s.[25]

By the fall of 1901, Harvard had won only two of the previous seventeen football games with Yale, and had not scored a point in three of the last four games with its prime rival. Only the spring before, Harvard had been tricked, it believed, when Yale changed its rules of eligibility to allow a law student, J. S. Spraker, to be admitted to the Yale Law School without an examination after he had failed to get into Princeton. Harvard students claimed he was brought into Yale only for athletic purposes. Spraker's winning of the high jump provided the points necessary for Yale to win the annual dual track meet. Harvard students, upset over Yale's chicanery, then successfully challenged the eligibility of one of Yale's football players early the next fall. Yale was, predictably, upset. It was then Yale's turn to question the eligibility of a member of Harvard's team. On a Wednesday preceding the annual Harvard-Yale football game, Ira N. Hollis, chairman of the Harvard Athletic Committee, received a telegram from Walter Camp, Yale's unofficial athletic boss and titular football coach. It read:

> So much unsolicited evidence comes into our hands that Cutts taught football at the school from which he was receiving a salary that we find it difficult to prevent trouble and stop stories, both of which we desire. Can you give us necessary material to answer strong prima facie case.[26]

Oliver Cutts was a 28-year-old, nearly 200-pound, second-year law student when he played right tackle for Harvard that season. Cutts had attended and played football for three seasons at Bates College before graduating in 1896. He then was hired to teach mathematics at Haverford Grammar School near Philadelphia and did so until 1900. Though he helped coach the Haverford football team and worked with students in the gymnasium, he was evidently not paid for that service. As a law student during his first year at Harvard, he did not play because Harvard had a rule prohibiting first-year law students from playing. The next year, though, the Harvard team welcomed him. On the morning of the Harvard-Yale game in 1901, Yale's Walter Camp produced one more bit of evidence from a Yale graduate stating that Cutts did receive a salary commensurate with his joint service as teacher and athletic instructor. The Harvard Athletic Committee met for about four hours that morning, and in a close vote declared Cutts eligible to play, primarily on the statement of Cutts's principal at the Haverford school who claimed Cutts was not paid for athletics and was thus an amateur. The game was played, Cutts starred, and Harvard won by the biggest score in its early history against Yale, 22–0.

Yale would not let the controversy die. Shortly before Christmas, Yale presented new evidence to President Eliot; a copy of a check showing that Cutts had received payment for privately teaching boxing while at Haverford—thus making him a professional. [27] With this information the Harvard Athletic Committee met in early 1902 and declared Cutts ineligible. [28] Chairman Hollis was disgusted with the insinuations by Yale that his committee had been deceptive in its dealing with the Cutts case. He said that Yale, not Harvard, had been the "worst sinner" for not cooperating in the movement to produce needed rules and regulations in athletics. Said Hollis: "While very little change has been made in the rules, the yearly meeting has been productive of much good in better understanding of the motives and intentions of various participants. Only Yale," Hollis emphasized, "has refused to take part in these discussions."[29]

The Cutts case, though, finally motivated President Hadley of Yale to take some initiative for his student-run athletic program. He called for a joint undergraduate rules conference concerning eligibility. [30] Out of the meetings came the 1903 Harvard-Yale eligibility agreement. This called for bona fide, amateur undergraduate students to have only four years of eligibility, with transfer students residing for one year before participation. No graduates were to play, and lists of eligible athletes were to be sent three weeks prior to the contests, with all protests being made two weeks before the event. [31] The existence of written rules of eligibility was a move to bring about more ethical play. One might argue, though, that it was evidence of the lack of the gentlemanly attitude in sport, for if Yale and Harvard had had true gentlemen, the spirit of fair play would have dictated the correct action.

While Harvard and Yale continued to question each other's athletic motives, Yale kept winning—especially in football, where it shut out Harvard for the next six years. The Harvard-Yale controversy boiled over in a closely contested game of the 1905 season, when a Harvard man, Francis Burr, was attempting to "fair catch" a Yale punt. Under the rules it was legal for Yale to attempt to play the ball. A Harvard player who was on the field at the time of the incident, later reported that a Yale player, James Quill,

> leaped into the air with his arms aloft and in a parallel position, to intercept the ball just as it was about to fall into Burr's arms. Quill missed the ball and, in his descent, fell on Burr with his elbow resting on Burr's nose. Burr fell to the ground somewhat dazed. The blood spurted from his nostrils. But it was not a cowardly attack. Any good player, in an effort to prevent a fair catch, would have used the same method as Quill employed. Of course, it was too bad that his elbow got in the way of Burr's nose.[32]

One would have expected the Harvard player to have been biased in his report of the game. He felt, though, that the Yale player had not been brutal, but had played "a piece of good football." Harvard fans saw it differently. They believed that the Yale player had deliberately and flagrantly disabled the Harvard man. A storm of protest grew at Harvard at the same time that the death of a Union College player in a New York University game stirred the NYU chancellor to call a meeting of colleges to either abolish or reform football. Harvard alumnus, Richard Henry Dana, after condemning the Yale "brutality," asked President Eliot "if a flood of light" on football "would not force a reform."[33] LeBaron Briggs, dean of the Harvard Faculty of Arts and Science, believed that despite incidents such as the Quill affair, Harvard-Yale games should not be stopped. "I am not yet so pessimistic," he wrote Eliot, "as to believe that students of different universities cannot play against each other as gentlemen."[34] The Harvard overseers, though, believed that the game of football was "essentially

bad in every respect." The "trickiness and foul play" encouraged in many colleges should be condemned. The
overseers asked: "Is it not time for the larger and more
important universities . . . to cry Halt?"[35] President Theodore Roosevelt, who only several months before had helped
settle the Russo-Japanese War, jumped into the athletic
malaise of 1905 in an attempt to save the game which he
thought best developed moral character. As a Harvard partisan who graduated from that institution in 1880, he corresponded numerous times with President Eliot trying to
convince him that football should be reformed rather than
abolished as Eliot desired. When Eliot, the overseers, and
the Harvard faculty called for the suspension of football at
Harvard early in 1906, Teddy Roosevelt wrote in private
that Harvard was "doing the baby act. . . ."[36]

The long-smoldering controversy between Yale and Harvard over the nature of college athletics was heightened by
an article published in the *Harvard Graduates' Magazine* on
the heels of the Quill controversy. In an unsigned article,
Yale and its administration were condemned for cringing
"before the athletocracy." It stated that Yale was only
seeking general educational publicity by linking its name
with Harvard in athletics. Further, and central to the theme
of this paper, there was a charge that despite Harvard's
sportsmanlike attitude toward athletics, "the temptation to
imitate the practices which have brought victory to their
opponents has sometimes proved too strong." The basic
philosophy of athletics in the two institutions, the article
emphasized, are different. "Harvard is pledged to the
proposition that athletics in a university shall be subordinated to the real purpose of a university, that they shall be
engaged in for recreation, that contests shall be waged in
a spirit of sport, and that the standard shall be that of gentlemen." Yale, it stated, had "persistently opposed every at-

tempt to curb, or regulate, or purify athletics." It suggested breaking athletic relations with Yale, an institution which had consistently promoted an "anything to win" policy.[37]

This was not a new charge, for a decade before, Harvard had broken relations with Yale over its attitude toward winning. The Harvard crew coach in 1895 claimed that Yale had deprived Harvard of many victories "by their 'anything to win' methods. The alternative," the coach believed, "is to cease doing business with them for a time . . . or descend to the same methods. They do not seem able to act like gentlemen."[38] In fact the charge had been made numerous times since Harvard had set up its first faculty athletic committee in 1882. More often than not it was the faculty and administration rather than Harvard students who made the charges. William Thayer, editor of the *Harvard Graduates' Magazine*, noted this in 1905 after the scathing article on Yale had been published and reactions had surfaced. In a reply to President Eliot, Thayer remarked that "Harvard authorities have been struggling to set a higher standard, which our athletes cannot hope to reach unless they give up making concessions to competitors—Yale first of all—who avowedly prefer a lower standard. To judge from discussion of the past four weeks," Thayer believed, "our athletes resent the suggestion that they have ever had, or ever wish to have a higher standard than Yale's."[39]

What was Harvard to do? Should it set higher standards of athletic conduct or should it play by the rules established by most American colleges, which stressed excellence and winning? The Harvard president, faculty, corporation, and a few alumni favored the English upper-class system of gentlemanly sport. Most of the student body and an increasing number of alumni favored beating Yale and showing its athletic superiority. The dean of the Harvard Faculty of Arts and Sciences, LeBaron Briggs, said in 1908: "The students love their athletics and their college and dislike seeing their chance of victory diminished by the shifting policy and restriction not subjected to by other colleges."[40] The Harvard faculty kept condemning what it believed were the evils of college athletics. The faculty even tried to pack the joint athletic committee, which had three members each from the faculty, students, and alumni. In 1907, the faculty voted that its three members would be the dean of the Faculty of Arts and Sciences, the dean of Harvard College, and the dean of the Lawrence Scientific School. The Harvard Corporation concurred.[41] Once on the committee, the deans all felt it was "a profound mistake," and recommended an athletic director and a return to the previous faculty representation.[42] The director of athletics was created as the Eliot era came to a close, and was given the title of Graduate Treasurer of the Harvard Athletic Association. One could hardly expect an athletic director to not promote winning.

Other changes rather quietly altered the emphasis at Harvard from a system based on the English spirit of athletics to one that emphasized winning in the American tradition. The failure of the Harvard authorities to preserve the British amateur spirit is evident in at least three occurrences during the early 1900s. First, Harvard alums of the class of 1879 gave $100,000 to build a football stadium. President Eliot, who in 1896 suggested holding contests with no permanent seating arrangement, decided by 1901 that a permanent football stadium would prevent the campus from being "defaced by unsightly banks of cheap wooden seats."[43] A stadium was erected in 1903 that could seat nearly 40,000 spectators. By building the first concrete stadium in America, Harvard motivated other colleges to increase the size of their stadiums and to commercialize and professionalize sport more than in the past. It would be difficult to remain amateur in spirit if the outward manifestations of sport were commercial and professional.

Second, the emphasis upon winning and athletic excellence became obvious when the Harvard Corporation began to award scholarships not only for scholarly achievement, but also for athletic performance. This is a difficult concept to prove historically, but there is evidence that Harvard began to grant athletic scholarships around the turn of the century. The Harvard Athletic Committee in 1903 raised the question: Should the George Emerson Lowell Scholarships be given to students showing excellence in athletics but only mediocre work in scholarship? According to the university catalog, the Lowell scholarships were to be awarded at the discretion of the president and fellows, with the provision that "excellence in classics or in athletics is recommended as desirable." The athletic committee chairman wrote President Eliot as follows:

I understand that one of them is usually awarded to a student who has exhibited special excellence in the classics, the other is awarded to a deserving student who has shown excellence in athletics. This latter was held last year by Mr. O. G. Frantz, who during the previous year had held a grade of C in his studies. To outsiders, it might seem that the University is insincere in permitting a man who holds this scholarship to play on an intercollegiate team, and I think that the precise reason for awarding the scholarship should be carefully defined, so that we may not be misunderstood. I call your attention to an account of a publication in one of the New York papers as to how Harvard is in the habit of procuring trained athletes.[44]

The fact that "Home Run" Frantz, a stalwart on the Harvard Nine, received the scholarship with little evidence of scholastic achievement indicated that excellence in athletics was beginning to have meaning for Harvard. President Eliot penciled a comment below the letter he received from the athletic committee: "Corporation have accepted the trust and propose to execute it." There is little proof, however, that athletic scholarships were common at Harvard. In fact, of those who held scholarships at Harvard in the early 1900s, very few were on athletic teams, and those who were played little.[45]

The hiring of a professional coach was a third indication that emphasis upon winning and excellence were creeping into Harvard. Possibly the most important of Harvard's policies attempting to maintain the British upper-class notion of sport was the preservation of amateur coaching. No issue in competitive athletics at Harvard was more fully discussed. Resolving the controversy by actually hiring a professional coach was probably the act most responsible for promoting winning and excellence at the expense of the British spirit of amateur athletics.

Harvard's Archibald Coolidge saw it more clearly than most. Coolidge was the grandson of a wealthy Boston Brahmin merchant. A graduate of Harvard, class of 1887, a member of the Harvard faculty and of the athletic committee, Archibald Coolidge, like the British upper class, favored amateur coaching and the belief that winning was not the "chief object of sport"; it was rather "sport for sports' sake." In a 1906 article titled "Professional Coaches," Coolidge agreed that continuous losses to Yale pressured Harvard to consider a professional coach. After the Harvard Athletic Committee voted for a five-year contract for a crew coach in 1904, and a highly paid position for a football coach in 1905, Coolidge expressed despair at having abandoned a standard the committee had "always tried to maintain." He asked whether "technical perfection [was] more important than true sport."[46]

Harvard had finally succumbed to the lure of the professional coach. It had taken almost a generation. Less than half a year after the Harvard Athletic Committee was created in 1882, it voted to fire the Harvard baseball coach, who was a professional and not a Harvard alumnus. At the same time, the crew was forced to agree to use only Harvard graduates as coaches, not allowing the team to hire outside professionals.[47] In the 1880s and 1890s, the committee sometimes wavered on the question of hiring professional coaches. In 1888, committee members agreed to allow John G. Clarkson (pitching star of the Chicago White Stockings) to coach baseball for several seasons, and in 1892, they allowed Timothy J. Keefe (his peer from the New York Giants) to coach pitchers.[48] The committee allowed the football team to employ a professional wrestler as a football trainer, provided that the team employed "a reputable physician" to supervise the team's health.[49] The same year, the committee asked President Eliot if he opposed hiring William A. Bancroft for three years as crew coach for a total salary of $10,000. Eliot pressured the committee to reject the idea, saying that he would make a public statement giving reasons for "disclaiming all responsibility for it" if the appointment were made.[50]

By 1900 almost all major colleges had begun to hire professional coaches for sports they considered important. Harvard students and alumni felt they could no longer bear the cross of this aspect of amateurism. Stated one student enthusiast: "The undergraduates want a man who will stand in the same relation to athletics at Harvard as that which Mr. Camp holds to athletics at Yale."[51] William Blaikie, Harvard crew member of the class of 1866 and New York City lawyer, sent President Eliot a twelve-page letter on the same subject. He suggested hiring a crew coach for $3,000 a year. "Suppose you *do* it, and Harvard *wins*," wrote Blaikie, "will you ever grudge the effort?"[52] After wavering, the Harvard Athletic Committee hired a crew coach for

$2,000 per year in 1904, and in 1905, the football team was given permission to hire William Reid as coach for $3,500.[53] At the same time the alumni were given permission, because of "extraordinary expenses," to raise an additional sum of $3,500, enabling Reid to receive a higher salary than any Harvard professor.[54] "It is perhaps superfluous to add," wrote a disgruntled Archibald Coolidge, "that this remainder was almost instantly guaranteed."[55]

The fight for the professional coach was not quite over. With the crisis of 1905–6, the Harvard authorities set up a Joint Committee on the Regulations of Athletic Sports to represent the Harvard Corporation and the overseers. This committee suggested that "professional coaching be done away with as soon as possible."[56] The Harvard Athletic Committee listened, but defeated a motion to abolish all paid coaches after the year 1909–10. They would agree to amateur coaches only if Harvard's "important rivals" would do the same.[57]

Harvard, in fact, hired Percy Haughton as its football coach in 1908. Haughton had been criticized as early as 1902 by a booster of Harvard athletics, LeBaron Briggs, dean of the Harvard Faculty of Arts and Sciences. Even Briggs could not countenance Haughton's attitudes in athletics. He said: "Things that Percy Haughton did in baseball almost everybody would condemn."[58] Haughton, whose attitude emphasized winning and excellence, held secret practices from the middle of October to the end of November in his first year of coaching as he readied the team for the Yale game. For the first time in seven years Harvard defeated Yale, 4-0. The British attitude of sports for sports' sake took a hind seat, and during the next decade, Harvard lost only two football games to Yale. In crew Harvard lost only 3 of the next 12 meets, and in baseball Harvard won a majority of its games from its closest rival, Yale, over the next ten years.

Much of this appears to have been the result of professional coaching and the abandonment of British ideals of sport.

The Harvard attempt to preserve gentlemanly sport in the British tradition had failed by the end of Eliot's era in 1909. It had been unsuccessful, it appears, because that system had not produced what was important in American society—excellence and winning. The gentlemanly restraints Harvard had placed on its athletics—generally imposed by the athletic committee, president, and governing boards—had thwarted attempts to perfect varsity athletics to the level achieved by its chief rival, Yale. It is suggested that Harvard authorities were trying to impose a system of values on American colleges based upon an upper-class notion that, for the most part, did not exist in America. If America were "born equal" or "born free"—as Alexis de Tocqueville suggested in the 1830s, and as Louis Hartz has effectively shown more recently—we can better understand why a more open society would produce excellence and winning based upon performance. America's lack of an effective aristocratic class with a belief in gentlemanly sports, such as England had produced, stymied Harvard authorities in their attempt to follow the British model. By the first decade of the twentieth century, the Harvard model gave in to the demands of American society, and Harvard began to strive for excellence and winning in athletics.

Notes

1. Henry D. Sheldon, *Student Life and Customs* (New York: D. Appleton and Co., 1901), p. 53; T. Cook, "Some Tendencies of Modern Sport," *Quarterly Review* 99 (January 1904): 141, 151; James F. Muirhead, *The Land of Contrasts: A Briton's View of His American Kin* (Boston: Lamson, Wolffe and Co., 1898), p. 117.
2. Endicott Peabody, "The Ideals of Sport in England and America," *American Physical Education Review* 19 (1914): 277–82.
3. Ibid., 277.

4. Alexis de Tocqueville, *Democracy in America*, vol. 2 (1840; reprint ed., New York: Vintage Books, 1945), p. 108.

5. Louis Hartz, *The Liberal Tradition in America* (New York: Harcourt Brace and World, 1955), passim.

6. H. J. Whigham, "American Sport from an English Point of View," *Outlook* 93 (November 1909): 738–44; Barrington Moore, Jr., makes a similar point in his *Social Origins of Dictatorship and Democracy* (Boston: Beacon Press, 1966), pp. 487–91.

7. Charles W. Eliot, "Inaugural Address," October 19, 1869, Harvard University Archives, p. 22. (Hereafter cited as HUA.)

8. Henry James, *Charles W. Eliot: President of Harvard University 1869–1909*, vol. 1 (Boston: Houghton Mifflin, 1930), pp. 80–81.

9. As quoted by John W. White et al., "Athletic Report," June 12, 1888, p. 12, HUD 8388.3B, HUA.

10. Guy Lewis, "America's First Intercollegiate Sport: The Regattas from 1852 to 1876," *Research Quarterly* 38 (December 1967): 642.

11. *A History of American College Regattas* (Boston: Wilson, 1875), p. 27.

12. John W. White, W. S. Chaplin, and Albert Bushnell Hart, "Harvard College Report of the Committee Appointed to Consider the Subject of College Athletics, and to Report Thereon to the Faculty," June 12, 1888, pp. 10–11, HUD 8388.3B, HUA.

13. Ibid., pp. 12–14.

14. J. W. White, W. E. Byerly, and D. A. Sargent (athletic committee), letter to the faculty of Harvard College, Dec. 2, 1884, in the athletic committee minutes, Nov. 25, 1884, p. 55, HUA.

15. "Overseer Athletic Abuses Committee Report," ca. April 1888, 10 pp., HUD 8388.5, HUA.

16. John W. White et al., "Harvard College Report," 1888, pp. 24–27.

17. John W. White, chairman of the athletic committee, "Annual Report, 1889–1890," to Charles W. Eliot, ca. March 1891, Charles W. Eliot papers UAI.5.150, Box 262, "1891, Jan.–Mar.," folder, HUA. (Hereafter cited as the Eliot papers.)

18. M. H. Morgan, acting secretary of the Faculty of Arts and Sciences, Harvard, letter to J. B. Ames, chairman of the athletic committee, March 20, 1895, Eliot papers, Box 264, "1895, Jan.–Mar." folder, HUA.

19. James Barr Ames, chairman of the athletic committee, letter to the Harvard Faculty of Arts and Sciences, Feb. 25, 1895, Eliot papers, Box 264, "1895, Jan.–Mar." folder, HUA.

20. Charles W. Eliot, "President Eliot's Report," *Harvard Graduates' Magazine* 9 (March 1901): 452.

21. "Report of the Brown University Conference on Intercollegiate Sports," Feb. 18, 1898, HUD 8398.75, HUA.

22. William James, Jr., "Sport or Business?" *Harvard Graduates' Magazine* 11 (December 1903): 225.

23. John Richardson, letter to Charles W. Eliot, July 16, 1908, Eliot papers, Box 202, "Athletics," HUA.

24. John A. Blanchard, ed., *The H Book of Harvard Athletics, 1852–1922* (Cambridge: Harvard University Press, 1923), pp. 141, 296, 456.

25. From 1825 to 1909, Yale enrollment grew from 582 to 1,236; Harvard grew from 766 to 2,265, as found in Allen L. Sack, "The Commercialization and Rationalization of Intercollegiate Football: A Comparative Analysis of the Development of Football at Yale and Harvard in the Latter Nineteenth Century" (Ph.D. diss., Penn State University, 1974), p. 81.

26. Ira N. Hollis, letter to Charles W. Eliot, Jan. 23, 1902, Eliot papers, Box 143, HUA.

27. Arthur T. Hadley, Yale president, letter to Charles W. Eliot, Dec. 18, 1901, Eliot papers, Box 117, folder 260, HUA.

28. Athletic Committee Minutes, Jan. 10, 1902, p. 417, HUA.

29. Hollis, letter to Eliot, Jan. 23, 1902.

30. Arthur T. Hadley, letter to Charles W. Eliot, Dec. 14, 1901, Eliot papers, Box 117, folder 260, HUA.

31. "Agreement with Yale," *Harvard Bulletin*, March 18, 1903, p. 1.

32. Karl F. Brill, "Football Revelation Period," newspaper clipping, Nov. 1905, HUD 10905, HUA.

33. Richard Henry Dana, Lawyer, letter to Charles W. Eliot, Dec. 18, 1905, Eliot papers, Box 209, "Dana" folder, HUA.

34. L.B.R. Briggs, letter to Charles W. Eliot, Dec. 4, 1905, Eliot papers, Box 204, "Briggs" folder, HUA.

35. "Report of the Overseers Committee," *Harvard Graduates' Magazine* 14 (March 1906): 497.

36. Theodore Roosevelt, letter to Edward Deshon Brandegee, March 7, 1906, in *The Letters of Theodore Roosevelt*, vol. 5, ed. Elting E. Morison (Cambridge: Harvard University Press, 1952), p. 46.

37. "From a Graduate's Window," *Harvard Graduates' Magazine* 14 (December 1905): 216–23.

38. R. G. Watson, letter to Charles W. Eliot, July 26, 1895, Eliot papers, Box 138, "1283" folder, HUA.

39. William R. Thayer, letter to Charles W. Eliot, Dec. 31, 1905, Eliot papers, Box 252, "William R. Thayer" folder, HUA.

40. L.B.R. Briggs, "Athletic Sports," *Harvard Graduates' Magazine* 17 (June 1909): 697.

41. "Athletic Committee Minutes," *Harvard Graduates' Magazine* 16 (September 1907): 128–29.

42. L.B.R. Briggs, letter to Charles W. Eliot, May 14, 1907, Eliot papers, Box 204, "Briggs" folder, HUA.

43. Joseph H. Beale, chairman of the athletic committee, letter to Charles W. Eliot, July 8, 1896, Eliot papers, Box 128, "615" folder, HUA; and

Charles W. Eliot, "President Eliot's Report," *Harvard Graduates' Magazine* 9 (March 1901): 452.

44. Ira N. Hollis, letter to Charles W. Eliot, Jan. 16, 1903, Eliot papers, Box 110, folder 143, "Hollis Letters," HUA.

45. See Eliot papers, Box 270, "Nov. 1902" folder; Box 274, "Nov. 1903" folder; Box 276, "Dec. 1905" folder; Box 278, "Dec. 1907" folder, for scholarship holders, HUA.

46. Archibald C. Coolidge, "Professional Coaches," *Harvard Graduates' Magazine* 14 (March 1906): 392–95.

47. Athletic Committee Minutes, June 17, 1882, p. 3; Sept. 27, 1882, p. 5; October 4, 1882, p. 7, HUA.

48. Athletic Committee Minutes, Dec. 12, 1888, p. 202; Nov. 11, 1889; Dec. 15, 1890; and Jan. 26, 1892, p. 334, HUA.

49. Athletic Committee Minutes, June 16, 1890, p. 281, HUA.

50. Athletic Committee Minutes, Dec. 15, 1890, p. 300; and Dec. 18, 1890, p. 302, HUA.

51. H. A. Bellows, "Athletics," *Harvard Graduates' Magazine* 13 (March 1905): 473.

52. William Blaikie, letter to Charles W. Eliot, March 4, 1904, Eliot papers, Box 203, "Blaikie" folder, HUA.

53. Athletic Committee Minutes, Jan. 10, 1901, p. 404; and Jan. 6, 1904, p. 467, HUA.

54. Athletic Committee Minutes, Feb. 7, 1905, p. 21, HUA.

55. Coolidge, "Professional Coaches," p. 394.

56. "Report on Regulation of Athletic Sports," *Harvard Graduates' Magazine* 15 (June 1907): 646.

57. Athletic Committee Minutes, Dec. 6, 1907, p. 625, HUA.

58. L.B.R. Briggs, letter to Charles W. Eliot, Jan. 27, 1902, Eliot papers, Box 102, "Briggs" folder, HUA.

FOUR
Social Reform in Gilded Age Boston

Introduction

Urbanization and industrialization in Massachusetts generated a startling prosperity for some, and a deep-rooted poverty for countless others. A climate of opinion that promoted the popular belief in hard work, frugality, saving for the future, and education for the young, helped propel many manual laborers or their children into the ranks of the middle classes. Yet, the unevenness of income distribution, inhumane working conditions, arbitrary wage-cutting, seasonal layoffs, periodic depressions, disease, industrial accidents, and ethnic and racial prejudice, kept many Massachusetts citizens poor, and promoted downward mobility for others. The reaction of the privileged classes to the new urban poverty was a mixed bag of racial hatred and paternalistic humanitarianism.

Some Brahmins, like Gamaliel Bradford of Boston, confessed to a feeling of "terror" when confronted with the "low-browed, dirty, hard-handed animal sons of toil." Kindled by fears of racial defilement and challenges to the social order, in 1894 Boston worthies such as Charles Warren, Robert de Courcy Ward, and Prescott Farnsworth Hall, founded the Boston Immigration Restriction League.[1] Others were to feel pity for the slum dwellers, while simultaneously dreading a breakdown of morality and an outburst of rampant vice that was thought to be a by-product of tenement life. Boston's crusade for social reform was born out of the desire to uphold the moral order, to bring the

downtrodden and wayward back to the Christian path, and
to redeem the poor through lessons of self-improvement.

Boston social reformer and journalist, B. O. Flower,
posited the problem distinctly for his audience of middle-
and upper-class sympathizers:

> It is difficult to over-estimate the gravity of the problem pre-
> sented by those compelled to exist in the slums of our populous
> cities. . . . From the midst of this commonwealth of degradation
> there goes forth a moral contagion, scourging society in all its
> ramifications, coupled with an atmosphere of physical decay—
> an atmosphere reeking with filth, heavy with foul odors, laden
> with disease. . . . The slums of our cities are the reservoirs of
> physical and moral death, an enormous expense to the state,
> a constant menace to society, a reality whose shadow is at once
> colossal and portentous.[2]

To be kept in mind, however, was the difference between
the "worthy poor"—those workers and their families who
were faultless victims of depression or accident—and the
"unworthy poor," the paupers who eagerly embraced idleness and vice and who tried to live off charity. The worthy
poor were to be given aid by the creation of a "community of
charitable societies," run by experts who would anticipate
the "legitimate" needs of the poor.

Boston ministers, such as the Reverend Edward Everett
Hale, preached to the prosperous citizenry to heighten their
social awareness and to enlist them in the noble quest to improve tenement conditions.[3] Illegal vice, liquor, and gambling were to be ferreted out and kept from the reach of un-
suspecting and naive workers. To that end, in 1878, Boston
philanthropist Robert Treat Paine and Ministers Edward
Everett Hale and Phillips Brooks, among others, established
the New England Society for the Suppression of Vice.[4]
The dualism of minister as moral uplifter and social reformer is artfully recounted in the essay by Ivan Steen.

Steen explores one of Boston's most popular, and long-since forgotten minister-reformers, the Reverend Henry Morgan. Morgan was both "a friend of the poor" and one who "launched a crusade to improve the moral climate of Boston."

Besides personal redemption and charity, other social reformers directed their efforts toward environmental rehabilitation. One such approach was to introduce settlement houses in the slums. These were to be laboratories for collecting sociological data that would lead to efficient social change. Robert A. Woods, founder of Boston's South End House, clarified his personal motives when he wrote: "There comes to many that challenge of responsiblity for the common good, which is the very life of democracy, and without which, as recent solemn warnings have assured us, our great cities will rush to industrial and moral disaster."[5] The settlement-house movement not only awakened middle- and upper-class young men and women to the "problem of the poor," it also opened new opportunities for the first generation of college-educated Boston women.

Vida D. Scudder and Emily Greene Balch, together with several other women, abjured the suffrage movement as too self-centered and selfish; they sought instead to be useful to society's less fortunate. After graduating from Boston Girls Latin (1880) and Smith College (1884), Scudder went to Oxford, where John Ruskin opened her eyes to his vision of Christian Socialism. "The point of my desire was an intolerable stabbing pain, as Ruskin, and the rich delights of the place, forced me to realize for the first time the plethora of privilege in which my lot had been cast. . . . A desperate wish to do violence to myself drove me to the dirty garrets, to the strange meetings where the [Salvation] Army was in evidence."[6] "Conscience-stricken maidens," so dubbed by historian Arthur Mann, these women wished to justify their privileged positions by becoming involved in a host of humanitarian ventures. Thus, Scudder organized the founding of several settlement houses, including Boston's Denison House in 1892, with Balch as its first director.[7] In addition to slum rejuvenation, the poor were to be morally redeemed through exposure to higher culture, and were to become physically "cleansed" through indoctrination in better health habits.

The enlightenment and education of the masses would help the poor raise their own personal standards of behavior, generating concrete efforts at self-improvement. The founding of the Boston Museum of Art in 1870, for example, was not grounded on collecting original works of art for viewing by upper-class connoisseurs, but to educate and civilize the working classes of the city. The straightforward educational goal of the trustees explains their decision to purchase mainly reproductions and not originals. Trustee Charles Perkins wrote in 1870: "We aim at collecting materials for the education of the nation in art, not at making collections of objects of art." At its dedication in 1876, Boston's Mayor Samuel Cobb called the museum, "the crown of our educational system."[8]

The establishment of the Boston City Hospital in 1864, "for the honest, temperate and industrious poor," was based on the recognition that poor workers needed a place to recuperate from industrial accidents or disease.[9] New urban conditions deprived people of previously available "familial care" so common in rural/village communities. Overcrowded slum families, or the armies of single men or women living solitary lives in Boston's infamous "lodging houses," required safe, sanitary institutions in which to seek medical aid and to recover from illness. The movement to teach the poor better sanitary habits, thus preventing the spread of disease and inculcating a higher morality at the same time, is described by Marilyn Thornton Williams in her essay on the bathhouse movement in Boston. She maintains that "public baths were one of the solutions put forward during the Gilded Age as an answer to the problems rising out of a rapidly changing urban society."

Doubtless, social reformers were motivated to a great degree by fears of moral decay and genuine humanitarianism. Be that as it may, concentration upon reform-minded ministers and paternalistic Brahmins may obscure the total picture. The possibility exists that the ministerial efforts to improve slum life and eradicate immorality were simply palliatives that prevented meaningful reform and merely assuaged the guilt of those who benefited from the new materialism. Moreover, the role of the poor themselves in improving conditions, particularly as devotees of the efficient boss-dominated political machine, has too often been minimized. In an essay on the relationship between social reform and machine politics, Jack Tager attempts to delineate the crucial connection that existed among Yankee do-gooders and Irish politicians in Boston during the Gilded Age and the Progressive Era.

Determining the true identity of Boston's social reformers is complicated by their variegated social standing and their multitude of interests. Whether the social gospeler or exhorter against vice (Edward Everett Hale, B. O. Flower, Henry Morgan, W.D.P. Bliss, Joseph Cook, Nicholas Paine Gilman), the social-science-oriented academic and professional (Frank Parsons, Robert A. Woods, Edwin Meade, Francis A. Walker, Frederick Bushee), the feminist activist (Julia Ward Howe, Helena Stuart Dudley, Mary Morton Kimball, Vida Scudder, Emily Balch), or the first- and second-generation immigrant (John Boyle O'Reilly, Solomon

Schindler, Louis Brandeis, Mary Kenney O'Sullivan, James Michael Curley, John Fitzgerald), all were Bostonians who recognized that unregulated capitalism posed serious threats to the well-being of everyone in the Commonwealth.

Jack Tager

Notes

1. Gamaliel Bradford, *The Journal of Gamaliel Bradford, 1883–1932*, ed. Van Wyck Brooks (Boston, 1933), p. 85; Barbara M. Solomon, *Ancestors and Immigrants* (Cambridge, Mass., 1956), pp. 99–102.
2. Charles N. Glaab, ed., *The American City: A Documentary History* (Homewood, Ill., 1963), pp. 278–79.
3. Nathan I. Huggins, *Protestants against Poverty: Boston's Charities, 1870–1900* (Westport, Conn., 1971), pp. 36–40.
4. Roger Lane, *Policing the City: Boston 1822–1885* (New York, 1971), p. 214.
5. Robert A. Woods, ed., *Americans in Process* (Boston, 1903), p. 6.
6. Vida Scudder, *On Journey* (New York, 1937), p. 84.
7. Arthur Mann, *Yankee Reformers in the Urban Age: Social Reform in Boston, 1880–1900* (Cambridge, Mass., 1954), p. 217.
8. Neil Harris, "The Gilded Age Revisited: Boston and the Museum Movement," *American Quarterly* 14 (Winter 1962): 553, 557.
9. Morris J. Vogel, *The Invention of the Modern Hospital: Boston 1870–1930* (Chicago, 1981), pp. 6, 35.

Ministering to the Poor of Boston:
The Work of the
Reverend Henry Morgan

IVAN D. STEEN

Aaron I. Abell, in *The Urban Impact on American Protestant-ism, 1865–1900*, noted that before the mid-1880s, "the urban poor scarcely figured in Protestant missionary tactics, which continued to angle for the support of the enormous rural and urban middle class."[1] Although this has become the accepted view of the Protestant attitude toward the urban underprivileged, it is a position that ought to be re-examined, in that it is based on incomplete evidence. For example, scholars have failed to take into account the work of such clergymen as the Reverend Henry Morgan, the vigorous, self-styled "Poor Man's Preacher," who worked in Boston from 1859 until his death in 1884.

Henry Morgan was born in Newtown, Connecticut, on March 7, 1825. Four years later his father died, and for the next twelve years he and his mother lived in poverty. When Morgan was nearly sixteen years old he left home to get an education, which, up until that time, had been provided by his mother. With but the rudiments of formal education himself, Morgan, while still a teenager, got a job teaching school in rural Connecticut. During this time, he became a Methodist, and after seven years of teaching, he left that occupation to become an itinerant preacher and travel throughout the eastern United States. Resolving to make preaching his life's work, he attempted to obtain a license from a Methodist Quarterly Conference in Connecticut, but was turned down. At his mother's suggestion, Morgan, from this time on, called himself the "Poor Man's Preacher," and signed the letters "P.M.P." after his name. Morgan formed an independent church in Long Hill, near Bridgeport, and laid a cornerstone for a church building in 1857. Before long, however, he discovered the perils of preaching without a license. A "superannuated preacher" claimed that Morgan had built the church in his circuit, and demanded that he be awarded the pulpit. The man won his claim, and Morgan lost his church and the $1,000 of his own money that had gone into it. After preaching for a while in several Connecticut towns, he moved to Boston, where he was to spend the rest of his life.[2]

When he arrived in Boston, Morgan was unknown and without any friends to further his career. He preached in several Methodist churches but, because he lacked a license, he was prevented from continuing these activities. At this point, Morgan decided that inasmuch as the existing churches would not provide him with a pulpit, he would carry his message directly to the people. To do this, he rented Boston Music Hall, and delivered his first sermon there on February 27, 1859. His object, he told his audience, was "to present the gospel to the working-classes, and to open a mission for the poor in some part of the city." He was convinced that this could be "done by no one denomination, and by no common missionary arrangement." A major obstacle to reaching this group was the common custom of charging for church seats. True, free seats were made available for those who could not afford to pay, but Morgan considered this an unsatisfactory arrangement, for "the self-respect of an American mechanic will not receive as a gift what others purchase; and if he cannot compete with others in seat and dress for his family, he will stay at home." One way to overcome this problem was to do what Morgan was doing: preach in a hall, "where all seats are considered alike, and all persons are on a common level."[3]

Morgan was concerned that the style of preaching which prevailed in Boston's churches had no appeal for the workingman, for in making their sermons acceptable to the wealthier classes, clergymen made God's word "so palatable that the Devil himself might drink it without turning his stomach. . . ." Sermons were too formal, used archaic forms of language, and bore little relation to daily life. Instead, Morgan believed in using simple, everyday language delivered in an exciting manner, and employing illustrations that had meaning for the workingman.[4] Not surprisingly, the Boston *Atlas and Daily Bee* reported that Morgan was "essentially a *live* preacher, having all the spirit and energy of Henry Ward Beecher." Pointing out that Morgan had "much power" as a preacher, the reporter for the *Atlas* predicted that he would "be a great success." This "genuine specimen of a live, jumping, nervous Yankee," would "not fail to draw a crowd," the reporter concluded.[5]

Morgan's Music Hall sermons did draw large crowds, and he quickly became a well-known personality in Boston. Only a few months after he arrived there, an organization known as the Union Mission Society was formed by an interdenominational committee, and Morgan was offered the position of pastor.[6] He accepted, and the Boston Union Mission Society soon developed into a vital institution devoted to ministering to the poor. By the beginning of 1860, the city authorities granted this organization the use of the Franklin School building on Washington Street for their activities.[7] The next year, the members of the Union Mission Society established a new denomination, known as the First Independent Methodist Church, and this organization granted Morgan the ordination that the Methodist Episcopal church had refused him.[8]

Unlike many other churches of the time, this one was

"devoted especially to the poor; taking care of the bodies as well as the souls of men; and recognizing humanity as a predominant part of Christianity."[9] In addition to holding religious services several times on Sundays, the Union Mission conducted daily prayer meetings. But of greatest importance were its activities aimed at aiding the poor in the temporal world. Morgan was a firm believer in the virtue of honest work, so he did what he could to find employment for his parishioners. At first, he read job notices from the pulpit, a practice which drew criticism from other clergymen. In time, a regular employment agency was organized, where the poor might learn of situations without having to pay a fee. Similarly, the Union Mission did what it could to find homes for the poor, especially for those newly arrived from rural New England. Donations of clothing, new and used, were solicited, and the mission distributed these items to the needy. A "benevolent circle," made up of volunteers, met weekly to repair worn clothing. Later, a sewing school was established where young girls were taught to make garments which they were then permitted to keep. Among other activities undertaken by the mission were visitations to those who were ill, and later, the establishment of a singing school which performed concerts for young people. A course of twice-a-week lectures to young men was given by Morgan. And for a decade or more, the Union Mission held an annual picnic at Neponset or Nahant. Tickets for this event were sold at 25 cents for adults and 15 cents for children.[10] According to one advertisement, activities at these events included, "Singing, Swinging, Boating, Sporting, Declamation and lots of small talk," as well as "Music by Gardner's Band."[11]

Particular emphasis, though, was placed on aiding poor children, especially those who were unable to attend Boston's public schools because they worked all day. For such children, many of whom were newspaper boys, a night school was established. In its five years of existence, this school educated hundreds of poor children and attracted considerable attention. Much of the school's fame came as a result of the publication of Henry Morgan's immensely popular novel, *Ned Nevins, the Newsboy* (1866), which, supposedly, was based on the exploits of one of its scholars. [12] It appears likely that the success of the Union Mission's night school was a major factor in the decision of the Boston School Committee to establish a night-school system. When this was done, in 1868, Morgan's school was taken over by the city, and became a major component in the newly formed system. [13] Morgan was highly critical of the way the school committee ran this school. When it was operated by the Union Mission, volunteer teachers were used and the costs were very low, whereas the school committee paid its teachers and expended $20,000 to educate fewer than half as many pupils. He was convinced that schools that taught "Geology, Botany, Fancy Drawing, and Star-gazing, would not elevate the dangerous classes who could neither read nor write." Moreover, he argued that "hired teachers would have no heart to arouse boys of this class, especially teachers who had been jaded out in the day-school." What was needed, he believed, was "great heart, warm sympathies, entering into their distressed state, and great will, and physical force, to inspire them with ambition."[14] Morgan tried to reestablish his night school a year later, but after two years of operation he was forced to admit that he was having difficulty sustaining the school, primarily because he found it impossible to obtain good volunteer teachers when the school committee was paying its staff. [15]

Through his work with the Union Mission Society and through his public lectures, Henry Morgan was established as one of Boston's best-known clergymen. Formal recognition came in January 1868, when he was elected chaplain of the Massachusetts Senate for the ensuing year.[16] While holding this position, Morgan became acquainted with William Claflin, who was later to become governor of Massachusetts. Claflin was very favorably impressed by Morgan and his work, and suggested that his organization, which had been forced to vacate the Franklin School building, should have a permanent home. The Rev. James Freeman Clarke's congregation had moved to new quarters, and their old church at Indiana Place was about to be sold at auction. If Morgan was interested in obtaining this building, Claflin would provide him with financial backing. Morgan was interested, and he was the successful bidder for the building which soon came to be called Morgan Chapel.[17] From now on, Morgan's work was centered primarily on his church and its neighborhood; but as a speaker he could not be limited to this restricted audience. In addition to regular sermons and lectures at Morgan Chapel, he continued to utilize the facilities of the larger Boston Music Hall and other auditoriums, made guest appearances at Boston and suburban churches, and delivered series of lectures in New England, New York, and Pennsylvania.

Morgan continued to fulfill his self-proclaimed role of "poor man's preacher," while expanding his activities to encompass several other causes. For example, Morgan was a vigorous supporter of women's rights, and as early as July 1869, he invited several women to lecture from his pulpit.[18] Then, in February 1870, he began his "Woman in the Pulpit" series. Each Sunday until June, a lecture was delivered by a woman in Morgan Chapel. Among those who spoke were Mary A. Livermore, Jennie Collins, and Julia Ward Howe. At the end of June, Morgan himself delivered his strongest statement on the subject of women's rights. In this lecture at Morgan Chapel, he urged working women to demand wages equal to those paid to men for the same work. Noting that "radical changes demand radical efforts," he called for "one general, universal strike for women's rights."[19]

The rights of the male worker were also staunchly advocated by Morgan. This was displayed most clearly in a series of lectures to workingmen which he delivered in August 1877, especially in the lecture entitled, "Railroad of Life—Strikes and Strikers." In a fiery oration, Morgan took the side of the striking railroad workers in their struggle against their employers, and expressed his belief that "through this agitation labor will secure its rights."[20]

Morgan's concerns also extended to another powerless group, the insane. What especially disturbed him was how easy it was for someone to be committed to an asylum. He was shocked by the case of one of his parishioners, Theodosia Scott, whose husband had committed her to an asylum in Connecticut. Morgan was convinced that this action was unwarranted, and that whatever problems Mrs. Scott had were the result of her husband's treatment of her. Morgan espoused her cause and succeeded in having a citizen's committee investigate her case. The committee concluded that many of Morgan's charges were probably correct, but it was powerless to secure her release.[21] Morgan continued to be dismayed at a society which permitted people to be incarcerated unjustly, at times merely to prevent embarrassment to their relations. "Society," he wrote, "in its anxious regard for its own safety, frequently encroaches on the rights and liberties of its individual members."[22]

By and large, Morgan was opposed to public institutions, preferring that the dispensing of charity be a private endeavor. Most particularly, he saw little accomplished by placing people within the walls of asylums or reformatories.

There, no reform could be achieved; rather, public institutions simply removed those guilty of antisocial behavior from the purview of society—and at considerable cost to the taxpayer. "It is cheaper," he maintained, "to reform a man or child on his legs than to carry him in your arms; better to give him encouragement at home while helping himself, than feeding him and clothing him behind compulsory walls." The greatest value, then, would derive from the efforts of private citizens coming to the aid of society's outcasts and helping them adjust to their own environment. "Reforms, to be genuine, must be voluntary; and, in the midst of temptation," Morgan wrote. "There is no moral grandeur in abstaining from thieving where there is nothing to steal. There is no virtue in fasting where there is nothing to eat." Morgan was convinced that "whole communities aroused to philanthropic action will accomplish more for preventing crime and reforming the fallen than a few paid officials in costly institutions."[23] The problem, however, was to "arouse" the community; and Morgan devoted considerable effort to doing just that

By 1878, Morgan reached the conclusion that a deteriorating moral environment was at the root of many of Boston's social problems, and he made up his mind to do something about this situation. He believed that the best way to attack the problem was to alert the people of Boston to the dangers about them and thus sway public opinion to demand action against the moral transgressors. The rest of Morgan's life was devoted primarily to this moral crusade. He, and the investigators he hired, explored the seamy side of the city, and in writings and lectures he exposed the sinfulness of Boston.[24] In doing so, Morgan attracted considerable attention; more attention, unfortunately, than he gained from his work with the underprivileged. His health, which had always been fragile, seems to have suffered as a result of the extreme effort he poured into his crusade, and in March 1884, at the age of fifty-nine, Morgan died, apparently from pneumonia.

Morgan hoped that his work would be continued after his death. In his will, he provided that his church was to become the property of the Benevolent Fraternity of Churches of Boston, with the requirement that the pastor was to be a member of the New England Conference of the Methodist Episcopal church. This arrangement prevailed until 1912, when complete control was given over to the Methodists. Earlier, in 1895, Dr. Edgar J. Helms had been installed as pastor of the church, which was now known as Morgan Memorial. Helms, building upon the work of Morgan, turned the Morgan Memorial into a true institutional church. [25] This was the origin of what is known today as Goodwill Industries.

In his twenty-five years as Boston's "Poor Man's Preacher," Henry Morgan had become a very prominent citizen of his adopted city. He had written five widely read books: *Music Hall Discourses* (1859); *Ned Nevins, the Newsboy* (1866); *Shadowy Hand; or, Life Struggles* (1874); *Boston Inside Out!* (1880); *Key and Sequel to "Boston Inside Out"* (1883). He had lectured before many thousands of people; one of his lectures was so popular that it was delivered forty-five times in Boston alone. He had been a friend to the poor, helping them find jobs and homes. He had educated hundreds of street urchins. He had supported the causes of women, workingmen, and the insane. He had launched a crusade to improve the moral climate of Boston.

Henry Morgan is buried at Mount Auburn Cemetery in Cambridge in a grave located on Garden Avenue, not far from the Mount Auburn Street entrance. The substantial, but plain tombstone bears the simple inscription: "An Earnest Preacher and a Beloved Pastor of the Poor." As far as is known, the site is hardly ever visited.

Were there other preachers similar to Henry Morgan during these years? Although it is unlikely that any others engaged in identical activities, it is probable that other cities contained their own versions of Morgan. Such individuals, however, have been forgotten; for, if Morgan is in any way representative, they worked alone, among a largely inarticulate group, and then passed off the scene. Because they founded no major organizations or movements, and left no writings of theoretical or literary significance, they have been overlooked by scholars. But these men are worth ferreting out. Although it is difficult to assess the extent of the impact of a Henry Morgan, it would be foolish to claim that the thousands of working people who heard his lectures, read his books, or in some way were helped by him, were not affected by the experience.

Notes

1. Aaron I. Abell, *The Urban Impact on American Protestantism, 1865–1900* (Hamden, Conn.: Archon, 1962), p. 4.
2. Henry Morgan, *Shadowy Hand; or, Life-Struggles* (Boston: Rev. Henry Morgan, Morgan Chapel, 1874), pp. 13–243, passim.
3. Ibid., pp. 244–47.
4. Henry Morgan, "Preaching for the Times," *Music Hall Discourses, Miscellaneous Sketches, Minesterial Notes, and Prison Incidents* (Boston: H. W. Swett and Co., 1859), pp. 7, 9–11.
5. [Boston] *Atlas and Daily Bee*, Feb. 28, 1859.
6. *Boston Evening Transcript*, May 3, 1859.
7. Ibid., Feb. 11, 1860.
8. *Boston Sunday Herald*, April 19, 1861.
9. Ibid.
10. Boston Union Mission Society, *Fourth Anniversary Celebration of the Boston Union Mission Society, January 17, 1864, Fifth Anniversary of the Boston*

Union Mission Society, *Jan. 22, 1865*, Massachusetts Historical Society; Boston Union Mission Society, "Financial View of the Boston Union Mission Society, 1866," in Henry Morgan, *Ned Nevins, the Newsboy* (Fifteenth Thousand; Boston: Lee & Shepard, 1867); *Boston Evening Transcript*, July 16, 25, 1860, July 20, 1861, July 28, 1862, July 20, 1863, July 25, 1864, Jan. 29, 1866, Feb. 18, 1867, Jan. 13, 1868, March 1, July 17, 1869, Feb. 28, 1870, Jan. 9, 1871.

11. *Boston Evening Transcript*, July 20, 1863.

12. Ibid., Nov. 2, 1863, Feb. 27, 1867; Boston Union Mission Society, *Fourth Anniversary Celebration, Fifth Anniversary; Zion's Herald*, Oct. 24, 1866; *Boston Herald*, March 23, 1884; Henry Morgan, *Ned Nevins, the Newsboy*, 35th ed. (Boston: Shawmut Publishing Co. [1881]), pp. v, vi, 12, 48–52.

13. *Boston Evening Transcript*, Nov. 28, 1868; Morgan, *Shadowy Hand*, p. 322; Boston, School Committee, *Annual Report of the School Committee of the City of Boston, 1868* (Boston: Alfred Mudge & Son, City Printers, 1869), p. 12.

14. Morgan, *Shadowy Hand*, p. 322.

15. *Boston Evening Transcript*, Jan. 9, 1871.

16. Ibid., Jan. 2, 1868.

17. Morgan, *Shadowy Hand*, pp. 323–25; *Boston Herald*, March 23, 1884.

18. See notices in *Boston Evening Transcript* and [Boston] *Daily Evening Traveller* for July and August 1869.

19. See notices in *Boston Evening Transcript*, Feb.–June 1870; *Woman's Journal*, April 16, 1870; Morgan, *Shadowy Hand*, pp. 351–52.

20. *Boston Daily Globe*, Aug. 6, 13, 20, 1877.

21. Morgan, *Shadowy Hand*, pp. 393–414; *Hartford Daily Courant*, May 20, 1874.

22. Henry Morgan, *Boston Inside Out! Sins of a Great City! A Story of Real Life* (Boston: Shawmut Publishing Co., 1880), p. 411.

23. Boston Union Mission Society, *Fifth Anniversary*; Henry Morgan, *Ned Nevins, the Newsboy*, 4th ed. (Boston: Lee & Shepard, 1867), pp. 8, 17.

24. Morgan's efforts to achieve a moral reform in Boston involved delivering a series of very popular lectures, appearing before legislative committees, and publishing two books: *Boston Inside Out!; Key and Sequel to "Boston Inside Out"* (Boston: Shawmut Publishing Co., 1883).

25. Henry Morgan, Will, Probate Court, Suffolk County Mass., 1884, No. 71125; Eustache C. E. Dorion, *The Redemption of the South End: A Study in City Evangelization* (New York and Cincinnati: The Abingdon Press [1915]), pp. 31, 115.

Urban Reform in the Gilded Age:
The Public Baths of Boston
MARILYN THORNTON WILLIAMS

The inauguration of winter bath-houses for the free use of the people is something of a novelty in any city in this country, and Boston has the proud distinction of being the pioneer in the work, which is sure to be an important consideration in the growing demands of the larger municipalities in the near future.[1]

On October 15, 1898, the *Boston Herald* proudly reported the opening of Boston's first year-round municipal bathhouse, the Dover Street Bath. The opening ceremony was attended by over 500 persons, with "the Back Bay" well represented, as well as a "large number of men and women who [were] identified with educational and sociological questions of the city." Mayor Josiah Quincy, the leader of Boston's public bath movement and the main speaker, proclaimed, "The opening of this bath marks the full recognition by the city of its duty to bring within the reach of all, in winter as well as in summer, facilities for securing the physical cleanliness that bears such close relationship to social and moral well-being." This occasion marked the culmination of many years of effort by Boston sanitarians and social reformers to provide the poor with a means by which to attain personal cleanliness, a resource their crowded tenements lacked.[2]

Public baths were one of the solutions put forward during the Gilded Age as an answer to the problems rising out of a rapidly changing urban industrial society. The burgeoning urban slums of this era were perceived not only as an economic and sanitary problem, but also as a threat to the social stability and unity of the community. The slums, as sources of disease, poverty, filth, crime, and corrupt politics, epitomized the breakdown of order and morality. Yet, as Morton Keller has pointed out, Gilded Age social reformers were limited in their capacity to take remedial action against the slums. Their desire for governmental economy, their hostility to governmental activism, and their belief that the poor were responsible for their own condition or that poverty arose out of unalterable social or hereditary laws combined to produce a failure to take action. The major exception to this limitation was the area of public health, of which public baths were an important part.[3]

The movement for public baths in Boston illustrates in microcosm many characteristics of urban social reform in the Gilded Age. Municipal activism in this case was justified on the grounds that public health would be protected. Growing acceptance of the germ theory of disease in the 1890s by both American physicians and the general public helped support a scientific argument in favor of public baths. This new focus on the germ theory rather than on the filth theory of disease transferred attention from the environment to the individual as a source of contagion, thereby emphasizing the importance of personal cleanliness. The poor, Mayor Quincy wrote, were "a menace to their cleanlier fellow citizens whom they come in contact with on the cars and in the streets, and who unknowingly buy the products of their labor." Although public health reformers continued to press for a cleaner environment through effective garbage collection, street cleaning, sewer systems, and other means, they also understood the role of the infected individual as a bearer of disease.[4]

Well before the dissemination of the discoveries of bacteriology, however, bathing was associated in the American mind with good health. During the eighteenth century, the vogue for spas, mineral springs, and watering places reached the American colonies via England, and the popularity of these bathing places continued throughout the nineteenth century. The connection between bathing and health was reinforced in the mid-1840s, when the water cure developed by Vincent Priessnitz in Silesia became extremely popular in the United States as a treatment for almost all ailments. The water cure, or hydropathy, was based on the belief that water was the sustainer of life; treatments consisted of a variety of baths, wet compresses, steam, water massage, and drinking cold water. Other health reformers of the mid-nineteenth century, such as Sylvester Graham, also urged frequent bathing. Although the water cure craze declined by the onset of the Civil War, hydrotherapy, as it came to be called, persisted as a treatment for some diseases. Simon Baruch, an orthodox physician and a leader of the national bath movement, was a leading proponent of hydrotherapy. At the same time as the water cure phenomenon swept the United States, the development of water and sewage systems, as well as bathtubs with attached plumbing, made regular bathing an established middle-class habit.[5]

Public bath advocates, however, were not only concerned with providing the poor with a means to attain middle-class standards of bodily cleanliness and with safeguarding the public health. Like most Gilded Age reformers they felt that poverty was to a certain extent due to deficiencies in character. Public baths, they asserted, would provide a means to moral rejuvenation. Mayor Quincy declared that "when physical dirt has been banished, a long step has been taken in the elimination of moral dirt." Writing in a U.S. government publication, G.W.W. Hangar stated that public baths would stimulate a "feeling of self-respect and a desire for self-improvement," and "elevate the material and moral tone of the poorer classes." And John Paton, president of the New York Association for Improving the Condition of the Poor, saw cleanliness as not only indicative of good character, but as one of the hallmarks of civilization. He wrote in 1893, "There has ever been an important and interesting connection between cleanliness and civilization. . . . With very large classes of society cleanliness of person, apparel and home are inseparable from thrift, industry and prosperity, and it is the absence of this which distinguishes upright, honest poverty from the condition of the improvident, the depraved and the worthless."[6]

Although the bath reformers claimed that public baths would change the moral character of the poor, they never clearly explained how this would happen. Mayor Quincy proclaimed that if "all bathed regularly . . . the filthy tenement house would disappear, for clean people will not live in a dirty house. Crime and drunkenness would decrease, for men and boys who are now driven to the saloon might then find the home a fit place in which to spend an evening." The assumption was that the poor would change their ways once they were exposed to proper behavior in regard to bathing, and that other aspects of the middle-class way of life would soon follow.[7]

To Boston's public bath advocates, it was the duty of the city to build and maintain these baths. Mayor Quincy asserted that the city must do "for the people those things which it can do better for them than they as individuals can do for themselves," and that it was the duty of those "already washed" to furnish baths for the great unwashed. One alternative to public baths—requiring slum landlords to provide bathrooms for their tenants—was not considered by advocates of cleanliness. Perhaps bathrooms were believed to be too expensive to be included in low-rent dwellings, or such a requirement would interfere with the property rights of tenement owners. Another alternative— paying higher wages to the poor, thereby allowing them to afford homes equipped with baths—was never mentioned by the bath reformers. In the case of public baths, the choice was municipal activism rather than disturbance of the property rights or profits of tenement owners or employers.[8]

As a final rationale, both proponents also pointed to the existing municipal bath systems of European cities, especially those in Great Britain and Germany. By 1890, most cities in these countries maintained rather complete municipal bath systems to serve both the poor and the middle class (the latter, unlike their American counterparts, lacked bath accommodations in their homes). The Boston *City Record* in 1898 compared Boston unfavorably with Birmingham, England, a city which had approximately the same population as Boston in 1895 (ca. 496,000). Birmingham had four year-round baths opened between 1852 and 1883, as opposed to Boston's newly opened one.[9]

Boston's public bath movement began in the 1840s as the first wave of Irish immigrants flooded into the city. The overcrowding, lack of sanitation, and filth of the Irish slums of Boston produced the very high mortality rates reported by statistician Lemuel Shattuck from 1845 on. Sparked perhaps by the 1849 cholera epidemic, the Committee on Public Hygiene of the newly organized American Medical Association urged the establishment in slum districts of cheap public baths, based on the European model. Asserting that frequent bathing among the poor and laboring classes would remove "a prominent cause of disease, and contribute to their moral as well as physical improvement," the committee stated for the first time the major argument of the Gilded Age bath movement:

That uncleanliness and mental degradation are intimately associated with each other, is now generally admitted; hence in proportion as the body is kept cleanly, are the moral faculties
elevated, and the tendency to commit crime diminished.

In 1850 the Massachusetts Sanitary Commission in a report
prepared under Shattuck also recommended the establishment of public baths. The commission cited the fact that,
although Boston had twelve or more commercial bathhouses, the fees—ranging from twelve and one-half cents
to twenty-five cents per bath—were far too costly for the
lower classes. [10]

These first recommendations for public baths had little
effect for a decade, and it was not until 1860 that Boston
began its pioneering efforts to provide baths for the poor. In
that year the board of aldermen and the common council
appointed a joint special committee "to consider and report
what measures, if any, can be adopted to provide such facilities for cheap bathing as will induce all persons to avail
themselves of the means so provided." The report of this
committee, issued in 1861, was probably the first public
document in the United States on the subject of municipal
baths. It found the city of Boston to be very deficient in public bathing accommodations, and the few year-round private establishments to be beyond the means of the working
classes. The report urged that the city initiate some plan to
provide the people with an "opportunity for habitual and
economical bathing." Specifically it recommended cheap
plunge baths (small pools) for the use of men and boys, to be
set up on an experimental basis in different parts of the city.
Although nothing came of this recommendation, probably
because of preoccupation with the Civil War, the cause of
municipal baths was revived in 1866. [11]

In that year another joint special committee was appointed "to examine and report on the practicability of

establishing within this city one or more Bathing Places for the free accommodation of the public.'' At first the committee hoped to set up salt water baths for the summer, and warm and cold fresh water baths for the rest of the year; they found that year-round baths would be too expensive and concentrated on summer baths instead. The committee selected six locations, $20,000 was appropriated, and in June, five floating baths at river sites and one natural beach bath (the L Street Bathing Beach) were opened. [12]

The floating baths were wooden, docklike structures, the shape and depth of modern swimming pools, with dressing rooms located around the sides. Some had separate shallow areas for small children; river water was used to fill them. In their first summer of operation these baths were very successful, recording a total of 433,690 bathers. Boston's total population at the time was approximately 200,000. This success prompted the board of aldermen and the common council to appoint a joint standing committee on Bathing and Public Water Accommodations. In 1867, under this new committee, six additional floating baths were opened, four for the exclusive use of women and girls. By 1869 Boston was operating a total of fourteen floating baths during the summer months. In 1879 the joint standing committee was discontinued and the baths were placed under the jurisdiction of the board of health. In placing these baths under this jurisdiction, the municipal government was emphasizing their cleanliness function, although the patrons probably considered them mainly recreational. [13]

Several other cities, including New York and Philadelphia, followed Boston's lead in providing floating baths for their citizens. However, because floating baths often had to be closed due to pollution of the rivers by sewage, the problem of the year-round uncleanliness of the poor remained unsolved. They did, however, become an accepted part of the services a city should provide for its inhabitants and probably paved the way for popular approval of the idea of more expensive, year-round baths as a logical extension of municipal services.

Although the Commonwealth of Massachusetts provided the first step toward the establishment of year-round baths in 1874—when it passed a law permitting any town to purchase or lease lands, erect public baths and washhouses, and raise or appropriate money for these purposes—it was not until the early 1890s that year-round baths became a reality in Boston. [14]

The cause of public baths became more urgent by 1890 as new waves of immigrants flocked to the city's slums, and popular acceptance of the germ theory of disease made personal cleanliness an essential part of public health. There was no doubt that the poor, as Mayor Quincy observed, did "not bathe properly from one year's end to the other, because there are no facilities for bathing in their wretched and overcrowded rooms." Statistical studies confirmed this observation. A tenement house census conducted in 1892 by the Massachusetts Department of Labor revealed that of 71,665 families renting tenements, only 25.78 percent had bathrooms, and in one slum ward, less than 1 percent of the families had bathrooms. [15]

The need for year-round public baths was first publicized by Robert A. Woods, who became head resident of Andover House in Boston's South End in 1892. Believing that settlement workers ought to call attention to the needs of their neighborhoods, Woods and the residents of Andover House made regular trips to city hall to appeal to the city council for a public bath. The council listened to their requests but refused to appropriate the money. [16]

Woods, whom Arthur Mann has called "the philosopher and tactician of the university settlement," was born in Pittsburgh in 1865 of middle-class, Scotch-Irish, rigidly Presbyterian parentage. He graduated from Amherst College in 1886 and then attended Andover Theological Seminary. Rather than entering the ministry, however, Woods was attracted to the idea of service through the social settlement movement. In 1891 he went to England to study Toynbee Hall so that a similar establishment could be set up in Boston under the auspices of Andover Theological Seminary, with Woods as its head. [17]

Woods's approach to municipal reform was realistic and pragmatic rather than doctrinaire and monistic. As Mann has noted, Woods scorned the reformers

> who thought the millennium would come by throwing out the bosses and getting honest businessmen to run the city. . . . The question was not who ran the government but how it was run; the crucial municipal issue was to extend political functions to satisfy the needs of the poor, to give them baths, gymnasiums, sanitary tenements, parks, playgrounds, clean streets, industrial education.

Thus, municipal baths were only one aspect of Woods's campaign against urban poverty, but, in Josiah Quincy, who was elected Boston's mayor in 1895, he found an ally in his realistic political approach and, in particular, in his demand for baths. [18]

Josiah Quincy, a member of an old and public-spirited Boston family, was the third Mayor Quincy of Boston, for his father and great-grandfather had been mayor before him. Quincy was born in 1859 and was educated at Harvard and Harvard Law School. He entered politics in 1884, when as a Democrat he campaigned for Cleveland against Blaine. In 1886 and 1889 Quincy served in the state House of Representatives, where he was a member of the committee on cities and worked for the secret ballot law. He was chairman of the Democratic State Committee in 1891–92. In 1893 he was appointed assistant secretary of state by President Cleveland, a position from which he resigned to run for mayor of Boston. [19]

Raised in a tradition of "social paternalism," inspired by the progress of the great cities of Europe in meeting the needs of their citizens, and influenced by his "creative friendship" with Robert Woods, Quincy, as mayor, determined to bring to Boston a panoply of social innovations including public baths (which were probably his favorite project), playgrounds, public gymnasiums, boys' summer camps, public concerts, and free lectures. Although Quincy is usually considered a reform mayor, he did not attack the bosses but rather tried to work with them. He also cooperated with organized labor and with Boston's leading citizens and philanthropists whom he involved in the municipal government by appointing them to unpaid commissions. Quincy wrote of his vision of Boston as a community:

> The duty of a city is to promote the civilization, in the fullest sense of the word, of all its citizens. No true civilization can exist without the provision of some reasonable opportunities for exercising the physical and mental faculties, of experiencing something of the variety and of the healthful pleasures of life, or feeling at least the degree of self-respect which personal cleanliness brings with it. The people of a city constitute a community, in all which that significant term implies; their interests are inextricably bound up together, and everything which promotes the well-being of a large part of the population benefits all. [20]

In his inaugural address on January 6, 1896, Quincy promised to take action:

> The maintaining of public baths, open all the year seems to me to be a project for encouraging social and sanitary improvement by municipal action which promises large return for a comparative-

ly small expenditure, and I am of [the] opinion that the experiment of establishing such a public bath in a suitable locality
should be tried. I shall recommend such an appropriation to be
provided for by loan.

On January 20, 1896, Quincy—probably following the
precedent of New York City's reform mayor, William L.
Strong—announced the formation of the Mayor's Advisory
Committee on Public Baths, with Robert A. Woods as its
chairman. The committee was to investigate the subject,
estimate the cost, and recommend the best location. It
planned to visit New York City to confer with Mayor
Strong's bath committee, and inspect the People's Baths.[21]

The People's Baths was a very influential prototype public bath erected in 1891 by the New York Association for
Improving the Condition of the Poor. Located on the Lower
East Side and built at a cost of $27,025, these baths had
twenty-three showers and three bathtubs. Each bathing
compartment was divided into a dressing room and a
shower area, three and one-half by four feet each. Following this example, shower baths rather than tub baths became the norm for public baths in the United States, for they
were easier to keep clean and sanitary, used less water, and
took less time than tub baths. Dozens of bath advocates
from all over the country inspected the People's Baths.[22]

In addition to Woods, the membership of the Boston bath
committee included Dr. Edward Mussey Hartwell, who
was director of physical training in the public schools of
Boston. Hartwell was born in 1850 in Exeter, New Hampshire, attended the Boston Latin School, and graduated
from Amherst College in 1873. He received a Ph.D. from
Johns Hopkins in 1881, and an M.D. from Miami Medical
College in Cincinnati, Ohio, in 1882. Hartwell had taught in
high school in the 1870s and was an instructor at Johns
Hopkins from 1883 to 1891, when he became Boston's di-

rector of physical training. Hartwell was strongly in favor of public school baths and was also a prominent member of the National Municipal League, which was devoted to municipal reform. Hartwell wrote extensively on both municipal reform and public baths. In 1897 Mayor Quincy appointed him secretary of Boston's newly created Department of Municipal Statistics.[23]

Two women were also members of the mayor's advisory committee, Mary Morton Kehew and Laliah Pingree. Kehew, a very active social reformer, was president of the Women's Educational and Industrial Union, an organization founded to encourage both trade unionism among women workers and labor legislation beneficial to women workers. After the American Federation of Labor convention in Boston in 1903, Kehew organized the National Women's Trade Union League for the same purpose on a nationwide scale. Pingree was a former member of the Boston School Committee.[24]

Labor was also represented on the mayor's committee by two members, Edward J. Ryan, president of the Buildings' Trades Council, and Michael W. Myers, president of the Plumbers' Union. The seventh member was Edmund Billings, superintendent and treasurer of the Wells Memorial Institute, a social and educational club for young workingmen which provided them with space to meet, socialize, and hold informal classes, and which housed a small library and a gymnasium with hot and cold water baths.[25]

In April 1896, the Mayor's Advisory Committee on Public Baths, after studying New York City's People's Baths, issued its preliminary report. The report recommended that the city build its first year-round bath in the vicinity of Dover Street and Harrison Avenue in the heart of the slums of Boston's South End, that the bath be built on a 50-by-100-foot lot, contain at least forty showers, and accommodate

both men and women in absolutely distinct compartments
with separate entrances and waiting rooms. It also recommended that the bath be completely free to all, and that at
least $50,000—and preferably $65,000—should be appropriated for land and building. In May 1896, Mayor Quincy
referred the committee's recommendations to the Joint
Standing Committee on the Health Department of the
board of aldermen and the city council. [26]

The Joint Standing Committee also visited New York City
and was much impressed by the People's Baths. Their report to the board of aldermen and the city council was issued in June 1896, and their recommendations were similar
to those of the Mayor's Advisory Committee. They recommended that $65,000 (to be raised by issuing 20-year bonds
at 4 percent interest) be appropriated for a bath similar to the
People's Baths and that it be located on a 50-by100-foot lot.
They urged that the municipal bath be placed under the
jurisdiction of the board of health, but made no recommendation on the matter of whether the baths should be
free or cost a small fee. [27]

The Joint Standing Committee's recommendations were
the basis for a feature story in the *Boston Herald*, which also
contained pictures and descriptions of New York City's
People's Baths. In addition, the *Herald* editorially urged the
board of aldermen and the city council to take "prompt and
favorable action" on the committee's recommendations,
pointing out that other cities, including Chicago, Brookline,
Yonkers, and Philadelphia, were well on the way to con-
structing their municipal bath systems. The *Herald* also
recommended the building of school baths, noting that the
school board was already conducting cooking and sewing
classes and asking, "Is not cleanliness, rather than cooking,
next to godliness?" [28]

During the summer of 1896, plans for Boston's first

bathhouse advanced as the board of aldermen and the city council appropriated the $65,000 requested. Land was purchased at 249 Dover Street near the recommended site for $14,150, and Peabody and Stearns were chosen as architects. In November the architectural plans—which called for a 43-by-110-foot, two-story bathhouse with fifty showers (seventeen of them for women)—were approved and construction began. [29]

Controversy did arise during this time, however, over the provision of baths in the public schools. This involved the question not only of whether baths should be located in the public schools, but if so, whether they should exist for the exclusive use of school children or be opened to the general public after school hours. Dr. Hartwell had suggested that twenty-eight shower baths be included in the plans for two new school buildings to be constructed in the near future. The school board was divided on the issue and school baths were rejected outright by the schoolhouse committee, which was in charge of school buildings, for they felt it was not the duty of the school authorities "to bathe the children in the public schools because they may not be clean, for if this be granted, we see no reason why we should not clothe them if they be improperly clothed, or feed them if not properly nourished at home." In October 1896, the controversy was resolved, however, when the Joint Committee on Hygiene of the board of aldermen and the city council reported favorably on school baths, and such baths were included in the two new school buildings. These baths, however, were used exclusively by school children until 1906, when they were opened in the evening to the general public under the supervision of the baths department. [30]

Another controversy arose over the question of whether the baths should be free. Those who favored a fee felt that the baths should not be a charity. Others argued, in Mayor

Quincy's words, "that free baths would not pauperize the people any more than free textbooks and free public schools." In the end it was decided that Boston's baths would be free, for "it was felt that the charge of even one cent might keep away the very people who most needed bathing." There was a fee of one cent each for soap and towel, however.[31]

While Boston's first municipal bathhouse was being constructed, Mayor Quincy, with the approval of the board of aldermen, created a Department of Baths, headed by an unsalaried Bath Commission of seven Boston citizens appointed by the mayor for one- to five-year terms. The secretary of the Bath Commission was also the superintendent of baths and was a paid official. In addition to having jurisdiction over the new Dover Street Bath, the commission also operated Boston's fourteen floating baths, two swimming pools, its natural beach baths, public comfort stations, and a combined gymnasium and bath in East Boston donated to the city by Mrs. Daniel Ahl in 1897. The chairman of the Bath Commission was Thomas J. Lane, who cannot be further identified. Of the original Mayor's Advisory Committee on Public Baths, only Robert A. Woods was a member of the Bath Commission. Other members were two physicians, Dr. John Duff and Dr. Henry Ehrlich, two women, Mrs. Lawrence Logan and Mrs. Jacob Hecht, and Leonard D. Ahl. The bath reformers in general advocated this type of bath commission, and Quincy used unpaid commissions extensively during his administration.[32]

The Dover Street Bath, which opened formally on October 14, 1898, cost $86,000 to build and was typical of the large, imposing municipal bath. It was 43 feet wide, 110 feet deep, and three stories high. The first-story granite front supported upper stories of gray mottled brick with limestone trimmings, all of which was surmounted by an ornamental cornice of galvanized iron. There were two entrances and two waiting rooms, one for men and one for women. The waiting rooms had terrazzo mosaic floors and Knoxville marble walls, with marble staircases leading to the baths on the second floor. The men's section had thirty showers and three bathtubs, and the women's section had eleven showers and six tubs. Each bathing compartment consisted of a dressing alcove with a seat and a shower compartment. The partitions were of marble, as was the floor in the bathing section. The third floor was devoted to janitors' and matrons' quarters, and the basement contained a laundry for washing towels. At the opening day ceremonies Mayor Quincy defended this bath, which was far more elaborate than New York's model People's Baths:

> The expenditure which the city has made in erecting its first permanent bath-house of this substantial and ornamental character has been incurred with a broader end in view than that of merely providing facilities for the bathing of a certain number of persons. The number of shower-baths and tub-baths contained in this building could have been furnished at a much smaller expense. . . . The purpose of the advisory committee which planned this first central bath house—a purpose which met with my hearty approval and support—was to erect a building of such character and appointments that it would be worthy as an architectural monument of the city which owned it, and would raise the whole idea of public bathing to a high and dignified plane.[33]

The opening of the Dover Street Bath prompted the *Boston Herald* to urge editorially that permanent baths be established in every part of the city where needed, and to commend Mayor Quincy for the progress made in that direction.[34]

The Dover Street Bath, however, proved to be Boston's last structure built for the primary purpose of providing baths for those without such facilities in their homes. After

1899, municipal bath facilities were often combined with gymnasiums, and the emphasis shifted slowly from cleanliness to physical fitness and recreation. Several factors probably account for this change. By 1898 Mayor Quincy saw a close connection between bathing and recreation, as he asserted:

> It is . . . impossible to draw any line between the maintenance of an out-door bathing place in summer and an indoor bath in winter, or between a shower bath and tub bath, serving only the purpose of promoting cleanliness, and the swimming-pool which answers the further purpose of affording facilities for exercise and recreation.

Economy played a role, for combined baths and gymnasiums were less expensive than the Dover Street Bath, and one criticism of Quincy's administration was that his social reforms brought an increase in municipal indebtedness, and produced an "insolvent utopia." After the turn of the century, tenement-house reform required builders to install a toilet in each new apartment; most builders installed a bathtub as well, thus decreasing the need for public baths. Cities which concentrated on building baths for cleanliness alone experienced sharp declines in bath patronage by 1915, a trend that did not happen in Boston.[35]

In 1899 Josiah Quincy was not nominated to run for mayor by Boston's Democrats, for his attempts to concentrate executive authority and rationalize operations of the city government met with opposition by the city's Irish bosses. Yet subsequent administrations, both reform and boss-led, continued his policy of providing facilities for both cleanliness and recreation. Under Mayor Thomas N. Hart, a Republican who served from 1900 to 1901, four combined baths and gymnasiums were opened. And under Mayor Patrick A. Collins (1902–5), a Democrat and fiscal conservative, the Cabot Street Bath and Gymnasium—which had an indoor swimming pool and cost approximately $100,000—

was opened in 1905 in Boston's Roxbury section. However, in 1902, Collins did veto an appropriations bill which would have provided for additional baths and gymnasiums. Provision of these facilities resumed when John F. Fitzgerald, Irish-machine boss and Democrat, became mayor in 1906. Construction of seven multiple-use municipal buildings—which included municipal offices, a public hall, a branch of the public library with a reading room, a gymnasium, and shower baths—was begun during Fitzgerald's first administration (1906–7), continued under Republican Mayor George F. Hibbard (1908–9), kept on during Fitzgerald's second administration (1910–13), and endured under James M. Curley who became mayor in 1914. In 1912 the Bath Commission merged with several other commissions to form the Park and Recreation Department. This merger marked the official disappearance of the cleanliness function of municipal baths, and the definite connection of baths with recreation in Boston.[36]

Boston's public bath movement was thus a reform which had its origins and achieved its first success in the Gilded Age, and was continued during the Progressive Era. In some respects it was a typical reform measure of the Gilded Age, with its use of European precedents and with its emphasis on public health and moral rejuvenation through cleanliness. Yet it moved beyond the limitations of Gilded Age reform, foreshadowing the Progressive Era's assertion that it was the municipal government's duty to provide services that would, to quote Melvin Holli, "humanize the city environment" and "redistribute at least in part some of the amenities of middle-class life." This reform bears out the contention of historians Geoffrey Blodgett and Richard Abrams that Massachusetts had already achieved many of the reforms associated with progressivism by the time that movement was well underway.[37]

Whether or not Boston, under Josiah Quincy's leadership, was—as Blodgett maintained—"the cutting edge of urban reform in America," and whether or not Quincy's Dover Street Bath was "a monument to municipal socialism," is beyond the scope of this paper. Nevertheless, Quincy's administration did bring reform to Gilded Age Boston and did improve the quality of life for some of its poorer citizens. In this accomplishment, Quincy involved many groups of Bostonians not usually associated with reform in this era. Not only were upper- and middle-class reformers like himself and Robert Woods involved in the movement for public baths, but Quincy also enlisted the support of labor leaders and Irish ward bosses. Several physicians and women social reformers also were members of Boston's Bath Commission.[38]

Mayor Quincy himself became a leader of the national movement for public baths in the 1890s. He wrote extensively on the subject in social reform periodicals, and was one of the main speakers at a mass meeting on public baths held in Baltimore, Maryland, in November 1898. His efforts were most certainly effective in helping convince other American cities to follow Boston's example in providing public baths. By 1915, thirty-one American cities could boast of public bath systems.[39]

Although one can rightly take issue with Quincy's naive assumptions and extravagant claims regarding the efficacy of the gospel of cleanliness as a solution to the problems of the slums, the provision of public baths can be seen as a small part of the "search for order" in Gilded Age America. Cleanliness was associated with the characteristics of industriousness, thrift, punctuality, and devotion to duty which, it was felt, Americans must possess if they were to meet successfully the challenges of urbanization and industrialization.

Notes

1. *Boston Herald*, Oct. 15, 1898.
2. Ibid.; Boston, *City Record* 1 (October 20, 1898): 593.
3. Morton Keller, *Affairs of State: Public Life in Late Nineteenth-Century America* (Cambridge, Mass., 1977), p. 500.
4. Howard D. Kramer, "The Germ Theory and the Early Public Health Program in the United States," *Bulletin of the History of Medicine* 22 (1948): 240–46; James H. Cassedy, "The Flamboyant Colonel Waring: An Anticontagionist Holds the American Stage in the Age of Pasteur and Koch," in *Sickness and Health in America: Readings in the History of Medicine and Public Health*, ed. Judith Walzer Leavitt and Ronald L. Numbers (Madison, Wis., 1978), pp. 305, 309–10; Josiah Quincy, "Municipal Progress in Boston," *Independent* 52 (February 15, 1900): 424.
5. Carl Bridenbaugh, "Baths and Watering Places of Colonial America," *William and Mary Quarterly* 3 (April 1946): 152–58; Ronald L. Numbers, "Do It Yourself the Sectarian Way," in *Sickness and Health*, ed. Leavitt and Numbers, pp. 89–93; Harry B. Weiss and Howard R. Kemble, *The Great American Water Cure Craze: A History of Hydropathy in the United States* (Trenton, N.J., 1967); Harold Donaldson Eberlein, "When Society First Took a Bath," *Pennsylvania Magazine of History and Biography* 67 (January 1943): 30–48.
6. Josiah Quincy, "Gymnasiums and Playgrounds," *Sanitarian* 41 (October 1898): 306; G.W.W. Hangar, "Public Baths in the United States," in *Bulletin of the Bureau of Labor*, comp. U.S. Department of Commerce and Labor (Washington, D.C., 1904), 1252; John Paton, *Public Baths* (1893), p. 6.
7. Quincy, "Municipal Progress," p. 424.
8. Ibid.; Quincy, "Gymnasiums and Playgrounds," p. 309.
9. Edward Mussey Hartwell, "Public Baths in Europe," in *Monographs on Social Economics* 6, ed. Charles H. Verrill (Washington, D.C., 1901); Boston, *City Record* 1 (October 20, 1898): 597.
10. Oscar Handlin, *Boston's Immigrants* (New York, 1972), pp. 108–17; American Medical Association, *First Report of the Committee on Public Hygiene* (Philadelphia, 1849), pp. 479–80, 569; Joseph Lee, *Constructive and Preventive Philanthropy* (New York, 1902), p. 182.
11. Hangar, "Public Baths in U.S.," pp. 1275–76.
12. City of Boston, *Report on Free Bathing Facilities*, City Document no. 102 (1866), pp. 2–14.
13. Ibid.; Jane A. Stewart, "Boston's Experience with Municipal Baths,"

American Journal of Sociology 7 (November 1901): 417; Hangar, "Public Baths in U.S.," p. 1277.

14. Hangar, "Public Baths in U.S.," p. 1251.
15. Hartwell, "Public Baths in Europe," pp. 25–26.
16. Allen Davis, *Spearheads for Reform: The Social Settlements and the Progressive Movement, 1890–1914* (New York, 1967), pp. 174–75.
17. Arthur Mann, *Yankee Reformers in the Urban Age* (Cambridge, Mass., 1954), pp. 115–17.
18. Ibid., p. 121.
19. "Josiah Quincy," *National Cyclopedia of American Biography* 19 (1926): 435; *Boston Herald*, Jan. 6, 1896.
20. Geoffrey Blodgett, *The Gentle Reformers: Massachusetts Democrats in the Cleveland Era* (Cambridge, Mass., 1966), pp. 244–54.
21. *Boston Herald*, Jan. 7, Jan. 21, 1896.
22. New York Association for Improving the Condition of the Poor, *The People's Baths* (n.d.), pp. 5–6; *The People's Baths: A Study on Public Baths*, reprint from *AICP Notes*, no. 2, pp. 2–11.
23. "Edward Mussey Hartwell," *Municipal Affairs* 1 (September 1897): 603.
24. Elisabeth M. Herlihy, ed., *Fifty Years of Boston: A Memorial Volume* (Boston, 1932), pp. 218–19, 223; Robert Sklar, "Mary Morton Kimball Kehew," in *Notable American Women 1607–1950*, ed. Edward T. James, Janet Wilson James, and Paul Boyer (Cambridge, Mass., 1971), pp. 313–14; Boston, *City Record* 1 (October 20, 1898): 595.
25. Boston, *City Record* 1 (October 20, 1898): 595; Wells Memorial Association, *Annual Report, 1883* (Cambridge, Mass., 1883), pp. 2–5.
26. Boston, *City Record*, p. 595; *Boston Herald*, June 9, 1896.
27. *Boston Herald*, June 9, 1896.
28. *Boston Herald*, June 9, 10, 1896.
29. Boston, *City Record*, pp. 595–96; *Boston Herald*, Nov. 30, 1896.
30. *Boston Herald*, June 9, 1896; Mayor's Committee of New York City, *Report on Public Baths and Public Comfort Stations* (New York, 1897), pp. 59–60; City of Boston, Department of Baths (hereafter referred to as BDB), *Annual Report, 1906–7* (Boston, 1907), p. 2.
31. Quincy, "Municipal Progress," p. 424.
32. BDB, *Annual Report, 1899–1900* (Boston, 1900), pp. 2–4, 13.
33. Boston, *City Record*, pp. 593–95; *Boston Herald*, Oct. 15, 1898.
34. *Boston Herald*, Oct. 16, 1898.
35. Stewart, "Boston's Experience," p. 418; Josiah Quincy, "Playgrounds, Baths and Gymnasia," *Journal of Social Science* 36 (December 1898): 139; Blodgett, *Gentle Reformers*, p. 259; Lawrence Veiller, *Housing Reform: A Handbook for Practical Use in American Cities* (New York, 1910), pp. 111–12; M. T. Williams, "The Public Bath Movement in the United States, 1890–1915" (Ph.D. diss. New York University, 1972), p. 215.

36. Blodgett, *Gentle Reformers*, pp. 258–59; Martin J. Schiesl, *The Politics of Efficiency: Municipal Administration and Reform in America 1880–1920* (Berkeley, Calif., 1977), pp. 68–70; BDB, *Annual Report 1901–1902* (Boston, 1902), pp. 6–11; *Annual Report, 1905–1906* (Boston, 1906), p. 1; John Koren, *Boston, 1822–1922, The Story of Its Government and Principal Activities during One Hundred Years* (Boston, 1923), pp. 49–62; City of Boston, Park and Recreation Department, *Annual Report for the Year Ending Jan. 31, 1915*, p. 51; Herlihy, *Fifty Years of Boston*, p. 109.

37. Blodgett, *Gentle Reformers*, p. 282; Richard M. Abrams, *Conservatism in a Progressive Era: Massachusetts Politics 1900–1912* (Cambridge, Mass., 1964), pp. 2–3; Melvin G. Holli, "Urban Reform in the Progressive Era," in *The Progressive Era*, ed. Lewis L. Gould (Syracuse, N.Y., 1974), p. 141.

38. Blodgett, *Gentle Reformers*, pp. 243, 251.

39. *Baltimore Sun*, Dec. 7, 1898.

Reaction and Reform in Boston:
The Gilded Age and the Progressive Era

JACK TAGER

In 1904, when one could say with some assurance that the Gilded Age was past, a much displeased expatriate Henry James toured Boston, among other places, on a visit from Europe. To James, Boston was "an honored haunt of all the most civilized," and he found pleasure in the honesty and "indefinable perfection" of Park Street. Yet, he mourned that the Beacon Hill of his young manhood was gutted by the uncultivated drives of the moneyed classes, or, as he put it, "the commercial energy." He asserted that his very past had been "ruptured [by the] gross little aliens, [coming] up from as over the Common," and swarming down from the Statehouse, "in serene and triumphant possession [of his] small homogeneous Boston of the more interesting time."[1]

Doubtless, this xenophobic literary genius exaggerated his lament of a bygone Boston. But "the dreadful chill of change" had come to Boston as it went through the turbulent stages of urbanization. Once characterized by Charles Francis Adams, Jr., as "the best balanced commercial city in America," Boston had become a multitiered metropolis with hordes of diverse newcomers.[2] Once the floodgates had been lifted by the Irish, it was not long before the other "huddled masses" of Europe joined in the incursions that were to erode the once solid ranks of Boston Brahmin civilization.

Less heralded—indeed, Stephan Thernstrom called it

"neglected"—was the wave of internal migration of Yankee farmers who were forced off the land by an increasingly mechanized agriculture and attracted by the new factory system. This "urban safety valve for rural discontent" stimulated what Thernstrom suggested was "the prime cause of population growth in nineteenth-century America and the main source of urban growth."[3] The multiple opportunities for material advancement drew the farm lads from the moribund agriculture of New England to growing Boston. One such dispossessed and discontented migrant was Henry Morgan, the self-proclaimed "people's minister."

Professor Ivan D. Steen admirably describes the career of the Reverend Henry Morgan in his article in this volume, and in an earlier article in the *New England Quarterly*. By 1878 Morgan had shifted from his successful work in establishing missions and promoting the welfare of the Yankee working class, to a more dubious full-scale attack on moral turpitude in Boston. The enemies were the greedy property owners, lax law enforcement officials, untrustworthy newspaper editors, and nefarious churchmen, who allegedly condoned and benefited from vice. Drinking, gambling, and prostitution were mighty temptations for his constituents, and Morgan took up the cudgel against sin as defender of the spiritual and moral values of the native-born migrants to Boston. Thus, Morgan's mission of helping the Protestant poor and his attempt to rid the city of social evil are well documented.

The self-ordained and bombastic Morgan, however, was not typical of nineteenth-century Boston reformers. Brought up as an impoverished youth, refused entry as minister into the established Methodist church, forced to become an itinerant pastor without congregation or credentials, Morgan finally migrated to the city. A disgruntled outsider, he was part of the displaced Yankee cohorts cast out of their villages into an alien urban environment, strangers in their own land. These newcomers found it difficult to adapt to what Ralph Turner characterized as a vast experiment in cultural change, "a new structure of behavior and thought."[4] Ironically, it was the "evil" city that offered Morgan his only chance to gain the status of moral leader. Fueled with a deeply held belief in the spiritual/ethical values of the simple Protestant rural life, scornful of the "sinful" city, Morgan became the self-appointed protector of the dislocated native-born migrants.

A critical element in the self-boosterism of Morgan's new-found position as "poor man's preacher," was his attack on the Catholic church in Boston. "Aristocracy bows to the Roman yoke," he wrote intemperately, "and Beacon Hill kisses the Pope's toe. Tools of the Catholic Church finger the taxes, manage the appropriations, deliver the votes and sell to the rich corporations all the privileges they want."[5] Unlike staid Bostonians, such as Charles Eliot Norton who openly admired the Catholic church because "it exercised control over the Irish immigrant," Morgan eagerly revitalized the dormant Know-Nothingism of his fellow country-born WASPs.[6] The Yankee mechanics' long-held anti-Catholicism quickly came to life due to their daily competition with the "foreigners" for jobs, housing, and the benefits of urban life. Embroidering on rural Protestant America's moth-eaten tapestry of religious intolerance, Morgan fashioned for himself a makeshift urban pastorate in Boston.

With all his concern for the urban Yankee poor, and for all his blistering sermons on moral depravity in Boston, Morgan was an unusual representative of the urban social reformer. More generally, the urban "social controllers" described by Paul Boyer were typically middle- and upper-class paternalists seeking to replicate the "moral order of the village in the city." The Protestant City Mission groups, which attracted heavy business support, or the Charity Organization founders, perhaps the most potent force in the "moral-control" movement, were "social uplifters," the likes of Samuel Lane Loomis, William T. Stead, Charles Sheldon, Mary Richmond, Charles Loring Brace, B. O. Flower, Josiah Strong, Charles Parkhurst, and Josephine Shaw Lowell.[7] Neither does Morgan belong among the "swells" of Boston who were the notable "social reconstructionists," graphically portrayed by Arthur Mann. Thomas Wentworth Higginson, Julia Ward Howe, Wendell Phillips, Franklin B. Sanborn, Edward Atkinson, and Edward Everett Hale had all been abolitionists, temperance and penal reformers, and women's rights advocates who became natural Mugwump sympathizers.[8] Nor is it likely that the iconoclastic minister would have been an acceptable recruit among the fashionable Mugwump bolters of 1884. Moorfield Storey, William Everett, Richard Henry Dana, Winslow Warren, Edmund Wheelright, John F. Andrew, George Fred Williams, and Josiah Quincy were the college-bred, urban, middle-class "gentle reformers" described by Geoffrey Blodgett in his brilliant work on the Mugwumps in Massachusetts.[9] The country-born Reverend Morgan was shunned by his more delicate Protestant cousins of the town, permanently outside the charmed reform circles of Boston's "middle and upper class scions of old, well-established Yankee Protestant families."[10]

Appropriately, Morgan could be considered a marginal religious moral uplifter, always on the periphery of mainstream social reform groups in Boston. Not surprisingly, he was not listed among the many luminaries and social worthies invited to participate in the 250th anniversary celebration of Boston, in September 1880.[11] Perhaps Morgan was more akin to those whom Blodgett suggested took part "in rabid attacks on the [Catholic] Church fomented by New England fringe-groups."[12] Not content with a relatively successful urban ministry, Morgan turned to class/ethnic/ religious divisiveness as the means to promote his vision of a purer past. "Alas! Alas!" he wrote stridently, "the Boston of 1776 is no more! Puritanism has given way to modern paganism. Patriotism to greed. Devotion to sensuality. Sacrifice for self."[13] The Reverend Henry Morgan was more the reactionary than the reformer.

Morgan was typical of a long line of nineteenth-century Bible-thumping, antiurban fanatics who pointed out social evils without understanding their origin, and thus, were unable to deal with them adequately. As Ralph Turner stated, "From the cultural point of view, the mere criticism of a social order cannot be the basis of social reconstruction." Social evils, he wrote, "must be dealt with in terms of the potentialities of cultural change, implicit in the industrial city milieu." It was left to others, ex-Mugwumps like Josiah Quincy, who recognized that both personal ambition and societal achievement necessitated conciliation with the immigrant masses. It was the creation of a "new integrated culture," to use Turner's apt term, based upon a mutuality of class interest and acceptance, that was to make urban reform possible in Boston.[14]

One of the many activities that characterized urban reform in Boston was the bathhouse movement. Social reformers connected habits of personal cleanliness with issues of morality. Teach the poor to bathe regularly and you not only prevent disease, but you also inspire them with the virtues of sobriety, frugality, and hard work. Boston's first public bathhouse opened in 1898 during the administration of Mayor Josiah Quincy. The Brahmin Quincy was hailed as the major leader of the movement to uplift and purify the city's lower classes. Without doubt, Quincy wore the mantle of reformer, and bathhouses for the poor were part of his reform tactics. More important, however, was the remarkable coalition with the Irish politicians of his party that enabled Quincy to carry out a program of social reform.

In an article on Massachusetts Mugwumps, Gordon Wood was of the opinion that as much as the Irish needed the Yankees, the younger ex-Mugwumps like Quincy desperately needed the Irish. Matters of conscience aside, these young Democrats wanted the power that had been denied them as liberal Republicans. The minority Democratic party offered the opportunities for a political future. The *Boston Beacon* of 1893 declared: "After years of strenuous effort the Democratic Party of this state is divided into two factions, the aristocrats and the plebians." This unlikely alliance, ever tenuous and fragile, signified the emergence of a realistic community of interest. Quincy was representative of those aristocrats, wrote Wood, who wanted "to build a party and to win elections. Harvard College needed the Irish slums. Some could not face this political reality; others, younger more ambitious perhaps, not only accepted the slums but eventually catered to them."[15]

Josiah Quincy was elected mayor in 1895, in part because of his alliance with old-time boss Pat Maguire. Maguire's death in 1896 left Quincy to deal with the Big Four (as Curley called them): "Smiling Jim" Donovan of Ward Nine in the South End; Joseph J. Corbett of Charlestown; Patrick "PJ" Kennedy of East Boston; and Congressman John F. Fitzgerald. (Martin Lomasney was always at odds with Quincy.) Quincy skillfully created a *modus vivendi* with the bosses, and the resulting ad hoc board of strategy had one major purpose: the equitable division of Boston's patronage. "Patronage," wrote Geoffrey Blodgett, "had become the politician's balance wheel for ethnic equilibrium."[16]

The finished Dover Street Bathhouse, with its cost over-run of $21,000 and its resplendent terrazzo mosaic floors and marble walls and staircases, must have brought smiles to the faces of the Irish politicians and their friends in the construction industry. One must also wonder how many patronage jobs were engendered by the creation of a new municipal bureaucracy, the Department of Baths, with jurisdiction over Boston's baths, pools, beaches, gymnasiums, and public comfort stations. The Boston Finance Commission reported in 1909 that between 1895 and 1907, the number of city employees increased 59 percent, or two and one-half times more rapidly than the population, justifying the comment that "the payroll of the city was heavily padded."[17] It was patronage and political plums and jobbing that enabled Quincy to convince the Irish strategy board that social reform, including bathhouses, would benefit all.

The question remains, Who were the major bath builders (i.e., moral uplifters) in Boston and, more important, what were their motives for supporting social reform for the lower classes? Professor Marilyn Thornton Williams states in an essay in this volume that after Quincy, "subsequent administrations, both reform and boss-led," continued the baths/recreation movement. It appears as if Republicans, conservative Democrats, and machine politicians, shared a common vision of providing governmental services for the less fortunate. Yet the fact that bath building occurred during a particular mayoral administration does not necessarily demonstrate a commitment to public spending for social reform purposes, or, for that matter, an ideological thrust of any kind.

In some cases the role of the city council could prove more important than that of a powerless mayor who was unable to manage a cantankerous mélange of councilmen/aldermen of another party, or of a different constituency. A famous case in point was that of Boston's first Irish-born mayor, Hugh O'Brien. O'Brien's momentous election in 1884 coincided with attempts by good government groups to change the city charter. O'Brien worked hard to demonstrate the successful assimilation of the Irish into American life, and his administration was characterized by Geoffrey Blodgett as "an effort at conciliation, not defiance." In his chosen role as a moderate and an enemy of patronage, O'Brien favored tax incentives to lure business to the city, and he continually launched small-scale municipal investigations, dismissing entire city agencies when appropriate. It was Mayor O'Brien's official request, made in conjunction with the City Reform Association, that prompted state takeover of Boston's power to fix tax limits, because O'Brien "was tired of being held responsible for the increase of expenditures" that he could not control.[18]

In his interpretation of the political implications of the charter change in 1885, A. Chester Hanford declared that the new charter "marked the emergence of the principle of executive responsibility, but left much to be done." The power of the mayor "was not so much strengthened as at first appeared," largely because of the existence of "numerous popularly elected offices," and because all mayoral appointments had to be confirmed by the board of aldermen and the common council, the creatures of the Irish bosses.[19] Only broad-based, machine supported mayors, with influence and connections in the city council, could wield tangible political power in Boston.

Those Boston mayors between 1895 and 1917 that increased public expenditures for programs beneficial to the poor, revealed the connection between reform and patronage. The Brahmin Quincy, as previously noted, turned out to be a big spender. Boston city historian, John Koren, cited Quincy's administration as "assuredly progressive but also expensive." In contrast, Mayors Thomas Hart and George Hibbard, Republican conservatives, consistently slashed appropriations. Hart's victory in 1899 seemed to be a repudiation both of Quincy by the middle and upper classes, and of his "reckless spending of city revenues on recreational facilities." Koren wrote: "Discontent with the alleged too generous outlay of public money became more and more marked, finally ending in the election of a conservative successor." George Hibbard, described as a "parsimonious Yankee," who served from 1908 to 1910, was notable for his "determination to give the city a nonpartisan and strictly economical administration." A believer in "efficient, cheap government," he fired a thousand city workers, decreased departmental expenditures, and reduced the city's indebtedness.[20] Acting in the same conservative fashion as these cost-conscious Republicans was the city's second Irish-born Democratic mayor, Patrick Collins.

Perceived as a man of "probity, high ethics, economy," and much like Hugh O'Brien, Patrick Collins's "impelling desire was to ease the tension between Irish and Yankee in Boston." As mayor from 1902 to 1905, he was opposed to building baths, remarking that "benevolent Socialism has gone too far in Boston." Historian Thomas O'Connor commented that the Irish Collins "came to enjoy considerable Republican support because of his vigorous attempts to cut back on extravagance in city government." John Koren stated that Collins "deprecated the high debt" and was in favor of "rigid economy." Moreover, he "persistently objected to needless and questionable drafts upon the city's borrowing power for general improvements. . . . For instance, in 1902 he vetoed a loan order amounting to $2,494,300 passed by the City Council, containing over twenty appropriations for playgrounds, bathhouses, wardrooms, etc."[21] Thus, Patrick Collins, albeit an Irish Democrat, was not a follower of Quincy with his belief in spending for the poor. Emulation of Brahmin ways meant that Collins imbibed from the Yankee well of fiscal restraint.[22]

It can be argued that three of Quincy's successors, Republican Thomas Hart (1900–1901), Patrick Collins (1902–5), and Republican George Hibbard (1908–9) were all opposed in thought and deed to bathhouses, and to costly reform measures specifically catering to the needs of the great "unwashed" lower classes. In any case, the poor were dubious political allies who were not to be relied upon. As "goo goo" structural reformers, benevolent to business interests, these mayors worshipped the twin gospels of efficiency and fiscal moderation. Ironically, it was the self-interested John F. Fitzgerald (1906–7, and 1910–13) and James Michael Curley (1914–17) who, because of their devotion to patronage and the spoils system, were to become Boston's only social reform mayors of the Progressive Era.

Fitzgerald turned out to be a major "moral purifier,"͵ building more baths and recreational facilities than all the stiffnecked efficiency types with their adherence to fiscal restraint and cost-cutting. Moreover, during his first administration he startled the opposition by recommending the appointment of a special commission to investigate "wrongdoing" and inefficiency in city government. The result was the establishment of the Boston Finance Commission of 1909, and the charter change of the same year, a move toward centralization of power in the executive and long a goal of Yankee reformers. So distorted and lopsided is the historical picture of John Fitzgerald that one historian of Massachusetts in the Progressive Era suggests that "what Fitzgerald intended is something of a mystery." Contrary to general belief, during his second administration he submitted twenty-eight official requests for investigation to the now-autonomous Boston Finance Commission. John Koren added to his accomplishments: "He gave much time to city planning, motor fire apparatus, garbage disposal, playground extension, . . . laborers' retirement plan, the city hall annex and to new district municipal buildings . . . containing public halls, branch libraries, baths, etc." Additionally, "Honey Fitz" built the City Point Aquarium, the Franklin Park Zoo, plus, quipped Francis Russell, "numberless public convenience stations memorialized with his name."[23]

Also angering Brahmin and Yankee (and confounding historians), in 1915 James Michael Curley initiated a bill in the General Court calling for increased tax rates, but it was defeated "by the real estate interests." During his first administration the total city debt actually decreased by $5 million, and the number of city employees under control of the mayor was cut by 117. He worked for more home rule, the abolition of correctional institutions for boys, and more street construction. Curley, of course, gave himself credit for building more and better recreational facilities than anyone else. "In 1907 there was one bathtub for every 25 families in parts of the city. I led the fight," he said, "that established public bathhouses in the North End, Charlestown and in other congested districts."[24] For all the boasting of the "purple shamrock," Thomas O'Connor agreed and gave Curley credit "for a rash of citywide construction projects" that proved doubly beneficial:

> He enlarged the City Hospital, created a series of local health units, developed extensive beaches and bathhouses in South Boston, built playgrounds, stadiums, and recreational facilities in various parts of the city, extended the tunnel to East Boston, expanded the subway system, tore down slums, paved streets, and widened roads. Not only did Curley provide extensive and much-needed benefits for his grateful constituents, but the projects themselves provided the necessary jobs upon which his whole system of personal patronage depended.[25]

During the Progressive Era in Boston, strangely enough, it was Fitzgerald and Curley who took up Quincy's example of government spending for reform, not Robert Wiebe's "new middle-class" reformers "searching for order."[26]

Settlement worker Robert Woods, moral uplifter par excellence, understood the crucial connection between ethnic politics and social reform, and he called it a "community of interest." Woods saw the hygienic-moral virtues of bathhouses, but he recognized that meaningful reform went beyond paternalistic philanthropy. This sentiment was echoed by his fellow settlement workers in their study of poverty in the North and West Ends:

> Social reform, to be in the highest degree sound and permanent, must spring from the cooperation of all classes. Yet nearly all efforts at social reform lean to one side or the other. They are predominantly either exertions of certain public-spirited individuals in behalf of others, or else spontaneous unaided efforts of the mass in its own interest. In a few cases—and here lie the greatest possibilities—the two elements are combined more equally.[27]

In his own fashion, Josiah Quincy was the cultural integrator, the "mass communicator" unifying the divided elements of society.[28] Quincy served as the cultural link between the social reformers and the politicians, thereby promoting urban progress in decentralized Boston during a period of enormous social change.

Could moral order and economic progress be achieved in a divided Boston without cooperation among the contending classes? A recent study by Jon Teaford argues that "an informal détente" existed among the divergent population of nineteenth-century Boston. Joint contributions of businessmen, municipal reformers, and political bosses based upon a series of uneasy compromises, resulted in a remarkably well-governed city.

> Overall, prosperous Americans enjoyed public facilities at least equal to any in the world, and an especially well-governed city such as Boston probably surpassed all those in Europe in quality of services. Boston could boast of the world's largest and grand-

est public library, as well as a park system designed by Frederick Law Olmsted, the first subway in America, an innovative system of intercepting sewers, renowned public schools, and of course typically American abundance of water. Moreover, it was one of the few American cities to provide public baths, municipal lodging houses for the indigent, and relief payments to the noninstitutionalized poor. Its low-interest bonds sold well above par, while state law ensured that its taxes remained within reason. Despite the rhetoric about failure and incompetence, cities like Boston successfully met the challenges of the age.[29]

Boston could be proud of its many public achievements and high standard of municipal service. City government could provide improved public service so long as all groups in the community had their interests respected.

Thus, successful urban government was predicated upon the realities of political accommodation, not upon "scientific" concepts of efficiency or paternalistic notions of self-improvement. Josiah Quincy mesmerized and enthralled the entire city with a center-ring balancing act—juggling moral platitudes for proper Bostonians while simultaneously treading cautiously on the high wire of Irish political patronage. For a short time Mayor Quincy brought a measure of political and social harmony to Boston during the Gilded Age. After Quincy's final curtain, however, the only significant urban reform mayors to emerge in Boston during the Progressive Era was the Celtic duo of Fitzgerald and Curley.

Notes

1. Henry James, *The American Scene* (Bloomington, Ind., 1969), pp. 232, 234, 231.
2. Charles Francis Adams, Jr., "Boston," *North American Review* 106 (January 1868): 6.
3. Stephan Thernstrom, "Urbanization, Migration and Social Mobility in Late Nineteenth-Century America," in *American Urban History*, ed. Alexander Callow, 2d ed. (New York, 1972), p. 400.

4. Ralph E. Turner, "The Industrial City: Center of Cultural Change," in ibid., p. 182.

5. Ivan D. Steen, "Cleansing the Puritan City: The Reverend Henry Morgan's Anti-vice Crusade in Boston," *New England Quarterly* 54 (September 1981): 405.

6. Geoffrey T. Blodgett, "The Mind of the Boston Mugwump," in *Moralists or Pragmatists? The Mugwumps, 1884–1900*, ed. Gerald W. McFarland (New York, 1975), p. 28.

7. Paul Boyer, *Urban Masses and Moral Order in America, 1820–1920* (Cambridge, Mass., 1978), p. viii, and chaps. 9 and 10.

8. Arthur Mann, *Yankee Reformers in the Urban Age: Social Reform in Boston, 1880–1900* (Cambridge, Mass., 1954), chap. 1.

9. Geoffrey Blodgett, *The Gentle Reformers: Massachusetts Democrats in the Cleveland Era* (Cambridge, Mass., 1966), chap. 2.

10. Gerald McFarland, "The Mugwumps and the Emergence of Modern America," in *Moralists or Pragmatists?* p. 1 n.

11. *Boston Anniversary Memorial: Celebration of the 250th Anniversary of the Settlement of Boston, Sept. 17, 1880* (Boston, 1880).

12. Blodgett, *Gentle Reformers*, p. 34.

13. Steen, "Cleansing," pp. 386–87.

14. Turner, "Industrial City," pp. 184, 185.

15. Gordon S. Wood, "The Massachusetts Mugwumps," in *Moralists or Pragmatists?* pp. 95, 98.

16. Blodgett, *Gentle Reformers*, pp. 153–54, 155, 248; Francis Russell, *The Great Interlude: Neglected Events and Persons from the First World War to the Depression* (New York, 1964), p. 173; James Michael Curley, *I'd Do It Again: A Record of My Uproarious Years* (Englewood Cliffs, N.J., 1957), p. 27.

17. A. Chester Hanford, "The Government of the City of Boston, 1880–1930," in *Fifty Years of Boston: A Memorial Album*, ed. Elisabeth M. Herlihy (Boston, 1932), p. 101.

18. Blodgett, *Gentle Reformers*, p. 61; Hanford, *Fifty Years*, p. 91.

19. Hanford, *Fifty Years*, p. 90.

20. John Koren, *Boston 1822–1922: The Story of Its Government and Principal Activities during One Hundred Years* (Boston, 1923), pp. 55, 56, 20; Robert V. Sparks, "Thomas Hart," and Peter d'A. Jones, "George Hibbard," in *Biographical Dictionary of American Mayors, 1820–1980*, ed. Melvin G. Holli and Peter d'A. Jones (Westport, Conn., 1981).

21. Blodgett, *Gentle Reformers*, p. 55; Peter d'A. Jones, "Patrick A. Collins," in *Dictionary*; Thomas O'Connor, *Bibles, Brahmins and Bosses: A Short History of Boston* (Boston, 1976), p. 100; Koren, *Boston*, p. 58.

22. Blodgett, *Gentle Reformers*, p. 61.

23. Richard Abrams, *Conservatism in a Progressive Era: Massachusetts Politics,*

1900–1912 (Cambridge, Mass., 1964), p. 147; Koren, *Boston*, p. 62; Russell, *Great Interlude*, p. 181.

24. Koren, *Boston*, p. 63; Curley, *I'd Do It Again*, p. 68.
25. O'Connor, *Bibles*, p. 119.
26. Robert Wiebe, *The Search for Order, 1877–1920* (New York, 1963), p. viii.
27. William Cole and Rufus Miles, "Community of Interest," *Americans in Process*, ed. Robert Woods (Boston, 1903), p. 322.
28. Seymour J. Mandelbaum, *Boss Tweed's New York* (New York, 1965), pp. 6, 67.
29. Jon C. Teaford, *The Unheralded Triumph: City Government in America, 1870–1900* (Baltimore, 1984), pp. 311–12.

Contributors

DALE BAUM is associate professor of history at Texas A and M University. He received his doctorate at the University of Minnesota. His publications include *The Civil War Party System: The Case of Massachusetts, 1848–1876* (Chapel Hill, N.C., 1984).

PETER HAEBLER teaches history at Merrimack Valley College where he is also registrar. He received Bachelor's and Master's degrees from the University of Massachusetts at Amherst and his Ph.D. from the University of New Hampshire. He has published several articles on the French-Canadian experience in Holyoke during the late nineteenth century.

JOHN W. IFKOVIC is associate professor of history at Westfield State College. He received his Ph.D. from the University of Virginia. His publications include a biography of Jonathan Trumbull, Jr., and biographies of other figures important in the early American republic.

ALEXANDER KEYSSAR teaches history at Brandeis University. He received his doctorate in American Civilization from Harvard University. He has published several articles and is the author of *Out of Work: A Social History of Unemployment in Massachusetts*, to be published by Cambridge University Press.

THOMAS MC MULLIN teaches history at the University of Massachusetts at Boston. He received his Ph.D. from the University of Wisconsin. He is co-author (with David A. Walker) of the *Biographical Directory of American Territorial Governors* (Westport, Conn., 1984).

RONALD A. SMITH is professor of history at the Pennsylvania State University. He received his doctorate at the University of Wisconsin and has published several articles.

Contributors

IVAN D. STEEN teaches history at the State University of New York at Albany. He received his B.A., M.A., and Ph.D. from New York University and has published several articles and book reviews.

JACK TAGER teaches urban history at the University of Massachusetts at Amherst. He received his Ph.D. from the University of Rochester. He is the author of *The Intellectual as Urban Reformer: Brand Whitlock and the Progressive Movement* (Cleveland, 1968), and *The Urban Vision: Selected Interpretations of the Modern City* (Homewood, Ill., 1970), and several articles on urban history.

FRANCIS R. WALSH is a member of the history faculty at the University of Lowell. He received his Ph.D. from Boston University and has published articles on American ethnic history.

MARILYN THORNTON WILLIAMS teaches history at Pace University. She received her Ph.D. from New York University and has published several articles on American urban history, including a study of New York City's bathhouse movement.

Index

Liberty Party, 41
Lincoln, Abraham, 41
Livermore, Mary A., 204
Lockard, Duane, 69
Lodge, Henry Cabot, 32, 60
Logan, Mrs. Lawrence, 224
Lomasney, Martin, 237
Loomis, Samuel Lane, 235
Lowell, Francis, 11
Lowell, Josephine Shaw, 235
Lowell family, 10
Lowell, 6, 12, 14, 126, 135
Lyman family, 10
Lynn, 6, 14–15, 134

Maguire, Pat, 237
Mann, Arthur, 150, 152, 195, 218, 235
Marcotte, Antoine, 78–79
Massachusetts Department of Labor, 217
Massachusetts General Court, 32, 242
Massachusetts Sanitary Commission, 215
Massachusetts manufacturing company, 12
Matthews, Nathaniel W., 115
McClellan, George B., 44
McFarland, Gerald W., vii, 63 n
McKinley, William, 57–59, 61, 68, 83
Meade, Edwin, 197
Merriam, George S., 37
Merrimack Courier, 13
Merrimack River, 12
Methodist Episcopal Church, 201
Miami Medical College, 220
Migration, 4, 7–8, 10–11, 125–26, 233. *See also* individual ethnic groups
Morgan, Henry, 233–36; work of, 199–209 passim
Morgan Memorial, 207
Mount Auburn Cemetery, 207
Mount Holyoke College, 136

Mugwumps, 32, 39, 46, 51–52, 54, 235–37
Muirhead, John, 165
Myers, Michael W., 221

Nahant, 202
National Association of Professional Baseball Players, 128
National Municipal League, 221
National Trade Unions, 133, 135
National Women's Trade Union League, 221
Nativism, 13, 32–33, 73. *See also* Catholics, opposition to
Nelson, Henry Loomis, 68
Neponset, 202
New Bedford, viii, 6, 35, 101–21 passim, 135
New Bedford *Daily Mercury*, 103, 106
New Bedford *Evening Journal*, 110
New Bedford *Evening Standard*, 103, 106, 110
New Bedford Industrial Cooperative Association, 104
New Deal, 38
New England Society for the Suppression of Vice, 194
North Adams, 137, 139
Norton, Charles Eliot, 129, 234

O'Brien, Hugh, 239–40
O'Connor, Charles, 156
O'Connor, Thomas, 240, 242
O'Leary, Robert, vii
O'Reilly, Frederick Stimson, 127
O'Reilly, John Boyle, 148–63 passim, 197
O'Shea, Peter, 89
O'Sullivan, Mary Kenney, 198
Oliver, Henry K., 132–33, 145 n
Olmsted, Frederick Law, 244
Otis, Harrison Grey, 10, 15

Paine, Robert Treat, 194
Paper industry, 6, 16, 70, 82
Papyrus Club, 157